MICK FOWLER

NO EASY WAY

The challenging life of the climbing taxman

Vertebrate Publishing, Sheffield
www.v-publishing.co.uk

NO EASY WAY

Also by Mick Fowler

Vertical Pleasure
On Thin Ice

To my father, George, for starting me off;
all those I have had great days climbing with;
and, in particular, to Nicki, Tess and Alec who have had
to put up with my irrepressible urge to go climbing.

First published in 2018 by Vertebrate Publishing.

Vertebrate Publishing
Crescent House, 228 Psalter Lane, Sheffield S11 8UT United Kingdom.
www.v-publishing.co.uk

Front cover: The author on Mugu Chuli, traversing the frontier ridge to the descent. Photo: Dave Turnbull.
Photography by Mick Fowler unless otherwise credited.

A CIP catalogue record for this book is available from the British Library.

ISBN: 978-1-911342-74-8 (Hardback)
ISBN: 978-1-911342-75-5 (Paperback)
ISBN: 978-1-911342-91-5 (Ebook)

10 9 8 7 6 5 4 3 2 1

Design and production by Jane Beagley.
www.v-publishing.co.uk

Vertebrate Publishing is committed to printing on paper from sustainable sources.

Printed and bound in the UK by T.J. International Ltd, Padstow, Cornwall.

CONTENTS

PROLOGUE

'Your cancer … I've been asked to update your obituary.'

I read the email again.

It was from a reporter at *The Daily Telegraph* who was updating a draft obituary they had on file.

'It's quite an honour,' he continued. 'We don't do this for everyone.'

The email brought my mortality into sharp focus.

Sixteen years earlier my challenges in life had been rather different.

CHAPTER 1

The Competing Priorities of Life ...

'And what do you think have been your main achievements this year?'

It was 2002, end-of-year appraisal time and my tax office boss was going through the usual motions. There was no doubt in my mind that the most significant achievement of my year had been a successful expedition to climb an eye-catching ice streak on a mountain called Siguniang in China's Sichuan province. I was really pleased with the way Paul Ramsden and I had found a way through the legendary Chinese bureaucracy and spent six days climbing a fantastic new line. For this we won a Piolet d'Or, the mountaineering world's equivalent of an Oscar, at a lavish ceremony in Paris. There was a hesitation as I wondered whether or not this might be a good achievement to mention.

'I think your paper on discounts for unmarketability was very useful,' my boss prompted, 'and your work embedding a Lean way of working in the office has been much appreciated.'

Climbing left my mind as I was dragged into my working world. I have always kept the different aspects of my life very separate, even to the extent of being called 'Mike' at work, 'Mick' in my climbing life ... and 'Michael' when in trouble at home.

My job at the tax office had varied a lot since I joined in 1977. At that time the Inland Revenue had offered the best salary with which to replenish my bank account in between summer climbing trips. I worked in a north London 'collection' office, knocking on people's doors and asking them to pay outstanding tax. The job was only meant to tide me over between trips, but when the time came to head out for another summer in the Alps, it was suggested that I could take the time off as a combination of flexi-leave and annual leave and save myself the hassle of looking for a job when I got back.

This tempted me to stay and on my return I was unexpectedly propelled up the promotion ladder.

The job was often tedious but fitted well with climbing and so I just kind of stayed with it. Part of my role involved visiting tax offices around the country to assess their staffing needs. Wherever possible I rented accommodation from climbing friends and joined local climbing scenes, giving me an introduction to numerous obscure climbing areas that I would never otherwise have visited.

I also viewed London as a pretty good place for a climber to live. That might sound odd, but its sheer size and diversity meant there was a sizeable pool of adventurous people to draw from and finding like-minded partners for whatever obscure activity one might want to pursue at the weekend was never a problem.

The advent of family life made me view things differently. Nicki and I married in 1991 and our first child, Tess, was born in 1992. Weekend visits to the country became trickier and moving to a place where climbing venues were more easily accessible seemed an attractive proposition. As it happened, fortune shone upon us, and the tax office made a decision to move specialist jobs out of London and to a site in Nottingham. I successfully applied for a job in the Inland Revenue's shares and assets valuation section; we decided that Nicki's job of restoring watercolours for London galleries could be carried out anywhere, and we ended up buying a large wreck of a house in the small town of Melbourne, twenty miles to the west of Nottingham and much closer to the great outdoors and the Peak District than London.

The house reputedly dated from the 1600s and I vividly remember walking in and looking up to see straight through to the inside of the roof. But where I saw only hassle, Nicki saw 'potential', as the estate agents say, and after nine years of effort had scoured every architectural salvage yard within a 150-mile radius and restored the house to something like its former glory. It was long, hard slog but eventually Nicki's efforts were such that they featured in *Period Living* and *Traditional Home* magazines in the UK and *The English Home* magazine in the USA. My DIY and building skills, however, are woefully inadequate and my efforts at art and design even worse. This meant that my contribution tended to be leaving early and returning late to marvel at how piles of 'junk' were transformed into beautiful useable items. Quite a few climbing friends got involved in various stages of the project. I recall Andy Cave perched on the ridge of an outbuilding asking for advice on pointing ridge tiles and Bert Simmonds sticking his foot through a ceiling and spilling limewash into his eyes such that he had to be taken to hospital.

Our second child, Alec, was born in 1994 and as work and family commitments grew it was perhaps inevitable that climbing trips would become less frequent. I enjoyed all forms of climbing, from technical rock to Scottish winter to alpine-style mountaineering in the Himalaya. It was the weekend climbing that was the most difficult to maintain. I very much wanted to be around and immersed in family things at weekends and, even when I did arrange weekends away, I found that they were always vulnerable to last-minute changes of family plans and to irresistible pleas along the lines of 'Oh Dad, please, please, please can you go away a different weekend?' Faced with such pressures it was perhaps inevitable that my rock climbing standard gradually declined. Curiously, the decline in my winter climbing standard was not so marked.

I managed to keep some semblance of fitness, meeting up with a group of friends once a week to do something that made us breathe heavily. In the summer that meant rock climbing, but in the winter when the evenings were dark, it could involve anything from caving to kayaking, running, cycling or, if we were short on ideas, the climbing wall – although this was very much a last resort. The other exercise that fitted in well was fell racing. With the Peak District so close there were numerous races to choose from and although I trailed along near the back of the field, my efforts did seem to help with the speed of my walking and the non-technical side of mountaineering.

The one area of climbing I was determined to keep up was my greater-range climbing. The retrospective pleasure from greater-range successes and trips like Siguniang was delightfully enduring compared to weekend action. And, importantly, the organisation required was such that dates were known well in advance and family and work activities could be planned around them. When the children were young, I organised trips on alternate years, but this changed to shorter trips every year as they grew up, squeezing expeditions into the few weeks' leave I had each year.

My boss was still waiting. I pushed mountaineering thoughts to the back of my mind, looked at him closely and heard myself telling him about the terribly difficult cases I had settled, the vast amount of yield (tax collected) I had secured and the horrendous management challenges I had overcome. It all went very well and I left the room content to be awarded a bonus.

But, internally, I was *most* satisfied to have succeeded on Siguniang and to have completed another year of safely juggling work, climbing and family life. And that is what this book is about: the ups and downs and stresses and strains of fitting the little-understood urges of a greater-range mountaineer into the well-understood challenges of being a family man with a full-time job. There truly is No Easy Way.

Chapter 2

Grosvenor – 'The Dangers of Cupping'

I have a bulging file at home where I keep bits of information that might lead me to 'interesting' objectives for the future. Every year I pore over the accumulated possibilities and choose the most urge-inducing objective based on a list of points that must be satisfied for the truly perfect mountaineering trip.

The ideal objective should:

- have a striking line leading directly to the summit,
- be unclimbed,
- be visible from afar,
- be technically challenging,
- be objectively safe,
- be on an eye-catching mountain,
- be in a remote, ethnically interesting area,
- be somewhere I haven't been before,
- have an aesthetically pleasing – and different – descent route.

It was 2003, the year after that memorable tax office appraisal, and my list had brought me to Sichuan province in China, to the town of Chengdu where I was lying face down in a massage parlour grimacing at the floor through a hole in the bed. The bony undulations of the Fowler body had initially made it difficult for the masseur to get a seal, but now he was making progress he was clearly keen to maintain the impetus. The suction pump was operated with great enthusiasm and the pain was becoming excruciating. I glanced sideways at the bed next to me where Neil McAdie was also face down. He too had opted for 'cupping' and his back sported eight 15-centimetre-diameter transparent suction pads through which I could see his skin sucked up to form tight fleshy lumps which stood proud like enormous inflamed sores. Perhaps testing the pain threshold was what Sichuan full-body massages were all about? Either way, it seemed unmanly to whimper and so I suffered in silence.

As usual we were a team of four, climbing as two pairs. My partner, Andy Cave, was an established all-rounder whose company I had enjoyed on trips to India and Yukon. Originally from a tight-knit mining community he had started his working life down the delightfully named Grimethorpe pit in Yorkshire and had used the free time afforded by the miners' strike of 1984–1985 to discover the joys of rock climbing and the outdoors. From there he shocked his family by breaking generational links with the pit and went on to become a top-flight climber, climbing guide, part-time lecturer in mining dialects and motivational speaker. His rise from the claustrophobic pit to clear mountain air is brilliantly written up in his award-winning book *Learning to Breathe*.

Neil McAdie and Simon Nadin were not so well known to me but were good friends of Andy's. Neil, on the bed next to me, worked in the outdoor retail trade while Simon was in the roped access industry and was the first ever winner of the world indoor sport-climbing championships.

The fact that we had all availed ourselves of a Sichuan full-body massage was Andy's fault. He had been insistent that the British Mount Grosvenor expedition would benefit from this special treatment. But Andy and Simon had taken the only places in the massage parlour that boasted 'fully qualified' masseurs, leaving Neil and me to visit the seedier-looking and less frequented establishment next door.

Afterwards we compared our experiences. There was no doubt about it: 'cupping' in the unqualified establishment left a deeper impact. Neil and I sported large blood blisters on our lower backs, whereas Andy and Simon were relatively unscathed. Carrying a rucksack would have been excruciating and, much as I am a firm believer in trying (almost) everything once, unqualified Sichuan massages are perhaps best left until the climbing and trekking is over. Even then, be prepared to explain the curious lingering marks to loved ones back home …

But we had not come to China to sample the Chengdu massage parlours. Our objective had been to make the first ascent of Mount Grosvenor, an unclimbed 6,376-metre peak in the Daxue Shan range, which appeared to tick every box on my list. The highest peak in the range is Minya Konka, the most easterly 7,000-metre peak in the world. Although the climbing history of Minya Konka is well documented, we could find remarkably little information about the surrounding mountains. Our best photograph was a black and white shot from *Die Großen Kalten Berge von Szetschuan*, a 1970s German book by Eduard Imhof. It showed a spectacular peak with a steep and shady north-west face sporting a series of rock ribs separated by icy couloirs. The thirty-year-old photograph looked very exciting, and so the four of us had come to Sichuan to see what it was all about.

'What do you think is going on?'

Neil's question was a good one. We had been stationary at the side of the road for over two hours and absolutely nothing of note had happened. Four buses to Kangding had left Chengdu that morning at half-hourly intervals and, being keen, we had caught the first one. Now the following three were readily visible in the enormous snaking queue that had formed behind us.

'The road is closed until 5 p.m.,' announced an authoritative Irish lady – the only Westerner we were to see between Chengdu and base camp.

And it was. There were eight or so hours to waste. Simon, a keen photographer, passed the time poking his lens into every interesting scene he could spot. Andy did his best to learn an ethnic dice game and Neil and I just sort of mooched about, spending much of the time bouncing dangerously on a flimsy, wooden-slatted footbridge.

The Chinese just kind of accepted it without looking bored at all. Most of them, certainly the bus drivers, must have known that roadworks meant that the road was always closed until 5 p.m., so why they had joined the queue at 9.30 a.m. was difficult to understand.

'The bus company haven't been told to change their timetable,' explained our interpreter, Lion, helpfully.

Five o'clock came and, sure enough, the queue started to move. Lion gathered a bit more information from officials and it transpired that traffic was allowed one way on alternate days. We were lucky that this happened to be a Chengdu to Kangding day. If it hadn't been, our eight-hour wait would have been twenty-four hours longer.

The roadworks were truly amazing. This was steep mountain country, a world apart from the flatlands of the Sichuan basin and populated by endless hairpins and murky grey rivers thrashing their way through steep-sided valleys. The road building was a 150-kilometre eye-opening mix of basic labouring and high-tech machinery. Thousands of ant-like labourers were living under plastic sheets at the side of the road and moving rocks into place by way of buckets on either end of a wooden pole over their shoulders. Conversely, at one point a gorge had to be crossed and seriously expensive equipment was much in evidence. The obvious availability of almost unlimited cheap labour and high-tech machinery seemed to say a lot about the rapid improvement of transport systems in the more remote parts of China.

Deep into the evening our bus was still bouncing painfully over the amazingly uneven surface. Eventually we came to a gasping halt at Kangding bus station, where a doctor in a white gown sprayed disinfectant in our direction. As Sod's law would have it we had chosen to visit at the time of a serious outbreak of Severe Acute Respiratory Syndrome (SARS). Between November 2002 and July 2003, 774 people had died – the majority in south China – and here in Kangding there was a palpable feeling of concern, with a large number of people wearing face masks. As we stood there being sprayed it felt as if the great unwashed were arriving.

Lion – we never did discover his proper name – had been a very useful interpreter the year before when I had visited the Siguniang area of Sichuan. But that was his home territory where he had been dealing with locals that he knew and trusted. Here, where he had no contacts, he appeared continually concerned and was close to being a hindrance.

'Don't use these horsemen,' he advised. 'They are not trustworthy.'

This was all very good but in the (very) sleepy hamlet of Laoyulin, half an hour's taxi ride from Kangding, there was not exactly a lot of choice. Lion was devoid of alternative suggestions. Negotiations over the price were interspersed with him regularly pointing out how shifty the men looked, how he could see it in their eyes, how their attitude made him nervous, how they kept changing the price. On and on it went. It was as difficult to keep our negotiator negotiating as it was to secure a sensible deal. But eventually hands were shaken, six horses were rustled up, and we were on our way. Within a hundred metres the loads had fallen from one horse.

'You see – they are unreliable,' announced Lion smugly.

Several load adjustments and perhaps two miles later we left the road and headed up the valley, which we guessed would lead us to Mount Grosvenor. I say 'guessed' because the trouble with exploratory trips in the pre-Google

Earth era was that you were never quite sure. The sketch maps we had managed to get hold of suggested we were going in the right direction but the horsemen didn't seem to recognise Mount Grosvenor from our photographs and, perhaps unsurprisingly, the name prompted equally blank looks. (As far as we could work out the name was dreamt up by the American team that surveyed the area and made the first ascent of nearby Minya Konka in 1932.)

Having set out late in the afternoon we failed to reach any good camping spots before night fell and ended up pitching our tents right in the middle of the track – which would have been fine if the night traffic hadn't been so heavy.

'Didn't sleep a wink,' groaned Neil. 'What the hell was going on?'

'Caterpillar fungus hunters,' retorted Lion, in what we were beginning to recognise as the usual Chinese way of responding to questions: in a direct and to-the-point, yet confusing manner.

By a memorable series of hand signals our horsemen conveyed the message that caterpillar fungus is much revered in Chinese medicinal circles as an aphrodisiac. The fungus itself is curious. The caterpillar buries itself and then, for reasons we never quite got to the bottom of, a green shoot starts to grow out of it. The fungus hunters dig up the whole lot, and we were told the market price for ground-up caterpillar was around $2,000 per kilo. But why these people felt it necessary to thunder up and down the track in the middle of the night was not clear to us.

As we continued up the valley the popularity of fungus hunting became more and more apparent. At 3,800 metres there were fifty or so tents in which whole families had based themselves for the full fungus-hunting season. I could hardly believe it. We had expected solitude at base camp but it was clearly not to be.

Unfortunately Mount Grosvenor was nowhere near as obvious as the fungus hunters. When the horsemen stopped and refused to go any further we were on a flat, grassy plain at about 4,000 metres and had still not set eyes on it. Lion had to leave immediately to return to Chengdu and we settled down with a sense of uncertainty. Not only were we not sure where our mountain was, but our decision not to employ a base camp guard was feeling suspect, bearing in mind the number of people around.

At least the next day was clear and, forty-five minutes or so above base camp, we were able to stand atop a moraine crest and see our objective for the first time. How the horsemen had not recognised it from our photograph was beyond us, but it was a relief to see that we had been dropped off in a reasonable spot, if not the best. Amid the adjusting of zoom lenses and the clicks of shutters Grosvenor looked to be a steep pyramid with the north-west face sporting a spectacular collection of mixed lines. All four of us agreed that it was all very exciting and definitely scored well against my list of essential criteria.

Acclimatising is a painful precursor to climbing at altitude. I work on the basis that a couple of head-throbbing nights at 5,300 metres or so is enough to prepare the body for technical climbing at altitudes around the height of Grosvenor. This probably conflicts terribly with expert advice on the subject but I take the view that technical climbing at altitude is a slow process for me and height is gained so gradually that any further acclimatising can be done while climbing. Here though, there was a slight problem in that there was nowhere obvious and easy that would enable us to reach an altitude of 5,300 metres. The foot of the face was perhaps 5,000 metres and the obvious peaks on the far side of our base camp valley rose to only just over that. There was nothing for it but to acclimatise by ploughing over these 5,000-metre humps and hoping for the best. It transpired that the snow was appallingly soft and we frequently sank up to our waists. The exertion required was extreme and after long sessions of heavy gasping we convinced ourselves that we must have sucked in so much 5,000-metre air that we were as acclimatised as we would have been if we had been able to stroll up to 5,300 metres. That was probably nonsense, but optimism is important and, having spent a couple of nights up high, we descended to base camp.

Down in camp there was a gradual realisation that all was not well. The first clue was the chocolate bar wrappers scattered around the tent. A closer review revealed more serious problems. Andy's glasses had been broken (fortunately he had a spare pair) and just about all our base camp food had gone. Only unappetising-looking seaweed, bought out of interest more than anything else, and a few sorry-looking vegetables remained. To add insult to injury our pan had been vandalised beyond repair.

I took time to contemplate what remained and whether we could make do with what was left. Andy's reaction was more immediate.

'Shouldn't take too long to stock up again in Kangding. It's about a twenty-eight-mile round trip and a taxi ride. If two of us go down tonight we will be back again by tomorrow evening.'

The Cave energy levels are clearly not those of a normal man. I made half-hearted noises about how I was sure that seaweed would keep us going for a day or two, after which we would be climbing and could live on mountain rations that had not been taken. Neil however was equally hunger-stricken and keen to accompany Andy. And so it was decided. Simon and I stayed at base camp munching seaweed while Andy and Neil jogged off into the distance.

Much to my surprise the next evening saw the jogging team return with a fine selection of food. Simon and I emphasised what a difficult time we had had surviving on seaweed and joined in a day of hearty eating. We then hid everything of value among large boulders near the tents and headed off towards Mount Grosvenor.

The snow conditions on the glacier leading to the face were as grim as on our acclimatisation outing and we jumped energetically from boulder to boulder in an effort to avoid the thigh-deep snow. But the weather looked reasonable and spirits were high.

As a result of much peering through binoculars Andy and I had decided to attempt a couloir line leading directly to the summit, whereas Simon and Neil were going for a mixed line that started further up the glacier and joined the west ridge about 500 metres below the summit.

The morning dawned crisp and clear but windy. For Andy and me the day was to start with a tedious 300-metre grind on forty-five-degree snow and it was a relief to finally come across a steepening and get out the ropes. I like roped climbing and sometimes try to avoid demoralising myself by breaking down the number of expedition days spent doing so compared to the number spent travelling, acclimatising and sitting out bad weather. This was our fifteenth day away from the UK and the first time we had uncoiled our ropes. They were both brand new and snaked out pleasingly as Andy dealt impressively with near-vertical sections of thin ice. Within ten metres of my starting to climb I had pierced one rope right through the core with the pick of my axe.

By now the previously blue sky had changed to a dull grey and snow was falling heavily. A couloir, albeit a broad one, was not the best place to be. The climbing was easy but frequent heavy sloughs of snow prompted caution and persuaded us to trade time for safety and dig deep to find solid ice into which we could arrange secure ice-screw belays. Several times the snow slides were so heavy that communication was impossible for minutes at a time. Eventually we managed to move out of the couloir and gain the snow shelf that was the site of our intended bivouac. The shelf slanted more steeply than it appeared from below and we soon discovered that the snow was not deep enough to cut a nice, comfortable ledge. An hour or so of dithering and excavating saw the tent pitched with perhaps one third of the floor space overhanging the ledge. It didn't look ideal.

'It'll feel better once we are inside,' I commented. Andy gave a doubtful look.

I was wrong. Inside was not better. Well, it was for me, but Andy ended up with a spot of floor bother and a sleepless night. The morning was one of the very few when I have seen the Cave body looking listless.

The clear morning skies showed that we had gained a lot of height the previous day. Above us was what looked to be the hardest section. So far the climbing had been almost exclusively on snow and ice, but now the angle steepened and the climbing became more mixed for 200 metres or so. Through the binoculars it had looked to be Scottish grade V or so; difficult but not too extreme – exactly the sort of climbing we liked.

The first real pitch looked straightforward: solid granite interspersed with streaks of ice and resting places. But I was soon reduced to removing my sack with a growing feeling of insecurity as the 'ice' turned out to be useless powder and what had looked to be a reasonable steep step succumbed only to precarious, unprotected climbing up a disintegrating rock nose. Still, we were making progress, trending diagonally right towards the back of the fault line that we hoped would contain enough ice to unlock this steep section. But we were slow. When we reached the fault line in mid-afternoon, we had only gained about ninety metres of altitude.

Above us it was only seventy metres or so of steep ground until the angle eased into an eye-catching line of ice leading to just below the summit. If we carried on it looked likely that we would end up spending a night hanging from slings, but there was nowhere obvious to bivouac where we were and we both felt that a decent night's sleep would help. Our progress had been so slow that our previous bivouac spot was really not that far below. We are both naturally decisive characters, but an uncharacteristic dithering session resulted over whether to abseil down to it and climb back up the rope in the morning or make the best of what we had. In desperation I climbed up a few metres, but there was nothing of interest so that didn't help. At one point we started to rig an abseil, but the thought of losing all that height only to have to regain it in the morning was too much to bear. Eventually we decided to make the best of it where we were and spent the rest of the afternoon trying to hack a bum ledge out of a mixture of snow, ice and rotten rock. Up till now the rock had been reasonable granite, but here in the back of the fault line it consisted of rotten bits and pieces frozen together. It was dusk and our axes were very blunt by the time we had hacked out a ledge. It wasn't very good and would just about provide two sitting positions, one obviously better than the other.

'Suppose I'll go for the worst one,' I heard myself say, conscious of the uncomfortable hours that Andy had endured the night before. Andy did not demur. He had not looked his usual perky self all day.

We settled down as best we could, me wrapped in the tent fabric and Andy in a single bivouac bag. The best I could say was that the spot we had chosen was sheltered from rockfall. It was exposed to wind-blown spindrift that had a tendency to blast us at the most inopportune moments. Most importantly for me, part of the bum ledge sloped outwards so that I was forever hanging in my harness or fighting to get back on to the ledge. I have had worse nights, but this was not the best. Andy too professed to have had nights that passed quicker.

The morning was surprisingly cold and vaguely clear, although an array of threatening clouds peppered the sky. It was my lead. The angle steepened, and looking up I could see that a dry corner led to a niche at thirty metres, which seemed an obvious place to belay. Above it the corner reared back, overhanging and choked with powder snow blasted up by the frequent spindrift avalanches. We had hoped for ice but it was clear there was none. It all looked very challenging.

A few steep ice moves and I was at the foot of the dry corner. Close up, it was apparent that the rock was interestingly insecure. Placing a poor peg, I removed my sack and left it for Andy to worry about later. Above, the corner was acute enough to allow precarious back-and-footing, but crampons screeching on the smooth overlapping flakes of the left wall raised the adrenaline factor uncomfortably. Instead I decided to climb the left wall itself and then hopefully rest by returning to a back-and-foot position higher up. The trouble was that the wall was not exactly confidence inspiring. The curious undulating granite overlapped in little flakes like the scales of a huge fish. In places these scales projected outwards, allowing a crampon front point to be hooked over them. Even without a sack, the Fowler calves were soon finding this testing. More significant was the strain on the nerves. There appeared to be no reason on earth why these projecting flakes should support my weight. I could only assume that they were frozen in place by their inner ends, which made it impossible to judge how secure they might be.

'Watch me,' I squawked, moving gingerly from one to another.

I managed to place a very dubious peg before grinding to a halt perhaps five metres higher. At this point I could lean into the corner, but that meant putting an even more frightening outward strain on my single flake foothold, and I could feel the right side of the corner move beneath my back. Agitated noises from below reported that the resultant volley of rocks was not appreciated. This was all getting very uncomfortable. The right side of the corner was loose to the extent that any movement sent a shower of rocks downwards, whereas the left side was now devoid of projecting flakes. The only way on seemed to be by frictioning on the left wall with my back against the right one. I tried this a couple of times but achieved little other than more concerned shouts from below.

It wasn't a position I could hold forever. I looked up. The niche I had been heading for was only about ten metres above me, but it now looked distinctly unappealing. There didn't appear to be a ledge of any kind, and worse, what had looked to be promising cracks in the right wall were clearly useless and ready to crumble. A belayless, ledgeless easing of the angle did not inspire confidence.

A wave of middle age washed over me. This was not a place to be silly. My last runner was five metres below and it was a further ten down to my last decent gear. Physically I could have carried on but instead found myself gibbering back to my last runner and down to a shivering Andy.

'You have a go.'

We discussed the situation in an appropriately deep and meaningful manner. It looked as if the climbing got more difficult above my high point and the condition of the rock was very challenging. But it was probably only forty metres to where the angle eased and where success seemed pretty certain. Should we try harder? Andy had become very cold while I tried. We dithered. The loose rock, cold, difficulty and tiredness were pushing us inexorably towards a decision. Our willpower was flagging. We had lost our motivation. The slide to defeat had begun and the decision to retreat became inevitable.

With frequent breaks to stare back up we began to abseil. Somehow we just didn't want to go down. We felt we hadn't tried quite hard enough. At one point we stopped and roped up to start up an alternative line but it immediately became difficult and our hearts weren't in it. We carried on down. By mid-afternoon we were at the foot of the face walking away across the glacier. And looking back …

'What do you think?' I asked Andy.

'It's a good line.'

'Might be icier later in the year?'

'Might have to return one day.'

Neil and Simon had had much the same experience. The wind, cold, spindrift avalanches and generally indifferent weather prompted them to retreat well short of the summit. They too felt disappointed and nagged by a feeling that somehow they could have tried harder. The mental side of mountaineering can be as challenging as the physical side. Mount Grosvenor had won. But, as it turned out, not for long.

The exploratory mountaineering scene is a small one, and, shortly after our return, Roger Payne, then general secretary of the British Mountaineering Council (BMC), contacted me. He asked if it was OK with Andy and me if he and his wife, Julie-Anne, had Grosvenor as a reserve objective should the Chinese authorities not give them permission to attempt a mountain called Chomolhari on the Tibet/Bhutan border. With no immediate plan to return that was fine by us. As it happened the bureaucratic challenge for Chomolhari proved too much, and so just a few months after we had been there, Roger and Julie-Anne climbed close to the line that Neil and Simon had attempted and made a fine first ascent and traverse of the mountain.

Then, in 2010, the strong team of Kyle Dempster (US) and Bruce Normand (UK) climbed the line that Andy and I had failed on. They managed to bypass the horrifically loose corner by climbing a thick ice streak that had formed on the left wall and completed the whole line in one push. At least one other route has been climbed on the north side of Grosvenor since then.

Andy and I noted these ascents with interest. Naturally we were disappointed not to have succeeded, but regardless of the subsequent ascents, I am always wary of returning to a line I have failed on. To return to my list, I suppose I visit the greater ranges for two main reasons: to experience the ethnic pleasures of visiting new places, and to tackle climbing objectives that inspire me. To return to a place means that the first reason is missing and the risk of what I would regard as a totally unsuccessful trip is increased.

With such thoughts in mind I had been hesitant to put Grosvenor back in my box of objectives, and, in a way, I was grateful that these subsequent ascents made it an easy decision for me to drop any thoughts of returning.

Chapter 3

Kajaqiao – Hands Drawn Together in Prayer

Back in the UK after our attempt on Grosvenor, I was giving a mountaineering lecture in Edinburgh when I was unsettled by a comment during the usual question and answer session at the end. In response to a question about my next objective I openly wondered about the possibilities in east Tibet, and had just finished saying that I wasn't aware of any mountaineers ever having climbed in this vast area when a hand rose and a voice politely announced that it had just returned from a wonderful trip there. There's nothing like feeling silly in public. To say I was taken aback is something of an understatement. Having kept myself aware of developments on the remote mountaineering scene for many years, my initial reaction was one of disbelief. I didn't recognise the chap who had spoken, chose not to seek clarification in a public forum and gave a rather bland response along the lines of 'we must speak later'. With that I moved on to field rather more standard questions. But the response niggled and I couldn't concentrate.

Visits to the Qionglai range in 2002 and the Daxue Shan range in 2003 had opened my eyes to the mountaineering potential in China, and an increasing number of photographs of east Tibet published by the renowned Japanese explorer Tamotsu (Tom) Nakamura had begun to whet my appetite.

At the time I had managed to arrange my tax office responsibilities such that although based in Nottingham, I was responsible for the shares and assets valuation office in Edinburgh. That meant visiting Edinburgh about once a month and so during subsequent trips I got to know Adam Thomas and Phil Amos. It was Adam who had spoken during the lecture and as we chatted afterwards it quickly become clear that there was no misunderstanding.

Not only had they managed to visit the remote Nyainqentangla East range, they had gone with the intention of climbing Kajaqiao, an eye-catching peak that Tom Nakamura had described as the 'Matterhorn of the Nyainqentangla', and which was top of my provisional list of objectives in the area. Mistakes on their maps (pre Google Earth) meant that intervening ridges sprouted unexpectedly as they tried to approach from the south and they never managed to reach the foot of the mountain. But they were keen to return and it didn't take long for us to agree to make up a four-man team with the intention of exploring the area further and having a go at Kajaqiao from the north, where access appeared to be more straightforward.

The more I researched the more I came to appreciate the mountaineering potential of east Tibet and the work of Tom Nakamura. Tom was a senior Japanese businessman and when he retired he approached the exploration and mapping of east Tibet in the meticulous way that I could imagine him handling difficult business issues. He was instrumental in getting the *Japanese Alpine News* published in English, which has been a great benefit to exploration-minded mountaineers in the West. His visits to east Tibet seemed to result in a never-ending stream of photographs of spectacular unclimbed 6,000-metre mountains, of which he reckoned there were over 250 in the Nyainqentangla and Kangri Garpo ranges. There was more than enough here to last me a lifetime, but Kajaqiao was the one that cried out to be climbed the most and, despite all the other offerings, it stayed firmly as our objective.

As usual we arranged to climb as two independent teams of two. From the outset we knew the trip would be expensive and my climbing partners of recent years were otherwise occupied. The search for a suitable partner led to Chris Watts. In years gone by Chris and I had enjoyed two greater-range trips together. He had been my climbing partner on my first ever trip outside Europe, to Peru in 1982. We had a wonderfully successful trip, making the first ascent of the south-east buttress of a mountain called Taulliraju in the Cordillera Blanca range. Our second trip together in 1984 had not been so successful. That was my first trip to the Himalaya and our plan was to make the first ascent of a 7,329-metre peak in Pakistan called Bojohagur Duonasir. Suffice to say that our inexperience at altitude showed and the trip was punctuated by numerous retrospectively laughable incidents stemming from our naivety. The end result across the team as a whole was: a fractured vertebra, a boot dropped at a crucial time, a lucky escape with a breaking abseil sling, food dumps lost under fresh snowfall, an unsuccessful attempt to melt snow in my helmet and such a poor relationship with our liaison officer that he threatened to report us for 'littering the mountain' because we had been unable to retrieve a cache of three or four ice screws. Meanwhile a Japanese walking club attempting the mountain from the other side joined our line, walked very strongly beyond where we ran out of steam and succeeded in making the first ascent. All in all it was a most memorable trip for all the wrong reasons. I remember writing an article about it and receiving a letter from a prominent member of the Alpine Club complaining that I was an embarrassment to British mountaineering and should be ashamed of myself.

Anyway, that was over twenty years ago. Since then, Chris and his wife Siobhan had built a successful outdoor equipment distribution business and Chris had kept himself in top shape by pursuing his original passion of cycling, together with irregular winter climbing trips to Scotland. Chris and I had climbed a lot together in Scotland during the 1980s and had developed a trust that I felt sure would stand us in good stead for another greater-range trip. The fact that he had done very little mountaineering since Bojohagur somehow mattered little. I knew him to be focused, fit, dependable and determined. All in all, these are more important than technical ability when it comes to greater-range climbing.

As the months went by preparations proceeded and the mound of pre-expedition paperwork grew. The frequency of my visits to the Edinburgh office increased markedly as Adam, Phil and I got to know each other better and we spent many fine evenings climbing on the outcrops around Edinburgh. The staff in Edinburgh must have wondered why it was suddenly necessary for their boss to visit so often.

There was however a notable absence of a letter of authority from the Chinese authorities. In theory, all of Tibet was 'open' to foreigners at that time, although in practice specific permits were required to visit specific areas. We knew the authorities tended to issue them at the very last minute, but as the months went by concern gradually grew. A particular frustration in dealing with the Chinese authorities is that I have never been able to make contact with the decision maker; there is always a middleman who I never manage to bypass. In the case of mountaineers wishing to climb in Tibet, the 'middleman' is the China Tibet Mountaineering Association (CTMA) and the message from them was consistently along the lines of 'your application is being processed'. That was fine to begin with, but the week before departure stress levels were rising fast. Adam had resigned as a grants officer with the Big Lottery Fund and was staying in London; Phil was in Edinburgh, having booked four weeks' unpaid leave from his job as an environmental engineer; and Chris and I were in the East Midlands, packed and ready to go. The plan was that as soon as the all-important letter of invitation was received, Phil would fly down to London, visas would be issued and we would be on our way. That was perhaps an optimistic timescale, but Phil had booked his flight in advance. Eventually the crucial moment came. My phone rang and it was Phil.

'I'm packed and ready. Shall I leave for the airport?'

I opened my computer and checked my emails yet again. Nothing at all. Absolutely nothing. I had lost count of the number of emails I had sent over the last few days with no discernible progress. Much as no one seemed prepared to say 'no', it was equally apparent that no one was prepared to say 'yes'.

I stared gloomily at the screen. If the Chinese were not going to be decisive then we would have to be.

'Sorry Phil. It's not going to happen.'

And so the 2004 British Kajaqiao expedition ground to a halt before it had even begun.

We decided to meet and discuss alternative plans. We met at my place, drank beer, peered at my box file, checked flights and gradually realised that we had been so set on east Tibet that nothing else would do. We decided to defer until 2005 and hope for better luck then.

'At least these little problems keep the crowds away.'

This has become a stock phrase of mine. I can say it quite cheerfully when not caught in the thick of stress-related action, but right then I had to admit I didn't feel quite so appreciative of the bureaucratic lines of defence that play such a large part in keeping these peaks unclimbed.

Adam and Phil drifted back to Edinburgh. Adam managed to return to the job he had resigned from, Phil cancelled his unpaid leave and Chris and I were left to contemplate. Chris suggested that we head out to Grindelwald and have a go at the *Harlin Route* (direct) on the north face of the Eiger. The thought didn't particularly inspire me and I don't know why I agreed to go really. I had climbed the original north face route with Mike Morrison back in 1980 and remembered that the upper section of the direct looked to follow a natural and inspirational line, but that the lower section looked to lack a clear line, involve lots of aid climbing and was generally not very attractive. I had harboured vague thoughts about one day following an alternative route to the Flat Iron (a point about halfway up where the original and direct lines cross) and then following the direct from there. Perhaps that was in my mind when I agreed to Chris's suggestion.

We headed out to Switzerland in his people carrier. When we arrived in Grindelwald the cloud was down and the grey limestone walls of the lower section of the face were running with water. Enthusiasm levels were low. We hung around in a hostel drinking coffee and watching rather uninteresting games of ice hockey for a couple of days until, just when I was close to suggesting giving up, the temperature dropped sufficiently to keep the face frozen and we decided an attempt was worthwhile.

The direct route starts beneath the centre of the face and is the natural fall line for items dropped from higher up. It was rather disconcerting to find the base littered with a significant number of items that tend not to be dropped accidentally, such as old pieces of clothing. The history of the Eiger is a grisly one and, although it has lost much of its once-feared reputation, the relics of the past remain as a poignant reminder of epics gone by.

It became apparent that the temperature was not really cold enough and our ropes soon became wet and dirty. Every now and then the clouds parted and we could see the inspirational upper reaches, but we came to a point where the obvious way on was via a half-frozen waterfall that clearly would not take our weight. After an uncomfortably damp bivouac there was no improvement in conditions and all remaining enthusiasm evaporated. By evening we were back in Grindelwald. In an attempt to recoup something from the trip we walked up to the Schreckhorn hut, but our hearts were still longing for east Tibet and we were soon back at work in England.

The end result was in fact not all negative. I had saved fifteen days of my annual leave entitlement which I was able to bank, giving me extra flexibility for years to come. With my Himalayan trips taking about twenty working days (four weeks) I had long felt guilty about using so much leave on my annual Himalayan holiday. When I was in the lower grades the key to balancing the books with the family was the flexibility provided by the tax office's 'flexitime' system, which enabled me to work long hours when I liked and take a couple of days a month off in lieu. I also became paranoid about unnecessarily using leave. Expeditions would be run to as tight a timescale as possible and I would always return home immediately after the climbing had finished thereby saving days wherever possible. After reaching the dizzy heights of Grade 6 (Senior Principal) in 2000, life became potentially more difficult as flexitime was not officially worked at that grade and there was a long-hours culture that my fellow Grade 6s appeared very comfortable with. I negotiated a certain degree of flexibility with my bosses, but always wondered how much my peers spoke about me behind my back when Fowler's electronic diary was peppered with TOIL (Time Off In Lieu) entries which were notably absent from theirs. Leave arrangements were always a challenge, but saving those fifteen days as a result of cancelling the Kajaqiao trip certainly helped. Disappointed as I was not to get there I took the view that it is important to celebrate the good things that come out of unfortunate circumstances.

Exchanges with the CTMA continued throughout the following year and got as far as 'Beijing is considering … '. At least communication channels were open and they weren't saying 'no'. The decision had to be made. Should we put ourselves through the stress and uncertainty of trying again or should we choose somewhere more straightforward? Based on Tom's photographs and Adam and Phil's first-hand experience we sensed there was something very special in Tibet that would make it all worthwhile in the end; so we persevered. This time our efforts were rewarded. By mid-2005 the CTMA had secured permits from the police, army, local governor, Beijing bureaucrats and several others and in mid-September we finally arrived in the once forbidden city of Lhasa.

The arrangements for mountaineering in east Tibet were new to us. The only way to secure permits seemed to be to agree a lump sum fee with the CTMA to cover all in-country costs. At approaching $5,000 per head it was far from cheap, but the arrangement made arriving at Lhasa airport feel like being on a package holiday. Jimi, our liaison officer, and Tenzing, from the CTMA, were there to whisk us to our hotel and, at long last, to a personal meeting with YangZhen of the CTMA. After so many emails between us I almost felt I knew YangZhen as a close friend. She sat resplendent in a smart leather jacket as thousands of dollars were meticulously counted out.

'Couldn't we have paid in sterling?' I enquired, more to make small talk than for any other reason.

'Of course.'

I tried to stare calmly and not reveal my irritation that we had followed instructions and paid commission to convert our sterling into dollars when there appeared to be no reason for us to have done so.

'Have you been to Tibet before?' she enquired as her minions studiously turned over yet more dollar bills.

I was still lost in following the counting but Adam stepped in briskly to enthuse about their visit to the Nyainqentangla East range two years previously.

'How did you get to east Tibet?' she enquired. 'I have no record of any permits issued for that year.'

This was suddenly looking bad. I gave up following the counting and paid attention. Adam had moved on to explaining how they had arranged the trip through an agent who had been responsible for arranging all the necessary permits. I was expecting an awkward exchange but her response surprised me.

'You made it. You were lucky,' she said with a big smile.

This permit business was all very mystifying. I couldn't quite work out whether it was some big joke or a terribly serious matter. It crossed my mind that we shouldn't bother in future. But then I thought back. Without the necessary official invitation letters we wouldn't have even been allowed to board the Lhasa plane in Beijing, let alone get anywhere near Kajaqiao. It seemed that Adam and Phil's previous trip had been lucky enough to coincide with a rare period of less stringent regulation.

A couple of days later Chris and I peered curiously out of the window of our hotel in the town of Nagqu. This was a fair-sized town that we knew to be one of the coldest, windiest and highest in Tibet. It is best known for a huge nomadic gathering which takes place each year in August, when something like 10,000 nomads congregate on the vast grassland site and indulge in activities as diverse as horse and yak racing, tug of war, stone lifting and Tibetan opera performances. Today, it had a bleak and desolate feel. At an altitude of 4,500 metres the temperature stubbornly hovered below freezing and a dusting of snow blew around the courtyard. On the pavement a group of well-muffled yak herders with eye-catching fox fur hats leaned hard into the biting wind. There were few other people visible. At 6,447 metres the summit of Kajaqiao was about 2,000 metres higher. Whatever would the conditions be like up there?

The 250 kilometres of dirt track to the regional centre of Lhari built my respect for four-wheel-drive vehicles. After a full day driving through wild scenery, passing small mud-hut villages, a few nomadic tents and some impressively large piles of beer bottles, it was something of a surprise when the track suddenly changed to a concrete dual carriageway with street lamps down the centre and lock-up shop units down either side. This continued for a kilometre or so and then stopped as suddenly as it had started. There was no doubt about it: Chinese influence had well and truly arrived. On the pavement a group of nomads with traditional wrap-around yak-skin coats and red braids in their jet-black hair were busy cutting up a yak with an axe. The head had been removed and hung forlornly on pristine metallic railings opposite the Chinese shop units. It seemed a fine symbol of two cultures striving to live side by side.

The place had a wild feel and the prospect of spending a night was clearly causing Jimi and Tenzing some concern. It had to be admitted that it was a very curious spot. We were told that it was originally a sort of mobile village where animal-herding nomads from the plateau met each year to trade. They called their trading place Lhari and, gradually, it became a semi-permanent settlement.

'Wow. This place has changed,' announced Adam.

Two years previously they had found the road completely dug up, presumably in preparation for laying the tediously bland concrete highway. The fact that change was obviously coming fast was perhaps emphasised by the fact that the locals appeared not to understand the concept of a dual carriageway and simply treated it as two parallel roads, driving up and down whichever side took their fancy. To add to the faintly laughable atmosphere a police car cruised up and down with a loud hailer continuously delivering a message of some kind.

'Probably telling them to drive on the right side of the road,' commented Phil.

But Jimi and Tenzing seemed more concerned about security than the driving habits of the locals.

'Best not draw too much attention to yourselves,' they suggested.

We were travelling in two vehicles: a Toyota Land Cruiser and a canvas-covered truck. In the compound behind our very basic hotel the driver backed the truck up hard against a high wall and the Toyota was parked so as to block the exit. Nervous, and not wishing to risk losing any of our equipment, I volunteered to spend the night in the Toyota. I would say 'volunteered to *sleep* in the Toyota' but a combination of the altitude and adrenaline ensured that no sleeping took place. There seemed to be a wild club of some kind nearby which produced much raucous noise and a number of young men who urinated close to the lorry. Every time someone approached I would peer tensely into the darkness and strain my ears for the sound of equipment being removed from the truck. It seemed a threatening place and I couldn't help wondering how any robbers might react if I disturbed them. It was not the most relaxing night.

'Good sleep?' asked Chris chirpily as he banged on the window in the morning. I refrained from comment and stretched grumpily to welcome the day.

And a very bleak day it looked too. A dusting of snow had fallen and the skies looked grey and threatening. Back in the UK I had heard a rumour that a Swiss team bound for Kajaqiao had been turned back here, and so felt that today could be the bureaucratic crux of the whole trip. As far as I was aware we had all the right permits, but I knew full well that it would only take one difficult official to bring us to a grinding halt.

We pulled up outside the incongruous blue glass of the police station and Tenzing signalled that I should come inside with him. At the reception desk we were immediately of great interest and a throng of uniformed officers gathered to test their English.

'Where do you come from? How old are you? How many children?'

I tried to smile in an appropriately relaxed manner as they revelled in being able to communicate with this foreigner. Soon though I was led into a small room where a stern-looking official peered closely at the grand total of nine official documents that Tenzing placed in front of him. For a long time he stared blankly and I wondered if he even knew what he was looking for, increasingly fearing that incomprehension could lead to refusal. At length, and still without any facial expression, he gathered up the pieces of paper, said something to Tenzing and disappeared.

'What's going on?' I asked fearfully.

'It's OK. He's writing a letter of authority,' Tenzing almost whispered.

I decided to smile sweetly and say nothing else until we were back in the Toyota.

I seemed to stand smiling inanely for a very long time before the man returned and I was able to leave clutching a police letter asking the headman of the local village to arrange for our equipment to be carried to our base camp. It seemed odd that a police letter was necessary effectively instructing him to help, but Tenzing explained that caterpillar fungus collecting gave the local communities so much income that they might not be interested in portering for us without a little 'persuasion' from the authorities. I breathed a sigh of relief. With luck, all the bureaucracy was now behind us and all we had to do was find the mountain and climb it.

From the outskirts of Lhari we caught a glimpse of Kajaqiao's striking profile, forty kilometres or so away. But as the valley became more deeply cut and clouds shrouded the peaks it was far from clear exactly where it was in relation to us. It was crucial that the jeeps dropped us off at the right place – a small village called Tatse which our rudimentary map showed as being somewhere above the road directly opposite a short valley leading to Kajaqiao. Satellite navigation devices were relatively few and far between in 2005 but Adam, being young and technologically minded, had brought along a basic global positioning device that very vaguely charted our whereabouts. Through a combination of map reading, satellite signal and guesswork we called a halt in an area of meadow above the Yi'ong Tsangpo river. A few houses were visible a hundred metres or so above the road and we felt a certain amount of relief when their occupants confirmed that this was indeed Tatse and that Kajaqiao was somewhere up in the cloud.

Tatse has a population of about forty and is dominated by an immaculately kept monastery. The younger people in particular were friendly and very interested in what we were planning to do. They told us that Kajaqiao is pronounced 'chachacho' and the mountain is named after its likeness to hands drawn together in prayer. An elderly woman expressed concern that it would snow forever if anyone ever stood on the summit, but the younger occupants were enthusiastic at the prospect of us trying to climb it and told of a Japanese reconnaissance trip and attempt on Kajaqiao that we were not aware of.

We enquired about using yaks or horses to carry our equipment to base camp, but it seemed that since the introduction of motor vehicles animals are very rarely used for carrying anything and the associated skills are fast disappearing. I like to use yaks or horses as they tend not to argue as much as humans but, perhaps inevitably, it was decided that our only practical option was to use porters.

'I think ten will be enough,' announced Tenzing.

I looked around at the enormous amount of gear that he and Jimi had brought. There were huge gas cylinders, a massive marquee-style tent, several large yak steaks, numerous crates of beer … Ten porters seemed ridiculously inadequate. Tenzing obviously recognised the look of concern on our faces.

'We will have base camp here,' he reassured us, pointing just below the village to the meadows next to the river.

This was all very curious. With security in mind we had specifically clarified with the CTMA that Tenzing and Jimi would be staying at our base camp. Something had clearly been lost in the translation, but there wasn't much we could do about it now. It seemed that the policy of the CTMA was to have base camp at the roadside wherever possible.

Having pitched our tents we were immediately something of a local attraction. Just about all of the inhabitants of Tatse must have gathered to marvel at us. And we, of course, took the opportunity to marvel at them, in a mainly 'looking-at-each-other' encounter, as the translation services of Tenzing and Jimi were very limited. Much as they were both friendly and had a reasonable command of English I couldn't help but feel that they were not very forthcoming. Jimi was a mountaineer and clearly relaxed and happy to chat about mountaineering, but when the subject turned to almost anything else he became reserved and unwilling to go into detail. The difficulties we had getting permits had left me feeling that, much as the area was classed as 'open', the Chinese authorities didn't want to encourage foreigners. It might be that Jimi and Tenzing had been told to be reserved with us or it could have been that they were simply reserved characters. Either way, it was frustrating not to be able to gain a deeper insight into the culture and character of the area and its people.

Although we were around 300 kilometres from the nearest metalled road (aside from the one-kilometre concrete strip in Lhari) numerous young men had motorbikes. It appeared that they could put in a month or two of effort gathering caterpillar fungus and then be the idle rich, zooming up and down the dirt road for the rest of the year. Meanwhile the women carried on the traditional way of life and looked after the animals. It seemed that the police chief's concerns could be valid. Somehow though, Jimi and Tenzing managed to persuade ten people to act as porters. They promised to report for duty the following day, although as I lay in my sleeping bag listening to the patter of sleet on the flysheet, I couldn't help but wonder whether they would bother to turn up.

I was wrong to be concerned. The next day dawned bright and sunny and the porters arrived on time. It was clear that they regarded portering as something interesting, unusual and worth preparing for. Several wore what looked to be inappropriately clean and fashionable clothes and one sported a hair style which must have taken some time to prepare and would not have been out of place in a London nightclub. All were on motorbikes. Our bags were quickly scooped up and the bikes roared off down the road to a footbridge over the river a kilometre or so downstream. Recalling the concern about pilfering in Lhari the four of us did our best to run after them, but our efforts at running in big mountain boots were dismally slow and viewed with much hilarity by the group of children and womenfolk who had come to watch.

Once again, our worries were completely unfounded and the porters were excellent. Once over the bridge and loaded up it took only about six hours of uneventful, trackless walking to arrive at the site of the base camp used by the Japanese. The only evidence of their passing was a couple of roughly levelled tent platforms where we dumped our sacks before the porters helped us build a stone wall and arrange a tarpaulin to make a vaguely weatherproof kitchen shelter.

The mountains had not been visible from the valley and it was only on the final stretch to base camp that it became clear that there were two very spectacular mountains ahead, not one. The far one we recognised as Kajaqiao from Tom Nakamura's photographs, but Jimi told us that peak was called Manamcho and that the near one was Kajaqiao. The joys of adventure mountaineering are such that life can be a bit uncertain at times. With permit complexities in mind we chose not to delve deeper and decided to discuss the situation and make our decision on what to do after Jimi and Tenzing had returned to the valley and we had done a bit of reconnaissance.

Our acclimatisation explorations revealed more. And our suspicions gradually grew that Jimi was correct and that Tom's 'Matterhorn of the Nyainqentangla' was actually the 6,264-metre Manamcho. Kajaqiao had been hidden in Tom's photo but was actually higher, at 6,447 metres. We were spoilt for choice between two of the finest looking mountains I had ever seen – and both were unclimbed. We could hardly believe our luck.

It was considerably colder than we expected, even to the extent that the eggs the porters had caringly carried had frozen solid ... and were to stay that way for the duration. The amount of snow was also a concern. We awoke to perhaps twenty-five centimetres of new snow and by the time we were ready to attempt an ascent, a metre or so had fallen. This wouldn't have been so bad with plenty of freeze and thaw, but with the temperature continually below freezing the snow simply accumulated as deep powder. We had not brought snowshoes so travelling around was exhausting. Despite this, we managed to reach a glacier plateau at 5,300 metres from where we were able to get a better view of both mountains and glimpses of the numerous others that had reared their heads as we gained height. We knew for certain that every mountain in the area was unclimbed and, with the exception of Kajaqiao, had never even been attempted. We felt privileged to be in this exploratory mountaineers' paradise.

We had always agreed that we would climb in two completely separate teams, and after plenty of deliberation Chris and I decided to go for the mountain that appeared to be Kajaqiao while Adam and Phil would attempt Manamcho.

The deep snow and bad weather slowed us to the extent that it took two days of heavy panting to get to the foot of our chosen line. Crawling over large snow-covered boulders around the edge of a semi-frozen lake proved to be particularly trying. Clouds had prevented us from getting a good view from below but now, at 5,400 metres, we could see that the west face above us sported a series of left-trending couloirs leading up to the crest of the north-west ridge. The overall angle was not too steep, but it was hard to judge the difficulties.

Our first bivouac was a remarkably good find. Perched on the crest of a projecting rib of rounded slabs, I was surprised that the snow was deep enough for us to cut a very comfortable tent-sized platform. The day had been an exhausting one, largely because of the vast amounts of soft snow that had accumulated on the lower part of the face. Technical wading is not my favourite style of climbing. But we had made progress and as the evening sun bathed us we relaxed in the tent and soaked up the view. And increasingly impressive it was too. The skyline to the west was opening up with a myriad of tooth-like unclimbed peaks while down below we could see Adam and Phil, tiny dots moving almost imperceptibly across the huge snow plateau that borders the west side of Kajaqiao and Manamcho. They looked small and insignificant against such a majestic backdrop.

The ground the next day was steeper, which was good as it meant the deep snow that had plagued us would not stick. But sections that had looked easy transpired to be granite slabs covered with a dusting of powder, and so the day proceeded cautiously. There was nothing particularly difficult, it just all felt uncomfortably precarious and insecure. At one point I was reduced to calling a gibbering 'watch me' on ground that we would have moved together on if the snow had been nicely frozen. But this part of the world seemed not to be over-endowed with nicely frozen snow.

Nevertheless, by dint of judicious route finding the day progressed safely, if slowly, and ended with an open bivouac on the left bounding rib of the main couloir line.

'This is a crap bivouac ledge,' announced Chris emphatically.

We had put a lot of effort into the ledge, but I had to admit Chris's comment was disturbingly true. What had initially looked like a promising possibility for getting the tent up was ruined by an immovable block in just the wrong place. There had been nothing for it but to fashion a narrow nose-to-tail ledge out of a thin snow band. Fortunately, the clouds that had swirled around for much of the day lifted and a glorious evening had developed by the time we sat down to brew up and tuck into our evening meal of Chinese baby powder and fruit-flavoured sausages. This was one of two menu options, the other being noodles with a flavouring sachet. These were not meals we meant to choose but, after deciding to buy our food in the shops of Lhasa in order to avoid excess baggage costs, our Chinese and Tibetan had been exposed as woefully inadequate and we had failed to understand exactly what we were buying. On the bright side, both menu options were very light. And they were sufficiently unappetising for us to frequently fail to finish our meals, so the food was lasting longer than expected. That was handy, because all the grappling with powdery snow meant the climb was taking longer than planned. Despite the bland food and high discomfort level, we both snuggled down in good spirits, soaking up the remarkable view and looking forward to a good night's sleep.

It was some hours later that I awoke with a start. I had been wrapped cosily in the tent fabric but now it billowed around me like a huge sail and spindrift was blowing uncomfortably into my sleeping bag. Moving too hastily to rewrap myself resulted in my end of the ledge collapsing and me spending the rest of the night perched uncomfortably on the remains. Chris woke briefly to curse the spindrift that was being funnelled directly on to his head before settling down and snoring loudly. By daybreak I had given him several good kickings with no positive response. Over breakfast he did mention that he didn't feel he had had a good night's sleep, which was comforting in a perverse sort of way.

Time and time again I come back to thinking that willpower and determination are two key factors that dictate success or failure in the greater ranges. Now, with a bleak and windy dawn, both were tested to the max. The climbing was initially similar to the insecure scrabbling of the day before. Above, we could see that the angle increased slightly, which we thought might make things more difficult, and we made a hesitant and weary team as we debated the best line. But mountains are nothing if not surprising and as the angle increased the snow conditions improved. We were able to move faster and by the afternoon were enduring a biting crosswind on the ridge. The choice now was difficult. On the windward side the wind was fierce and the ground technical, whereas on the lee side the excitingly steep powder was potentially avalanche prone and exhausting to climb. We alternated uncomfortably, reaching an easing of the angle above a prominent ice cliff an hour or so before nightfall.

'Time for a snow hole,' Chris shouted above the now roaring wind.

Snow holes have always distressed me. Perhaps it is because I have never had the time to dig out a nice, spacious one, or perhaps I have latent claustrophobic tendencies which only surface when I am surrounded by snow. The last time I had spent the night in a snow hole was when Chris and I had climbed Mitre Ridge in the Cairngorm mountains of Scotland. Four of us had spent the day making the long walk in from Braemar and were keen to get an early start in order to complete our intended climb and walk out in time to get back to London for work the following day. Visibility was nil and the wind so ferocious that a night in a snow hole was deemed the best option. My recollection is that it took a couple of exhausting hours to dig one big enough and that it was impossible to prevent snow getting into my gloves and down my neck. The digging was a damp, exhausting and miserable experience. The night was just as bad. The hole had one entrance and the roof tapered towards the far end. The warmth of our bodies made it sweaty inside, the roof dripped and I was farthest from the entrance with the roof just above my nose. I tossed and turned, wondered what it would be like if it collapsed, and eventually turned round to a position where my head was lower than my feet but where the roof was at its thinnest. This markedly increased my physical discomfort level but did do a little to alleviate my concerns about being smothered. In the morning I exited at the earliest opportunity and was amazed to see two figures approaching through the mist. It turned out to be the well-known mountaineer Rick Allen and his wife,

Alison, who had walked in that morning. They must have had a very early start but looked much fresher than I felt. I pondered what a small world it is, wondered why we had endured such a night and vowed to avoid snow holes whenever possible.

But I digress. We were at over 6,000 metres on Kajaqiao and Chris suggested a snow hole with such enthusiasm that I found myself digging into the slope, even going so far as to lie on my stomach and hug vast quantities of snow against my body in my efforts to clear out what I had dug. Inevitably I sweated, snow ended up inside my clothing and I became damp, just like in the Cairngorms. The calm atmosphere in the hole was encouraging though. After an hour Chris pronounced it big enough, produced his sleeping bag, and settled down. I peered in. Length and width looked OK but the ceiling was flat and about fifty centimetres high. Hesitantly I decided to test my feelings before committing myself. It felt awful. A quick bit of experimenting revealed that even the weedy Fowler shoulders were broad enough to dislodge copious quantities of snow from the roof when I turned over. This snow tended to fall in my face and down my neck. I began to feel really cold and have flashbacks to that night in the Cairngorms.

'No way. Sorry, Chris. Can't do it.'

For me the last hour or so had been a complete waste of time and energy. I now had an urgent need to arrange something safe for myself or it was all going to go horribly wrong. Chris, who somehow appeared very comfortable in the snow hole, was very understanding and emerged to help. It was dark now and we struggled against the wind to erect the tent. After fifteen minutes we sat in the flapping fabric together. The hastily stamped-out snow platform was ludicrously uneven and the outer edge overhung the slope.

'Sorry, Mick. Can't sleep here.'

And so, as much as it might seem laughable, Chris ended up in the snow hole with me outside in the tent. Fortunately the wind dropped slightly, so at least my concerns about being blown away without Chris's weight lessened.

There was a volcano-shaped mound in the tent ledge and I curled myself around this in as comfortable a manner as possible. For a few hours all was well and I slumbered uneventfully until suddenly I was awoken by the awful sensation of my small volcano erupting and taking me into the air. All hell let loose. A heavy weight pushed me downwards and planted my face firmly into something hard and cold. This was a new experience. Fortunately I had a small torch around my neck, the light from which revealed that the tent was now upside down and the cold hard things against my face were the crossed poles that are normally at the top. My immediate urge was to escape from the icy prison, but there were a few things to be done before then.

I struggled to sit up and push the heavy snow off the tent. That done, the next priority was to take a photograph. It is important to record such situations so they can be fully savoured later. But with the snow partially removed I could feel the wind gusting wildly. Jumping out hurriedly would risk the whole show being blown away – not a good idea. I was sleeping in all my clothes, including my Gore-Tex shell, so all I had to do to prepare myself was put my boots on. It was while I was doing this that I came across Chris's inner boots. This was a worry. He must have only put his outer boots on when he helped me erect the tent. But where was he now? Clearly the tent had been hit by a snow slide. What had happened to the snow hole? Whatever his situation, he would certainly need his inner boots at some point.

Having located the entrance zip I emerged, stood on the tent fabric, cursed the situation that had ended up with us sleeping apart and scoured the slope above for signs of the hole. The narrow beam picked out nothing but windswept snow and snowslide debris. There was no sign of the substantial entrance we had dug the evening before. Securing things as best as I could I started to search the slope. I had only taken a few steps when a faint but urgent shout pierced the wind.

'Fowler! Fowler!'

And then, after contact had been renewed via a tiny hole: 'I'm stuck. Fucking well get me out of here.'

The weight of the snowslide had caused a section of the roof to collapse, leaving Chris disorientated and partially smothered. From outside it was easy to grab his extended hand and pull him to safety. But it turned my stomach to look in at the partially collapsed roof. In the confusion Chris had been unable to find his head torch and I could only imagine how terrifying it must have been milling around in the dark in such constricted circumstances, aware that there could be further collapses and not knowing in which direction the surface was closest.

Together we retrieved items from the remains of the cave, dug out the tent, put it the right way up and squeezed inside. It was good to be together again. Checking everything took time but, remarkably, nothing appeared to be lost or damaged.

It was light by now and I was uncomfortably aware that the hours had slipped past quickly. The wind seemed stronger than ever, we were in the cloud and it was one of those situations where a negative decision could be made all too easily. We decided to contemplate over a hot drink and half a chocolate bar. In the end two hot drinks were decreed to be worthwhile, after which we had gathered our wits such that we could recognise that there was nothing really wrong apart from the weather and some frayed nerves. There was no pressing reason to retreat. Like-minded thinking is crucial to Himalayan success. Onwards it would be.

The north (lee) side of the ridge was steeper than the day before and consisted of bottomless powder, a section of which had slipped down and caused us so much grief in the night. Fearful of a bigger avalanche, we were forced on to the rocky crest, which was technically challenging and outrageously windy. Nevertheless, clearings in the cloud revealed that we were making progress. Some maps show the height of Kajaqiao as 6,447 metres and others as 6,525 metres, but by mid-afternoon the 6,264-metre Manamcho was below us and we knew we couldn't be far off. It seems incredibly old fashioned now, but at about 6,300 metres my camera ran out of film. The wind and spindrift meant that changing the roll was out of the question. Fortunately, for the first time ever, I had packed a cheap, lightweight spare.

The final section to the base of the summit slope proved memorable. A shallow gully came up from the right and its far side was steep and technical mixed ground, blasted full force by wind-driven snow. It was with some relief that I completed this section and found a small but secure belay. Above me a snow overhang protected the summit slope. We were nearly there.

'Your nose!' I screamed.

Chris had arrived at the belay and what I could see of him looked mystified at my concern. Goggles fully covered the top part of his face and his balaclava the bottom part. In between, his nose was fully exposed and sported a white patch the size of a small coin. Being engrossed in the technical climbing in wild conditions he had no idea that his nose had started to freeze. I had never seen anything like it and could hardly believe it had happened so quickly. And with a fully exposed open slope above I feared that continuing could make matters worse. The thought of going down was even mentioned. But bodies are remarkable things: a further protective layer, a few deep breaths through the nose and a healthily pink glow returned. Lesson learned – these conditions demanded great respect.

Chris had an altimeter that read 6,500 metres as the slope started to ease off. The highest point was still five metres above us but we were aware of huge cornices overhanging the other side and had an uncomfortable feeling that we were pretty close to their breaking point. It was 6.30 p.m. The skies had cleared a little on the final section and I optimistically hoped for a glorious panoramic view. But the views east and north were obscured by the cornice and those to the north and west were hampered by inconvenient clouds. The wind still howled incessantly. My hopes for indulging in a photographic frenzy were dashed as I fought bravely to hold the camera still while taking shots which I knew were destined to be blurred and unremarkable. After not very long at all we retreated to our last ice screw and abseiled into the gathering gloom.

By nightfall it was snowing hard. The bergschrund at the foot of the slope overhung seriously at one point and looked to give protection from the waves of spindrift pouring from above. Somewhat nervously, we pitched the tent in the protected bowels of the crevasse, belayed ourselves well and did our best to settle down. But settling down can be tricky when heavy waves of snow keep roaring overhead. We managed a flavoured noodle meal and a cup of tea before it started to become clear that, much as it was not hitting the tent directly, the snow was building up against the outside wall and gradually pushing us into the crevasse. The thought of ending up hanging inside a tent inside a crevasse was not appealing. By the time we had finished our second cup of tea there was no doubt that the first of many digging-out sessions was necessary. That might sound straightforward but inevitably results in lots of snow entering the tent and, ultimately, the sleeping bags. I have been known to protect my sleeping bag by leaving it stuffed away while I survive the night wrapped in every available piece of clothing. Here though, the attraction of a warm bag was too much. It was really cold; the night before had been awful and we were on the way down with hopefully less severe nights to come. But by morning I had lost count of the number of tent-clearing exits that had been necessary and I couldn't deny that dampness prevailed and my bag was in a sorry state.

A full day of abseiling in heavy snow took us more or less down the line of our ascent. I never really like abseiling in the Himalaya – putting all that faith in a single abseil point time and time again – and so I breathed a sigh of relief when we were on walking territory again.

'Whooooahh!'

Suddenly I was riding a wave of snow. The slope had avalanched; I could hardly believe it. One minute I was waist deep in the snowslide debris at the foot of the face and the next minute the debris itself had avalanched. Mountains can be surprising places. The slope wasn't steep and the angle eased not far below but nevertheless the experience was memorably unpleasant. I found myself floating along amid waves of cotton wool snow and coming to a halt after a hundred metres or so with my legs held surprisingly firmly. Chris shouted that he would wait until I had extricated myself and got away from the fall line. It felt faintly ridiculous digging myself out while my partner watched from a distance, but all seemed calm; I wasn't hurt and as much as further slides were unlikely, it felt better to be safe than sorry.

That night was decidedly chilly. Our sleeping bags had suffered badly and the damp down had frozen into balls of ice. The bags were a shadow of their former warm and cosy selves. We were eight days out from base camp, tired, and the dropping snowline gave a clear indication that winter was approaching. We were both keen to get down as fast as possible.

The easiest way down was via a thirty-degree snow slope, but our snowslide incidents had reminded us of the dangers, so we chose to abseil straight down a steep couloir to the main glacier. The slope at the top was steep and open and we felt certain that it would avalanche with the slightest encouragement, thereby safely scouring the gully. It perhaps goes to emphasise how difficult avalanche forecasting can be that despite our best efforts, we were unable to start a slide and ended up abseiling down ground we judged much more likely to avalanche than the slopes we could have walked down. At least we felt relatively safe and secure attached to the abseil rope which we judged would hold us if waves of snow should rush past.

The wade to base camp was long and exhausting but by the end of day nine we had rejoined Adam and Phil. They had reached about 5,800 metres on Manamcho but had been stopped by the wild weather and low temperatures. Despite this, they were still smiling. Exciting mountains have that effect on people. And I was left with the germ of an idea. Even though I don't like to return to places I have already been to, the north ridge of Manamcho, the mountain Tom Nakamura had christened the 'Matterhorn of the Nyainqentangla', was beginning to give me quite an urge. As we bounced back along a direct route across the plateau to Lhasa I contemplated that east Tibet was probably the most culturally interesting area of spectacular unclimbed mountains I had ever visited.

I knew I would be doing my best to return.

Chapter 4

The Goody Gash – Scottish Sea Cliffs at Their Best

While my children were at school my climbing was generally restricted to one mountaineering trip per year and one evening per week. That wasn't really a problem as I managed to keep a reasonably high level of fitness and was keen to spend as much time as possible at home enjoying family life. But in 2006, I still had a surplus of leave saved from the aborted trip to Kajaqiao, and Steve Sustad persuaded me that a week rock climbing in Scotland was in order.

Stephen was my main Himalayan partner before he decided to give up visiting cold places and instead focus on trying to derive equally memorable experiences from activities ranging from horse riding to wild and remote rock climbing trips. Ever adventurous, he is not the sort of man who normally looks uneasy when surrounded by steep, intimidating stretches of rock. But on this particular occasion, despite having bounded gleefully down a dripping parallel-sided gully cleaving a 200-metre-high Scottish sea cliff, Steve was looking disconcerted.

'It's my glasses,' he explained as I slithered down the greasy rock and vegetation to within hearing distance. 'They fell off. I think they are down in that grass. But I can't see to see them.'

This was not a problem we used to experience in younger years. Additional challenges confront the exploratory climber as the years pass by and, after some deliberation, the rope came out and the sighted member of the party (glasses on) made a tricky traverse to spend some time precariously poking about in fulmar-vomit-splattered grass. If I was unsuccessful then 1,500 miles of driving and accumulated family credit points would have been wasted. But luck was with us; smelly but intact glasses were recovered and Steve was once again able to get a good look at our intended line.

'Shit! Not sure whether that's better or not!'

We were on the Isle of Hoy in the Orkney Islands off the north coast of Scotland. Hoy is best known for the Old Man, a fabulous 140-metre rock tower that graces the north-west coast of the island. We, however, were at the south end on a remote and infrequently visited headland called the Berry. The Berry is cleaved by a 200-metre-deep gully, the Gash, which it is possible to descend to sea level with only a short section requiring a rope. In the dark and dank depths the terrain is steep with unstable, slimy rocks, slippery grass and, perhaps most disconcertingly, enthusiastic fulmars. These birds are Britain's undisputed experts at projectile vomiting. Why some chose to live in such an inhospitable place was beyond us. That said, I suppose some humans tend to hang out in some pretty odd places. It's a funny old world.

The aim of our efforts was the 170-metre-high north wall of the Gash and in particular a dead-straight 100-metre crack which we had spotted piercing the upper section. Viewed from the top of the south side the line looked to be on clean, good rock and offered a compelling objective. But now we stood near the bottom, Steve's comments, said in jest as they were, looked to contain more than a grain of truth.

Over the years Steve and I have found that we derive enormous amounts of pleasure from weaving about on steep, inhospitable terrain trying to escape self-induced commitment. Occasionally we have tended to enhance the degree of commitment still further by choosing lines that necessitate a swim to get to the start. As a non-swimmer Steve finds such climbs particularly memorable. Here, much as it was disappointing that the access did not involve swimming, the swooping fulmars and crashing waves in the deep, narrow confines of the Gash were enough to heighten the atmosphere and guarantee an experience which would likely stand the test of time. And the tide was coming in, so there was always the possibility that we would be forced to abseil into the sea.

Eighty metres or so of challenging activity was necessary to reach the start of the crack line. The rock looked steep, green and slimy and it was not at all clear where to go. An easy ledge looked to provide an obvious traverse pitch to start. Thereafter it looked to be a choice of extremely loose and green corners or extremely steep and greasy walls. I led out along the ledge, Steve led the corners and then we were at a point where further walls seemed to bar the way forward.

It was while I was looking around wondering where to go that I noticed that our ropes had slipped off the belay ledge and were resting solidly on a fulmar, which was still sitting resolutely on its egg. Fulmars might be unpopular due to their propensity to puke on climbers but they are indeed remarkable birds. In human terms, this bird had the equivalent of perhaps 2,000 metres of rope resting on it. If I was a bird I would fly away rather than allow myself to be pinned down in this way, but fulmars are made of sterner stuff. Having defensively covered both ropes with putrid vomit this one moved on to pecking at them so violently that I felt more concern for our ropes than the bird.

But there were other things to worry about. A ten-metre green and greasy wall looked to guard access to a horizontal break. After several up and down efforts, I concluded that i) the wall was overhanging, ii) the rock was loose as well as green and greasy, and iii) my ability was going to be severely stretched. Most importantly though I concluded that the protection I had finally managed to place would probably hold a fall.

'Trying again.'

Steve gave me a withering look which I interpreted as a wish that I had got on with it ages ago.

I would never claim to be an elegant climber, but as the crack I'd just lunged a hand jam into began to open at the same time as a large foothold broke off, my movements were indeed less than fluid. Steve seemed to find this very amusing.

'Thought you were off there,' he cackled as I arrived at the relative security of the horizontal break.

Routine climbing led out over the void to our left and up to the foot of the crack which we had by now inexplicably christened the Goody Gash.

Close up the Goody Gash was very different to what we had expected. From a distance we had thought it would be a fist- or leg-jamming crack, tapering after fifty metres or so to a hand/finger crack. Now we found ourselves peering into a deep, wet chimney which led up through overhangs before disappearing out of sight. Precarious-looking blocks wedged in the main overhangs looked likely to add interest. Steve moved the belay to one side as I hesitantly made progress. The blocks were indeed interesting. Several very large ones were clearly supported solely by a crumbling ten-centimetre-diameter block. Fearing the consequences of trying to trundle them, I sneaked past as quietly and carefully as possible. Having taken a fine stance above the overhangs it soon became clear that Steve did not share my concern. Blocks rained down into the base of the Gash, 100 metres below, sending fulmars wheeling in surprise at such a noisy assault.

'Pat spends ages cleaning when he is seconding,' wafted up from below as Steve recalled the actions of the legendary Pat Littlejohn, his usual new-route partner nowadays. This was an approach I had not considered before. We explored the issue further as an enthusiastic Sustad reached the stance. Some first ascensionists abseil down and clean routes thoroughly before they start to climb. I had done that on occasion but, logistical considerations aside, it just didn't seem the right thing to do on the adventure-climbing scene. Knowing what was coming in advance would, we agreed, destroy the challenge – and it is a degree of uncertainty that gives such climbing its appeal. But what about the second cleaning new routes during the climb? Could that deprive future ascensionists of the challenge of dealing with loose rock and thereby reduce their level of enjoyment? We were high enough to just catch the sun now and sat there absorbing the rays while contemplating the complexities of the desirability or otherwise of new route cleaning.

'Bummer that I couldn't shift those big ones,' announced Steve, his disappointment clear.

Conversely I found myself speaking in favour of future climbers coming this way being able to experience such a key feature of the pitch.

Above us the crack cut through an overhang and then, from what we had seen from the opposite side of the Gash, narrowed for a long section leading to the foot of a deep final chimney. But, as we now knew, the scale was deceiving. Everything was so much bigger than it had appeared.

Being half American, Steve flowed easily up a desperate-looking offwidth section and plugged into what turned out to be a long stretch of fine jamming crack. The occasional piece of rock or clump of vegetation sailed past but, judging by the chirpy noises from above, all was well. Soon a shout indicated that I should stir from my sunny slumbers and exert.

The pitch was excellent and led to Steve, who was lying down soaking in the sun on a horizontal break, enthusing about the pleasures of Scottish sea cliffs and pointing gleefully up at the final section.

We were about thirty metres from the top, but what we had expected to be a wide chimney was in fact a gaping gash perhaps five metres wide. A crack up the back corner gave some hope, but it did not exactly look an easy finish.

Steve, though, appeared to have little concern other than to find the warmest, most comfortable spot on the break he was belayed in.

It is one of those wonderful feelings in climbing when a pitch turns out to be much easier than it looks – and this was one of those pitches. Awkward but well-protected climbing led to a large capping roof where, just as all looked bleak, a hidden, fulmar-free ledge allowed an easy exit to a short finishing groove. Elation!

I can't honestly say that the retrospective pleasure of such climbs is as enduring as that enjoyed after a big mountain climb, but the rarely visited nature of the cliffs, the challenges of getting there, the uncertainties inherent in the climbing and the sense of achievement on getting up a long-anticipated objective ticks a lot of the criteria boxes I have for greater-range objectives.

And it is amazing what great memories the smell of fulmar vomit can induce.

Chapter 5

Manamcho – I've Never Seen a White Man Before ...

I always knew that I would have to return to east Tibet if the opportunity arose. That image of unclimbed Manamcho lurked at the back of my mind, even while contemplating the retrospective pleasure derived from climbs like the Goody Gash. The opportunity came quicker than expected when I applied to the China Tibet Mountaineering Association and, with remarkably little delay and hassle, was given a permit to attempt Manamcho in 2007.

The October weather on Kajaqiao had been very cold and stormy, and as collapsing snow holes, turned-over tents and avalanches were to be avoided if possible, it was decided that we should try our luck in the spring. That way there was also less time for the Chinese to change their minds regarding the permits.

Three of the original four-person Kajaqiao team couldn't make it. Chris was back into his original pastime of enthusiastic cycling and was training for a non-stop road race from Paris to Brest and back. Adam Thomas had changed jobs and was in the Congo braving sweaty hostilities working for Médecins Sans Frontières, while Phil Amos suffered much internal anguish before finally deciding that commitments at home and at work were such that he couldn't make it. But finding a team was never going to be difficult. I would climb with Paul Ramsden and our companions would be Steve Burns and Ian Cartwright.

Paul and I had last climbed a big mountain together in 2002 on my first trip to China when we climbed Siguniang in the Sichuan province. A health and safety consultant based in Nottingham, Paul's job ranged from delivering dry lectures about health and safety legislation to considering whether or not the James Bond team were safe to drive expensive cars over frozen Icelandic lakes. His wife, Mary, ran the sales side of her family's wine merchant business. This helped to make the Ramsdens excellent dinner guests.

Paul and I had got to know each other, and Steve, through a small Nottingham-based group that irregularly met up to play together on Wednesday evenings. Steve is three months older than me, but as a retired, keen and dedicated action man he has managed to maintain a higher rock-climbing standard. His other activities have a delightful feel of eccentricity to them: embarrassing his family by stripping to his underpants to clean out his garden pond, bemusing winter dog walkers by engaging in solitary wild swimming in the River Trent and being spotted with a sheep in his car while only wearing underpants. The witty anecdotes arising from such behaviour make for fine banter and Paul and I were confident that he would be great company in Tibet.

Ian was a long-standing friend of Steve's and a member of the Williams Formula One support team. Based in Oxford, he had been on a couple of Himalayan trips with Steve, and Paul and I were confident that the four of us would gel together as a good team.

With the contacts and understanding of the system gained on the Kajaqiao trip, the process of negotiating the price of the trip was pleasingly straightforward. With weeks to spare permits were in place, arrangements finalised and excitement building.

Physically, access to Lhasa, once the 'Forbidden City', felt almost unethically easy. Having left England at 5 p.m. on a Friday and arrived in Lhasa at 4 p.m. on the Saturday, the tourist brochures advertising 'remote adventure holidays' to Lhasa seemed rather short of the mark. It was also difficult to imagine anything being forbidden there. Neon signs flashed bold advertisements, shiny boutiques lined the city centre streets and plastic palm trees threw shade on the entrance to the Lhasa Playboy Club. Mountaineers approved by the CTMA were put up at the Himalaya Hotel, an incongruously plush establishment once graced by Michael Palin and featuring lift carpets which stated which day of the week it was. I suppose this might have been useful if the staff remembered to change them. But they didn't.

This time the CTMA designated just one man, a softly spoken Tibetan called Dawa, to accompany us as our liaison officer. The vast majority of mountaineering trips authorised by the CTMA head in the direction of Everest, and Dawa, like Jimi and Tenzing on the Kajaqiao trip, was used to big expedition base camps with lots of people around and other liaison officers to socialise with. An expedition that consisted of four people and a base camp with a tarpaulin stretched over boulders for a kitchen was a completely alien concept to him. He had never been anywhere near the Nyainqentangla East range and clearly wondered what the hell he was going to do with himself while we were off climbing. At least Jimi and Tenzing had each other for company. We sympathised with Dawa's predicament.

Two jeeps and two drivers had been allocated to our expedition. One driver was young, speedy and fun; the other was middle-aged, stern and formal and wore pristine white driving gloves. I ended up in the vehicle with Pristine White Glove Man. Soon though we had a puncture and his refined demeanour slipped badly as he squirmed under the vehicle to access the spare. By the time he had fought with greasy wheel nuts his gloves never looked quite the same again. I pointed at them and expressed sympathy but it was clear his day had been ruined. He was really grumpy.

The well-surfaced road to Nagqu rises to over 5,000 metres and as we rose on to the Tibetan plateau some of the contrasting sights of modern China were plain to see. A huge army convoy passed us heading towards Lhasa, while in small, basic roadside settlements young men played snooker on outdoor tables against the backdrop of the remarkable engineering feat of the Beijing to Lhasa railway. The railway was all but complete when I passed in 2005 but the grand opening by Chinese President Hu Jintao had taken place on 1 July 2006 and now, in April 2007, we could marvel at trains crossing the wild expanse of the plateau on sections of track raised on pillars to keep the heat from the trains melting the permafrost.

Reaching 5,072 metres at the Tanggula Pass, it is the highest railway in the world and it had only been open for two months when, on 28 August 2006, the first passenger died on the train. Admittedly he was a seventy-five-year-old man travelling against doctor's orders, but the incident is a reminder of the very real risks of travel at altitude. The authorities have gone to great lengths to minimise these risks and passengers on the railway are not allowed on the highest section unless they have a passenger health registration card and have signed to confirm that they have read a high-altitude information leaflet. Paperwork aside, every passenger has their own oxygen supply and every train has a doctor.

Being aware of this, I was rather conscious of the fact that we had arrived in Lhasa from sea level and the next day were driving, with no oxygen, doctor or health registration card, at an altitude of about 5,000 metres. We commented flippantly on how good this was for acclimatisation while also being aware that, if anything should go wrong, it was not exactly easy to lose altitude quickly from the plateau.

Nagqu was as bleak, windswept and miserable as I remembered. We stayed at a different hotel to the one from the Kajaqiao trip. This one seemed to be frequented mainly by poorly looking travelling officials suffering badly from the altitude, and so it was surprising to find that every room came with packets of complimentary condoms. Mind you, judging by the covering of dust on the packets, they saw little use.

Although the accommodation was quite plush, the level of personal service was truly appalling. In the restaurant Dawa did his best to attract attention but the staff completely ignored him.

'They just don't care,' he announced, exasperation evident in his voice.

That did seem to be the case. The level of rudeness really was remarkable. Staff would turn their heads towards us, clearly recognise that Dawa was asking for service and then turn back to their conversations without even acknowledging that he existed. It happened time and time again until we eventually gave up and went to a shop across the road to buy snacks to keep us going.

Two days out from Lhasa our jeeps drove under the 'Welcome to Lhari' sign and pulled to a halt on the vividly remembered concrete dual carriageway. Vehicles were still driving in both directions on both sides of the road. Again, we were put up in a different hotel to my previous visit. This one had a secure-looking car park, so I felt able to enjoy a night inside rather than adopt the role of a rather poorly prepared vehicle guard. The hotel occupied rooms above a row of shops and was noteworthy for having yak dung stoves in the bedrooms and no toilet facilities whatsoever.

Like Jimi and Tenzing eighteen months earlier, Dawa suggested that it might be best if we didn't draw unnecessary attention to ourselves, so we stayed in the hotel and peered out of the window across the dual carriageway. It was twilight, the mist was down and the snow flew horizontally. A yak and a dog faced up to each other over the contents of a bin while two old Tibetan ladies swept the concrete gutter with twig brushes. We stayed concealed, marvelling at the bleak outlook, until Dawa reappeared triumphantly with the permits. He was looking distinctly more relaxed.

'We can leave first thing tomorrow!' he announced, a beaming smile spreading broadly across his face. Pleased, but still not acclimatised to Lhari's altitude of 4,500 metres, we spent the night clutching our heads and occasionally urinating into a plastic bowl. In the morning, in common with other guests, we emptied the contents of the bowl out the back windows, thereby adding to the frozen urine mountains littering the car park. Fortunately none of us had to enquire about the usual procedure should a crap be needed.

Reaching Tatse, this time without a letter of instruction from the local police chief, the locals took some persuading to act as porters. The first people we asked turned out to be builders from Shigatse, about three days' drive away. They were here, we were told, because the local people were so rich they couldn't be bothered to build their own houses and paid others to do the work for them.

'They are too rich,' moaned Dawa. 'Thousands of yuan in the bank.'

We had paid an all-in price to the CTMA and so were able to sit back and relax in an appropriately stress-free manner while Dawa persevered with negotiations. Eventually, albeit looking a little glum, he signalled success and the focus turned to settling in for the night.

With Dawa on his own I wondered where he was expecting to stay while we were climbing. Tenzing and Jimi had had each other and plenty of crates of beer to while away the time. Not only was Dawa alone, he appeared to have little personal equipment. I never saw a tent, food or stove. At length I asked the inevitable question while keeping my fingers crossed that there hadn't been some terrible misunderstanding.

'Where will you be staying?' I enquired.

'I think perhaps the monastery,' he answered, waving vaguely in its general direction.

The monastery stood proudly on a rocky bluff overlooking Tatse and we walked up to it together. On the way we passed a water-driven prayer wheel shrouded in ice. There only appeared to be one monk in residence and, although they had not previously met, he greeted Dawa like an old friend. I could only guess that the culture of just turning up and staying was perfectly acceptable – no advance booking necessary. Steve and Ian were off exploring, but Paul and I were invited in for Tibetan tea. Paul paled. The Ramsden taste buds seem generally resilient but Tibetan tea is an acquired taste. A mix of yak milk, butter, salt and tea, it doesn't really taste like Western tea at all.

Jimmy Chin, an experienced American explorer, described it as 'having a smell like the inside of a cheese cave but with a hint of yak fur; sort of like wet dog but a bit more earthy with undertones of barn.' Smell and taste aside, the offer of tea is more than just a casual welcome – it is offered as a customary greeting and it risks deep offence to not empty the drinking bowl and show appreciation. But emptying the bowl was difficult as our host took every opportunity to refill it, even after the smallest sip. Poor Paul. The next hour was clearly excruciating for him.

The end result appeared to be no offence taken and a good outcome for Dawa.

'I can stay here for the duration,' he told us happily.

A good relationship with those at the monastery was good for us too. It was the first time that either of us had been in a small, remote monastery and we were keen to understand more about how it all worked. Back in the UK I had read that the time before and during the Cultural Revolution had been tough for the Tibetan monasteries, with reported numbers reducing from around 6,000 to fewer than ten. We gathered that even this remote place had been caught up in the mayhem and only in relatively recent times had draconian rules been eased and authority granted to increase the size of the monastery. The monk gave us a brief tour before it was somehow decided that it was necessary for us to be blessed before we set foot on the mountain. This involved sitting cross-legged for a very long time in the ornate surroundings of the inner sanctum. I never did quite grasp the detail of what was going on and after much chanting one of my legs had very much fallen asleep, but we were classed as ready for action.

Since my last visit, a footbridge had been built across the Yi'ong Tsangpo river exactly where we needed one, saving us from any running along behind bike-driving porters. It also meant the walk to base camp was even shorter and we found intermittent tracks through the low bushes and gained height quickly. There was far less snow plastering the mountains than on our previous trip, but, conversely, there was more snow around our base camp site and the walled kitchen shelter we had caringly constructed eighteen months earlier was choked with winter ice. Knowing that there was no wood anywhere near base camp we had carried up a couple of poles to act as an upright and a ridge. A plastic sheet draped over these made it vaguely weatherproof and the discovery of a pleasingly flat stone to act as a table made it feel almost homely. Moving this stone to the kitchen shelter seriously aggravated Paul's long-standing back problem, but as our chef and kitchen guru he was well pleased with the end result.

There were only seven bags carried up by the porters, so in theory it should have been an easy job to sort ourselves out.

'Anyone seen the bag of vegetarian food?'

Ian is a strict man in this respect and had carefully overseen food purchasing in Lhasa to ensure that he was well catered for. However, it appeared that his carefully bagged purchases had somehow disappeared, with the result that he could either return to Tatse and search for them or resign himself to losing more weight than expected. He chose the latter.

After the soft snow of 2005 we had decided to bring snowshoes. This made it more difficult to be within our twenty-kilogram baggage allowances and was a new experience for me. My competence level in using the things seemed on a par with my skiing ability and I kept on placing one snowshoe on the other and tripping over. Paul found this very amusing. I soon took them off in disgust, but again to Paul's amusement, had to concede that his acceleration into the distance was at least partially due to his using the things.

The lake that Chris and I had traversed with so much difficulty was frozen after the cold of winter. It looked dodgy to me but I deferred to Paul's professional judgement.

'Safe as long as you don't weigh a huge amount and go fast enough to create an ice wave.'

I weigh seventy kilograms and understood from Paul that it takes speeds in excess of twenty-five kilometres per hour to create a dangerous ice wave. All in all I felt pretty safe, particularly as Paul, who is heavier than me, had offered to go first. No waves or cracking occurred and the travel was blissfully easy compared to crawling over big snow-covered rocks round the edge.

It took two days to reach the head of the icefall above our base camp. Later, when acclimatised, it would take three and a half hours. It was here that our path diverged from the line followed to Kajaqiao in 2005. Then, Chris and I had climbed straight up above the icefall to the base of Kajaqiao's west face. This time our route lay across a snow plateau to the foot of Manamcho. In 2005, crossing this had taken Adam and Phil a whole day of wading. This time, acclimatised and with snowshoes, half a day was ample – even with me regularly tripping and falling over. Paul celebrated by stretching to do up his boots and once again aggravated his back. Thereafter the Ramsden body moved in a carefully robotic manner, frightening me occasionally with disturbing talk about the immobilising effect of previous seizures.

Our plan was to try and climb the north ridge, which had caught my eye from Kajaqiao and looked to be a wonderful and safe climb. But it rapidly became clear that climbing conditions were not good. The snow on one side of the ridge was sugary and soft while on the other it was powdery and hopeless for climbing. Some pondering ensued. The weather was not looking ideal, Paul's back was giving him grief and the conditions made us wary of obvious difficulties high on the ridge. After a full day of exploratory dithering we ended up back where we had started, having decided to give the north-west ridge a go instead. This was the line that Adam and Phil had tried in 2005.

In cloudy weather the next day we crossed a tricky bergschrund, climbed a fifty-five-degree ice slope and moved up steep mixed ground to gain Adam and Phil's high point. It was an exposed spot, and being caught there by challenging weather had prompted their retreat. Paul and I could not help but notice that the wind was rising and black clouds were approaching fast. Finding a flat knoll on the ridge, we decided to pitch our little tent and hide from the gusting snow while we still could.

To begin with all was well. We brewed contentedly, discussed the pros and cons of which food goes down best at altitude and relaxed. Having snuggled cosily into my sleeping bag I looked forward to a good night's sleep. It was not to be. By about 2 a.m. the wind was such that concerns other than sleep were beginning to surface.

'Perhaps it's worth you climbing on top of me?'

Paul had never made such a suggestion before. The problem was the wind. Our little flat knoll was a lovely camping spot, but very exposed with overhangs beneath us on the lee side. Our belays were five metres in front of the tent – if it were blown off the ridge we would suffer a painful pendulum into a jagged, rocky groove. Not a pleasant thought. We had considered the risks when pitching the tent but had tempted fate, optimistically relishing the prospect of a good night's sleep on a flat spot. We were even confident enough to insert the tent's little cross pole, presumably designed to increase ventilation but now creating a small sail. It was impossible to remove the pole without getting out of the tent and, being as the tent was clearly in danger of blowing away, the thought of removing one person's weight, albeit temporarily, was not appealing.

'Perhaps it will release the pressure if we open the ventilation flaps,'

I wondered out loud, noting that the two flaps were very close to each other at the top of the tent. Without further ado I unzipped them. Instead of the wind blowing straight through and reducing the pressure, my efforts unleashed a powerful blast of spindrift which immediately covered everything with a film of snow.

'Nice one,' commented Paul. I gave up the idea and settled back down on top of him.

The night was memorable but passed safely. Morning dawned drearily. The wind had dropped, but a peek outside suggested that a lot of snow had fallen. Mind you, within reason, conditions mattered little. The basic ethos we operate by is that we carry on unless there is an exceptionally good reason to turn back. And in fact the wind-blasted, snow-covered granite provided conditions very similar to those regularly experienced in the Cairngorms back home. Avalanches were not a threat, and with no pressing reason to retreat we focused on the ground ahead.

Gaining height gradually, we moved up the ridge. Difficulties consisted of short and steep rock steps that were difficult to avoid. One step was noticeably harder than the rest and it was my lead. To the horror of any ethical purists I was soon dangling forlornly from a skyhook – a small metal hook designed for aid climbing – which I find useful in situations where my strength runs out or my fingers need warming. Unfortunately I had caught my finger between the hook and the rock and bright red drops of blood dripped down to land near a bemused-looking Paul.

'I'll leave my rucksack here,' I grunted.

Soon I was grappling with the overhang above, searching desperately for the right nut to slot in a perfect tapering crack.

'Where's all the gear?' I cursed at my empty harness.

A calm voice from below had the answer. 'It's hanging from your rucksack gear loops ... '

It wasn't going very well. It is fortunate that greater experience allows one to get less flustered when incompetence occurs.

By the end of our third day above the bergschrund, our sixth from base camp, we were approaching the steep summit towers which looked likely to give the technical crux of the route. Our plan had been to join the north ridge at the apex of the north face and follow it to the summit while soaking up a splendid panoramic view – a sea of unclimbed and unexplored peaks. This now seemed an unlikely finale. Not only was visibility non-existent but the way ahead looked difficult. Ever optimistic, we sat and waited for a clearing in the cloud before finally giving up and descending half a pitch to try and bypass some steep walls via an exposed ledge line below the crest.

It was while descending that Paul made the discovery that some of the new snow hereabouts was overlaying smooth slabs, and prone to slide away. A ten-metre rope-testing slide added interest before we settled down for the night on a reasonable nose-to-tail ledge with me wrapped in the yellow tent fabric and Paul in a bright red bivouac sack. Somehow his sack was considerably smaller than his fully lofted sleeping bag, with the result that he looked like a well-inflated balloon. The wind was still blowing hard, but at least without the tent up I didn't have to worry about him asking me to climb on top of him.

Paul fidgeted uncomfortably in the constricted surroundings of his bivouac sack while I enjoyed the surplus fabric of the tent and started to snooze happily. Some time later I awoke, wondering what it could be that was pinning me down to the ledge. Surely Paul hadn't thought I was in danger of being blown away? I peered out cautiously to an eye-opening discovery. The wind had dropped but at least two feet of snow had fallen without waking me. Our ledge was banked out, I was almost buried and, of most concern, the temperature had risen to the extent that condensation from my breath was making the head area of my sleeping bag disturbingly damp. It might sound strange, but low temperatures often make for the most comfortable nights.

This change in temperature was remarkable considering that at base camp, about 1,400 metres below, night-time temperatures had been in the region of −10 °C. We could but wait and see whether the changes in temperature and wind speed would herald a further change in the weather. Perhaps we would have a glorious, clear summit day after all?

By daybreak the weather had indeed changed ... for the worse. The howling wind had returned and all but cleared our ledge of new snow; the sky was slate grey and visibility perhaps ten metres. All indications were that conditions were worsening. Paul greeted the day with a customary blunt Yorkshireman's assessment of the situation.

'One of the worst nights I've ever had. My back hurts, weather's crap, view's crap. Let's get up and get out of here.'

I had to agree. We felt that the top couldn't be much more than seventy metres above us but the way ahead looked hard and conditions were truly wild. Ice crystals massaged our faces in a manner that may have improved our complexions but was not conducive to pleasant climbing. The whole scene was reminiscent of a wild winter day in Scotland, with extra remoteness thrown in for added interest.

I led a pitch, after which Paul's challenge was to find a way up what appeared to be the final tower. Being unable to see much he first ended up at a cul-de-sac beneath a blank wall. Things looked bleak before he found a tricky mixed groove leading to an easing of the angle. A wildly windy ten metres then led to a sudden knife-edge upon which appeared to be the highest point. We dutifully shook hands.

It was as we prepared for the ritual of summit photos that a brief clearing revealed the uncomfortable possibility that a corniced edge about forty metres away might be slightly higher.

'Shit.'

We looked at each other miserably while knowing exactly what we had to do.

The traverse was not difficult but the view from our new 'summit' was equally non-existent. Our summit photos could have been taken on any cold, snowy, misty and windswept spot in the world. And, looking back, it was debateable which summit was the higher one. And yet, somewhere out there in the mist, we sensed some of the finest unexplored peaks anywhere.

We abseiled into the maelstrom and began our descent. At one particularly wild point not far above the bergschrund I could just make out Paul, who had abseiled first, punching the smooth ice slope in frustration. I couldn't work out what was going on and it was only later that he explained that his back problem was preventing him being able to kick the slope firmly enough to get the front points of his crampons to bite. I hadn't registered that he was having such difficulty and felt rather embarrassed at not showing much appreciation or concern for what was clearly a serious problem.

By the time we were back on the plateau at least three feet of snow had fallen, but the skies had cleared and the weather was perfect. Sod's law had operated with perfect precision; the only really bad weather of the trip had coincided exactly with our climb.

Meanwhile Steve and Ian had sensibly waited out the weather and as we finally arrived at base camp they were just about to leave to attempt the first ascent of a peak our map showed as 5,935 metres, on the west side of the Manamcho/Kajaqiao plateau.

As the jeeps were not due to return for a few days, Paul and I had time to overcome any post-climb lethargy and spring into exploration mode. Having descended to Tatse and, for reasons not clear to me, been blessed again at the monastery, we set about hiring a jeep to have a look at the Manam valley, which leaves the main Yi'ong Tsangpo valley between Lhari and Tatse and runs up to the west side of Manamcho, presumably giving the peak its name.

We were immediately struck by its beauty. There were sparkling streams, hillsides dotted with grazing yaks and small but scenic local villages, all with a fabulous mountain backdrop. We were lucky that our jeep driver came from the valley, knew everyone and was happy to introduce us. We enjoyed tea with the local headman who stared at us intently before telling us that he had never seen white-skinned men before, except on his satellite television. He fed us dried strips of yak and said he would welcome us back to climb 'his' mountains. It felt a real privilege to be entertained in his house and to be invited back to climb in this fantastic area.

At the last house, well beyond the roadhead, we were invited in and the whole extended family gathered to marvel at the white-skinned men who had just climbed the mountain that dominated their valley. The thought that it might be possible to reach the summit had clearly never crossed their minds and they fired non-stop questions at us about the detail of our ascent. The photographs we showed them on our new digital camera screens were a source of great fascination. Word spread quickly and soon the cosy room was packed with people sitting around a huge yak-dung-burning stove with a long horizontal flue that acted as a radiator. Around us, most of the wall space was covered with intricate wall hangings and the main ceiling beam was colourfully painted. Their welcome was a joy to experience and soon extended to treating us to a fine stew, washed down with a never-ending supply of Tibetan tea. Naturally I felt obliged to alert our hosts whenever I thought Mr Ramsden's bowl was getting a bit low.

The headman told us that higher up there were two lakes: the Silli lakes. Local mythology has it that they are joined deep down below the surface. Our goal for the day became to visit the smaller, higher lake, and we left the final house with full stomachs and a relaxed stroll in mind.

We were unprepared for the magnificent view that greeted us as we crested the slope and could fully take in the beauty of the place. The lake itself was a glimmering white sheet of ice and all around it were spectacular mountains over 6,000 metres. None had ever been attempted and as far as we knew we were the first non-local people to set eyes on them. It was a mountaineer's and explorer's paradise. We walked slowly round the lake just soaking it all in.

Back down in Tatse we met Steve and Ian. Ian was distinctly slim, having somehow survived a couple of weeks without any vegetarian food, but they had been successful on their climb. They reported that the ascent had not been incredibly difficult and that the good weather had given them panoramic views of even more spectacular unclimbed peaks. Both were smiling in the way that suggested a pretty wonderful time had been had by all.

'What are the police doing here?' asked Paul, to no one in particular.

We had been having a final explore of the monastery and, sure enough, a glance down to the road showed two police jeeps parked next to the vehicles that had arrived to take us back to Lhasa. Dawa was gesticulating and clearly being called upon to explain something. A little discretion looked to be required and we decided it might be best to remain out of sight. Later he explained that the police had received reports of two unknown vehicles passing through Lhari and had given chase to check that all was in order. As it happened all was well and we had all the right permits, but the incident served as a reminder that visitors to this part of the world are treated with a marked degree of suspicion. Dawa had also purchased a huge, intricately carved chest of drawers which took up most of the space in one of the vehicles and about which he seemed very relieved to have had accepted as a police-approved acquisition.

Back in Lhari there was no longer any need to keep a low profile and we had some time to explore. Our popping into a shop to get some nibbles for the journey seemed to coincide with the end of the school day. Almost immediately crowds of children appeared, hemming us in and taking great delight in marvelling at the unwashed white-skinned men. We were clearly a major attraction and the sea of inquisitive, smiling faces stretched out across the pavement where, for some odd reason, nearly all the drain covers were missing. The twenty-foot-deep holes were not to be trifled with and it was with some relief that no accidents occurred and we all ended up safely back in the jeeps.

We had different drivers for the return journey and it soon became clear that although they were keen to return to Lhasa by the most direct route, neither of them had travelled this way before. From Lhari we travelled generally westwards on reasonable tracks until a fork prompted a halt and much debate. At length Dawa turned to me.

'They are asking which way you think is best.'

It became clear that they had no idea and were more prepared to trust my guess rather than their own. It is well reported that the Chinese do not like to lose face or be proved to be wrong. At least one of our drivers appeared to be Chinese so maybe it was the potential loss of face that was the root cause of the difficulty. Whatever it was it felt slightly bizarre that it was down to me to make what could be a fairly crucial decision. But it was difficult to know what to say. The plateau is pretty flat with few distinguishing features. I had travelled across it once in my life as a back-seat passenger eighteen months earlier. I stared meaningfully at the junction.

'I think perhaps to the left.'

And off we went with both drivers apparently very happy.

'Your fault if we run out of petrol in the middle of nowhere,' commented Paul.

It was already proving to be a pleasingly memorable holiday. What lay in store now could only be guessed at. A compass was produced from one of the bags (the only time it was used on the entire trip) showing that we were at least heading in roughly the right direction. In the far distance a range of hills blocked the way, but we would worry about that later.

After an hour or two we arrived at a small settlement of perhaps a hundred people. Most of the buildings were rudimentary and the place was remarkably filthy, with open sewage flowing freely. One building stood out from the others; it gave the appearance of a cube of blue glass panels and was the only two-storey structure in the village. A fine selection of particularly snotty and scruffy children rushed out to greet us.

'The school,' explained Dawa, having spoken with two young Han Chinese ladies who we were told had been incentivised to teach at this remote and inhospitable spot. Presumably they came from one of the big cities in China. Quite what they made of this place we could hardly imagine.

'I'd need a bloody big incentive to live here,' commented Steve.

'They say Lhasa is this way,' said Dawa beaming happily.

'Told you so.' I vainly sought appreciation of my Tibetan plateau route-finding skills.

Soon we were rising into the hills and Ian's altimeter was registering over 5,300 metres. Slushy snow lay on the ground and the track was getting increasingly icy. I was increasingly impressed by our vehicle and driver, but Dawa was beginning to express doubt about the direction-giving skills of those we had spoken to.

'Perhaps it's a bit like India,' I proffered helpfully. 'If you phrase the question such that the answer can be "yes" then that will be the answer you will get.'

Dawa looked concerned. His ornate chest of drawers was bouncing badly and the shock-absorbing bubble wrap was clearly close to its limit. Higher and higher the track rose until at last it crested a col and up above us we could see a huge opencast mine. The temperature was perhaps –10 °C, the wind was blowing and it looked a distinctly less comfortable place to work than a tax office.

We pulled over and got out to soak in our surroundings. This definitely wasn't the way we had come on my previous visit. But luck was with us. Looking down the far side we could just make out what looked like a better road with a couple of vehicles on it. Happiness flowed over our little party. There was some more difficult ground to cover but the road continued down the other side and we were back in Lhasa that night.

Two days later we were flying from Lhasa to Chengdu, looking down at the unclimbed mountain wilderness of east Tibet. Little did I know at the time that trouble would flare up in Tibet and I might never be able to return to the Nyainqentangla East range.

Chapter 6

Nottingham Castle 1 – Challenges Close to the Office

As Paul lived in Nottingham and I worked there, it was convenient for us to meet in my lunch break every now and then. Our favourite venue was Ye Olde Trip to Jerusalem, a watering hole apparently dating back to 1189 and reputedly the oldest inn in England. The fine beer and ambience was very pleasant, but the feature that attracted us was that the pub is built into the sandstone cliffs that support Nottingham castle. And I mean literally built into the cliff – several of the bars are caves hacked out of the soft rock and one has a desperate-looking and probably unclimbed jamming crack across the ceiling.

Drinking here, it was perhaps inevitable that the conversation should drift towards the nearby climbing potential. After all, the cliffs into which the bars are cut and on which the castle stands are very steep and about forty metres high. In fact, these cliffs have a fine mountaineering pedigree. After the first ascent of the South-West Face of Everest in 1975, Doug Scott – being a Nottingham man – was duly honoured by being granted the freedom of the city. After some clarification this honour was acknowledged to extend to freedom to climb on the 'no climbing allowed' cliffs beneath the castle, and so Doug was able to make the first ascent of many fine lines on these steep cliffs. His climbs attracted considerable local press coverage which his father kept and which Doug still has today.

But, Doug moved on, climbing became frowned upon, vegetation and pigeons prospered, and the cliffs slumbered in vegetated obscurity. Then, on Christmas Day 1996, water pressure from a burst pipe caused the retaining wall of the castle terrace to fail, and a large section collapsed.

There had been such falls before, notably in 1969 when a substantial rock buttress collapsed on to the road. To hold everything together, a patchwork of concrete structures and steel bands had been put in place. This time, the damage was close to the main castle wall and the cause of much consternation. There was much dither and debate between the environmentalists – who 'delight in a greening of the rock by natural tree growth' – and the geologically minded, who 'prefer the boldness of bare rock'. The bare-rock lobby prevailed and Paul and I closely monitored progress of a remarkably thorough deforestation programme.

To our amazement the vegetation clearing and renovation work lasted nearly ten years, and, by the time of our post-Manamcho lunchtime meetings, had revealed a series of fine crack lines in glorious golden sandstone that reminded me of my early days on the outcrops south of London. It also resulted in a new terrace; a steel frame inside one of the man-made caves that riddle the rock, and areas where the surface was reinforced with fibreglass were embedded with sand grains for a natural-looking finish. A further important result of the stabilisation programme was the appearance of a flake that gave the most prominent line on the newly cleaned area of rock. The contractors presumably felt the flake was unstable and, rather than try to remove it, had effectively pinned it to the cliff with a large number of steel bars which now spanned the crack and would clearly offer excellent protection.

At long last the contractors finished their work. With the rock clear of vegetation, workmen and – presumably temporarily – pigeons, this could be a chance of a lifetime. The time had come.

Being a city-centre location, a bit of discretion was required. A 5.30 a.m. Sunday start meant no one was around to pay any interest as I fought my way through nettles to the start of the first pitch. It soon became clear that the contractors had cleared off all the loose rock but had not considered clearing dust and debris from the holds. In the damp morning air the dust had congealed into a slippery mud and the climbing felt difficult and insecure. The first reinforcement bar was a fair way up and the possibility of failure was great as I carefully inched higher and higher until finally I could place a metal wedge in the crack and clip it into the rope to protect myself. A few feet higher I was able to thread a sling round the first bar and stand on it to bring up Paul. From here the crack steepened and became more difficult, but also safer as there were more reinforcement bars. A fine lead by Paul saw us established beneath overhangs, which I avoided with a traverse and a bit of thin slab climbing leading up to the newly constructed smooth walls supporting the castle balcony. Initial concern about a lack of belays was resolved when I discovered that the drainage holes in the wall were just the right size for our camming devices. The sun was shining by now and it was feeling a fine and memorable way to start the day.

I had never visited the castle grounds before and had not realised that they were so extensive and so difficult to escape from. We wandered around uncertainly. The main gate was a huge cast-iron affair that was firmly locked, and everywhere we looked the grounds were surrounded by vertical walls that dropped on to the streets of Nottingham. Eventually an abseil from a convenient tree branch made for a landing next to a statue of Robin Hood. By now early risers were about but a nonchalant stroll with all our clanking equipment attracted no attention. Back at the car we contemplated what great outings might be had so close to home.

I dare say the private nature of the climbing and the fragile rock dissuades most climbers. It perhaps says a lot that Paul and I both consider the unusual nature of these little adventures as being right up there among our most memorable exploits. I suppose it adds up to a similar approach to climbing more generally: seek out something special, accept the challenge on offer, try your best and keep climbing unless there is an exceptionally good reason to stop.

Chapter 7

Vasuki Parbat – The Judgement Game

BANG!

Paul and I were snoozing gently while retreating from Vasuki Parbat in the Indian Himalaya when our hanging stove disintegrated in front of us. The lid shot across the tent, the windshield buckled and the remains swung violently from side to side; a commotion of metallic noise filled the tent. It was not the best way to be roused from one's slumbers.

'What the **** was that?'

It did not take long to see the gaping hole in the tent fabric and find the small rock that had been the cause of the disturbance. We had failed on our climb and the mountain was clearly intent on helping us on our way.

The Chinese had refused my permit application. 'Beijing says no,' the email had said. Efforts to identify the decision maker in faceless 'Beijing' drew a blank and I was reduced to looking for an alternative objective. Luckily, about five years earlier Harish Kapadia, a wonderful, extra-helpful chap and acknowledged expert on everything to do with the Indian Himalaya, had sent me a disturbing CD entitled 'Objectives for Mick'. It contained twenty or so photos he thought I might find 'interesting'. One in particular caught my attention. It was an eye-catching image of a steep face with a single buttress-line cleaving the centre. For some years the image lurked in my subconscious and it readily came to the fore now. Paul was keen, and so, as 2007 became 2008, Harish's image found its way on to my screen saver where it provided a regular reminder for me to get on with organising a post-monsoon attempt.

It was nine years since my last trip to India and I had a niggling concern that the country's much vaunted economic growth might have diluted the aspects of India that I found so attractive. I need not have feared. The Indian boardrooms might be stashed full of cash but adhesive beard salesmen still paraded outside Delhi's Red Fort, the roads were still clogged with every method of transport imaginable, people still slept in the most remarkable places and there was still a vibrant feeling of continuous activity and interest.

Much as the civil servant in me had previously managed to derive a degree of satisfaction from overcoming Indian bureaucratic challenges, I was – perhaps naively – hoping that surging economic activity would have brought about a reduction in the amount of red tape. I was soon to conclude that it had certainly not done so regarding mountaineering in the recently created state of Uttarakhand, and in particular in the Gangotri region where Vasuki Parbat is situated. Once this was thought of as a bureaucratically straightforward area and it was possible to climb on a set of permits one could organise from one's home country. Now, in addition to the usual permits from the authorities in Delhi, it was necessary to obtain permits from the local government and the forestry commission.

Brejish, our liaison officer, was a Brahmin, traditionally the highest caste in India's still-influential caste system. He enjoyed an endearing personality along with a persuasive aura of confident authority and proved to be a star at overcoming the numerous difficulties that potentially blocked our way. Banker's drafts were forced through at short notice, obstructive officials expertly overcome and rip-off merchants curtly dismissed. It was a credit to his efficiency that two days after leaving Delhi we were approaching the road-head at Gangotri. But at this point it became clear that Brejish's efficiency had included fastidiously memorising the small print of his responsibilities as a liaison officer. 'Sorry,' he announced. 'You can't take a photograph here.'

I looked at him mystified. We had stopped by a spectacular gorge spanned by an equally spectacular bridge a few miles short of Gangotri town. Rumour had it that Pat Littlejohn – who I had climbed Tawoche with in Nepal back in 1995 – had done some top-quality rock climbs here. It certainly looked an excellent spot for such activity and the bridge gave an excellent backdrop.

'Sorry,' repeated Brijesh. 'I will be in trouble if I allow the bridge to be in a photograph.'

'But you can probably see it just as clearly on Google Earth … ' I tailed off, deciding that picking an unnecessary fight with the liaison officer was not a great idea. We continued in a rather more hesitant photographic manner to the town of Gangotri.

Gangotri is one of those curious places where the population is almost entirely transient. Situated at an altitude of 3,100 metres on the banks of the Bhagirathi River (which joins the Alaknanda to become the Ganges a few hours downstream), it is the seat of the goddess Ganga and one of four sites on the much revered Chota Char Dham pilgrimage circuit. When we arrived it was packed with pilgrims, many of whom appeared to be queuing at the large number of water bottle shops that dominated the entrance to the town. But these were not what you might call normal water bottles. Hanging like ripe fruit outside the shops they came in every shape and size imaginable. I wondered for a moment whether the high level of interest might have something to do with preparations for the nineteen-kilometre walk from here to Gomukh, the snout of the Gangotri Glacier.

'Very popular,' announced Brejish, noting me taking photographs of a shop with a particularly large collection.

I looked slightly blank.

'Afterwards I will be taking water home for the family.'

It dawned on me that this was nothing to do with ensuring good hydration for the trek. It was all to do with collecting sediment-laden holy water and presenting it as a gift for drinking at a later date. The most pure – and most sediment-laden – water is said to be taken from the source itself, and later I was to witness the immense gratitude of Brijesh's parents when he presented them with a bottle of the gritty grey liquid.

An hour's walk beyond Gangotri, we noticed a smart official with a side parting and a fetching cardigan sat in a tin shack at the side of the track.

'Rubbish bond. Ten thousand rupees. Banker's draft only. And park fees.'

Our paperwork clearly showed that we had already paid park fees but this was apparently irrelevant. A sign announcing strict enforcement of the 'only 150 entry permits per day' rule caused a pang of concern about whether our porters would be allowed to continue. For some reason though, that potentially awkward issue was not addressed and it was the rubbish bond that became the sticking point. Ten thousand rupees amounted to approximately £150 and Mr Side Parting was most insistent that a banker's draft was necessary. But the last bank was in Uttarkashi about six hours away. This didn't look good. Brejish battled firmly, exercising his mobile phone (it's amazing where you get a signal in India) and harassed senior officials in various distant towns. And then, for some delightfully inexplicable reason, the problem disappeared as quickly as it had arisen. Tea was offered, cash accepted and we were free to go on our way. In retrospect, such encounters add to the Indian Himalayan experience. It is not always easy to see them that way at the time, though.

Soon though Brejish was apologetically reprimanding us again. The spectacular and instantly recognisable Bhagirathi peaks had just come into view and Paul and I were keen to take photographs.

'The rules say that you can only take photographs of the peak you have a permit for.'

This was a new one on me. With literally thousands of photographs of the Bhagirathi peaks on the internet this rule seemed so obviously ridiculous that I had to take issue with him. But it was to no avail. Much as we didn't have a full copy of the rules and regulations with us (probably too heavy to carry ...), Brejish stood firm. There was nothing for it but to be discreet and keep the relationship on a positive footing by promising to abide by this curious rule.

The Gangotri Glacier is an eye-opening example of glacial retreat. According to such revered institutions as NASA and the National Snow and Ice Data Center, it has retreated nearly one kilometre over the last twenty-five years.

As we arrived, people were seeking to maximise the value of their visit by collecting water as close as possible to where the water emerged from under the glacier. The snout is known as Gaumukh (cow's mouth) in Hindi and was rather spectacular: a vertical ice wall forty metres high, topped by large quantities of moraine. Unfortunately, not only did the ice show signs of collapse but the heat from the sun would release a regular cavalcade of rocks. Several people have died here, yet, despite clear signs, people were prepared to risk their lives to get close to the holy source. Paul, with his health and safety adviser hat on, was impressed with their dedication. We mentioned the risks to Brijesh, who asked if such behaviour was any different to trying to climb mountains.

Above the snout the going became tougher but the spectacular peaks of the area gradually revealed themselves in all their glory. And, three days out from Gangotri, we had our first good view of Vasuki Parbat.

'*Wow!*'

The normally reserved Mr Ramsden was impressed. Several buttresses soared up towards an overhanging headwall, which appeared to be broken by a single possible line. It looked as impressive as it had in the photograph on Harish's CD. What's more, conditions appeared favourable: a decent plastering of snow and ice on the face but none on the approach. Could this be too good to be true?

'And we are allowed to photograph it too,' I observed. Brijesh confirmed that this was indeed the case.

Our base camp was by a small lake called Vasuki Tal. A slight downer was that it was already occupied by a large Indian expedition that had just climbed Satopanth, a high but straightforward peak just to the east of Vasuki Parbat. I suppose I could be classed as selfish in that I prefer to be alone at base camp. Perhaps I have been spoilt with remote experiences in east Tibet and the like, but the close proximity of a large expedition complete with laptops, satellite telephone and assorted paraphernalia was not something I found appealing. That said, there was plenty of room; they seemed good company and the photographs they showed us made it clear that a descent we had considered down the east side of Vasuki Parbat looked distinctly unattractive. Early the next day they left to go down, and we became the sole inhabitants of base camp. The atmosphere changed immediately: it was just the mountains and us. *This* was what we had come for.

Forty-eight hours later only five centimetres of our tent poked out of the snow. Base camp had been transformed. I love snow at home. The very sight of it excites me and it doesn't take much for me to feel the need to play in it in some manner or another. My colleagues seem bemused when I enthuse about such challenges as getting the chains on and outwitting closed roads to reach the office. I suppose it's this mentality that enjoys big mountain climbs. It may not have quite the same level of difficulty, but it is in a similar vein.

Anyway, as much as I tend to regard snow as my friend in the UK, it did not have quite the same effect on me at Vasuki Tal. Here I yearned for firm, climbable snow and solid, well-frozen surfaces. A metre and a half of soft snow was exactly what I did not want.

Outside, unknown to us, Brejish was using a frying pan to dig a trench to our tent. There was a sound of scraping and scuffling followed by the entrance zip being pulled down and a small avalanche of snow entering.

'What are you going to do?' A twinge of concern was audible in his voice.

Paul and I lay in our sleeping bags. It had been snowing for nearly two days and we had already delayed the start of our acclimatisation by a day. A day might not sound a lot but on a tight timescale it is significant. We had allowed one week to get there, a week to acclimatise, another to do the route and a fourth to get home. We had three days' leeway and so one day lost was a concern. The truth, of course, was that we could only wait and hope.

'Be fine tomorrow,' we chorused glumly. Brejish looked around, unsure of what to make of our feigned optimism.

'Bed chai?' he suggested, to general noises of approval.

Some time later chai had not arrived. Some investigation was called for.

The cook tent had collapsed. Actually, calling it a tent gives rather the wrong impression. We hadn't expected to be in base camp for long, and this, combined with our enthusiasm for keeping expenses to a minimum, had meant we supplied our cook, Premsingh, with only a tarpaulin to stretch between a couple of boulders. Premsingh was an experienced operator, well used to harsh conditions, and he had been content throughout the sunny evenings of our walk-in. Now, with the temperature hovering around freezing and his kitchen smothered in collapsed fabric, his smile appeared a little forced.

Next morning the clouds had lifted just above base camp. The temperature had dropped below freezing and the previously damp kitchen had frozen solid. Bags of food and kitchen items protruded from the icy sidewalls and Premsingh's plimsolls were totally encased in ice. Remarkably, he was still smiling as he prepared an inspirational bowl of cardboard-like cornflakes for breakfast, although he did accept our offer to lend him a pair of walking boots. Things must have been bad.

Our plan was to follow our tried and trusted method of getting up high and then just lying around for a couple of days, reading and popping headache tablets while acclimatising. The terrain here appeared ideal: the easy east side of the Bhagirathi peaks rose up opposite our intended line and looked to give easy access to altitudes at least as high as we needed to acclimatise. Brejish and Premsingh stood outside their tent and waved goodbye until we had disappeared. The snow was so deep that this took a ridiculously long time. Their arms must have been exhausted by the time we dropped out of sight on to the Vasuki Glacier.

I had hoped that the fresh snow on the glacier would be easier to cope with but the opposite was true. The conditions were so bad that they reminded me of the Arwa Glacier, perhaps only twenty miles away in a straight line, where Steve Sustad and I had been reduced to crawling on all fours on the crust, pulling our sacks behind us after climbing the Arwa Tower in 1999. Here there was no crust but over a metre of soft snow covering a sea of boulders. With heavy sacks, balance was lost at nearly every step. It was all so exhausting that we resorted to a new technique for me. One person would break trail without a sack and the other would follow, carrying his in the freshly made trench. At half-hour intervals we would switch places, the first person retracing his steps to collect his sack and bring up the rear. Progress was ridiculously slow.

Eventually, early on our third day, we reached 5,100 metres at the foot of the face. We had gained a mere 300 metres in altitude and travelled perhaps five horizontal kilometres from base camp. We lay in our tent trying to convince ourselves that the heavy breathing it had taken to get to this point might be as good for acclimatising as lying still at our target altitude of 5,800 metres. We tried to go higher but the snow stayed uniformly appalling such that we only managed another 100 metres of height gain. That would have to do. The weather was now clearing and it was frustrating to think that, just a few days before, this glacier had been rubble-covered moraine and we could have moved easily to this spot in just a few short hours from base camp. But that was not to be and, with the time allocated for acclimatisation over, we had no option but to return to base camp and get ready to climb. We knew in our hearts that we were not well acclimatised, but convinced ourselves that by climbing slowly we would be able to acclimatise on the route.

Back at base camp the weather seemed to be changing again. Until now we had been too hot in our sleeping bags. Now we wore base layers and woke to find water bottles in the tent frozen solid.

'Be nice and cool at 6,800 metres,' commented Paul cheerfully – he being a man with a well-exercised penchant for climbing in sub-zero spots such as Antarctica and Patagonia in winter. I prodded my frozen bottle doubtfully, noted the heavy build-up of hoar frost inside the tent and packed some extra long johns.

'Winter is here now,' announced Premsingh helpfully while serving hot milk on more soggy cornflakes. It certainly felt that way. The skies had cleared and the day had that cold, crisp feel reminiscent of the European Alps in fine winter weather.

Four days later we were below the steepest section of our line and had cut a pleasingly level but narrow nose-to-tail ledge, hung the stove between us to melt snow for a brew and snuggled down to some reading. The snow conditions on the glacier had not improved but our tracks had been a godsend and we had easily reached the foot of the face in a day. And not only was the face steep enough for the new snow to have sloughed off, the vast quantities of snow that must have come down during the bad weather had compacted to form good, firm climbing conditions. I relaxed, feeling content and immersing myself in my book.

In a world where weight is so important it sometimes surprises me that we cut our toothbrushes in half but still carry superfluous weight in the form of reading material. I never used to do this, but five days stuck in a tiny mountain tent with Victor Saunders on Spantik in Pakistan in 1987 had been a turning point. It snowed incessantly and we left the tent only to go to the toilet. Even the normally garrulous Victor ran out of conversation. We lay in a mind-numbing silence. Eventually I didn't even bother to put my contact lenses in and just sat in a blur. The experience left a marked impression on us both and since then I have always carried reading material to sustain morale through periods of inactivity.

From our bivouac the walls above looked disturbingly challenging compared to their earlier appearance through binoculars. What we had hoped would be snow and ice providing enjoyable mixed climbing turned out to be powder snow stuck loosely to near-vertical rock or blasted up under overhangs. A snow and ice traverse leading to a tenuous vertical line near the right edge of the buttress looked to offer the best route, but the first section was devoid of ice and looked far from straightforward.

Normally we alternate leads, with both the leader and the second climbing with their sacks on. That is the style of climbing we most enjoy and it generally flows smoothly. It allows us both to enjoy the climbing and, equally importantly, have a good rest and admire the view from the stances. It didn't take long before this routine took a knock. Paul's first pitch turned out to be challenging to the extent that he was forced to abandon his sack. Sack hauling is the anathema of our style of climbing, particularly on diagonal pitches. When it was my turn to climb, not only was I soon teetering badly in the face of a nasty pendulum, but my efforts to control the sack were sadly lacking. All I could do was unclip it and vaguely control its pendulum. It promptly got stuck and was only freed by Paul pulling as hard as he could while I pushed from below. Paul's sleeping mat parted company from the sack in the struggle, and we were both exhausted by the time I reached the stance. I hate sack hauling.

Panting aside, our position was magnificent. Days away from anyone else, just the two of us halfway up a huge unclimbed face with steep ground all around and wild drops below. We savoured the position and then turned our attention to the tiny digital screens on our cameras, zooming in to our images of the face, trying to pick out the best line up the technical ground ahead. Unfortunately, as we had not been able to gain a good vantage point during our acclimatisation, the images were not overly helpful.

Out right still seemed best, and so off we went. The further right we traversed the more the ground fell away steeply beneath us as squeaky white ice carried us to where a pinnacle provided a wild bivouac spot right on the edge of a huge overhanging wall. Although the pinnacle itself was near vertical on all sides, its top had accumulated a knife-edge snow crest deep enough for us to simply chop the top off and pitch the tent. Inside it was easy to forget our surroundings. We could have been on a flat, grassy campsite; the only slight giveaway being the belay ropes that snaked out of the entrance.

I slept soundly, but the cold was getting to be a concern. My feet had been intermittently numb during the day and, although they looked pink and healthy when I peered at them in the evening, I could feel the first stages of cold damage. Paul's feet were cold too, despite him wearing boots designed for much higher altitudes.

But it was an incident first thing the next morning that really gave food for thought. Starting up a difficult pitch, I took my mitten off to use an undercut for twenty seconds or so. On removing my fingers I was shocked to see a blister on my middle finger. I warmed it immediately, but this was an unwelcome and frightening new experience I had not encountered in over twenty-five years of climbing in the greater ranges. I squawked about it to Paul who looked suitably subdued.

'My feet are cold,' he said forlornly. 'Eight-thousand-metre-rated boots, too.'

From my point of view I was uncomfortably aware that I was already wearing my biggest mittens. And at the back of my mind was the fact that I was increasingly suffering from cold hands in life in general. Swimming in the sea or driving home from the office in the winter months would result in white wooden fingers that were very difficult to warm. The sensation was quite different to what you might call 'normal' cold fingers. One day, for example, one of my little fingers would be wooden-white down to the first joint and below that, after a very clear demarcation line, be pink and healthy. The next day it might be fingers on my other hand being wooden-white to varying degrees while the finger that suffered the day before would be pink and resilient. I had done some research, self-diagnosed Raynaud's phenomenon and sought advice from my GP as to whether or not anything could be done to alleviate the problem. It seemed there was nothing much that could be done, but curiously the cold seemed not to affect me in quite the same way in the mountains. Even here at over 6,000 metres, the wooden fingers and white/pink demarcation lines were not present.

I wondered whether it would be warmer to get two sets of inners into one shell, but decided that the extra tightness might have the opposite effect and that this was not the place to experiment. I would have to make do with what I had and be careful. The pitch itself was fantastic: Scottish grade V right on the edge of a wildly exposed buttress leading to an excellent belay ledge. But we both increasingly felt that all was not well. The pitch had taken me ninety minutes to lead and we knew we were slowing down and gasping (even) more than usual. My trademark 'rest the helmet against the ice' move was becoming more and more frequent. However, the elation of making upward progress in such a fantastic position was such that neither of us voiced any concerns.

From what we could pick out on the screens of our cameras it seemed the best way ahead was to cross a rib to our left and traverse a hidden ice band left for fifty metres or so. After that it looked possible to gain access to a snow/ice slope and the end of the most difficult climbing.

It was not long before we had to conclude that small camera screens are not the best for detailed route-finding decisions. The first pitch of the traverse proved a lot more challenging and time-consuming than we had expected, but the real shock came on the second pitch when I reached the crest of a shallow buttress and it became clear that ground we had expected to lead easily upwards was, in reality, near-vertical rock with powdery snow stuck to it. Out left a much longer route, exposed to falling ice in the afternoon sun, looked a vague possibility, but my immediate thought was that we had gone the wrong way and should retreat along the traverse and try to climb a short rock buttress to gain the snow/ice slope.

And so back we went. The traverse back was difficult and time-consuming and when we had regained the buttress it was time to look for somewhere to spend the night. There were no options beyond a hanging or, at best, a sitting bivouac. This prompted the only major dither I can recall Paul and I having in the mountains.

Normally I would vote strongly for staying at our high point, but I knew I was tiring and that the cold was getting to me and giving cause for concern. After all the traversing backwards and forwards it was only eighty metres down to the pinnacle bivouac site where we knew we could pitch the tent and enjoy a sound night's sleep. Paul was keen to descend, have a good rest and return fresh the following morning. I dithered. We had two 7.5-millimetre, fifty-metre-long ropes and the idea of tying them together, abseiling on a single rope and then starting the next day with a long jumar back up was enough to prompt me to hesitate. Surely it would be best to stay where we were? But the sun was low in the sky and I could already feel the cold biting hard. Cutting a reasonable bum ledge might not be possible and would, at best, take a long time. The bivvy platform was ready and waiting. We discussed, traversed a bit in search of a possible ledge, failed to find one, discussed more ... and decided to retreat to the pinnacle. As I was abseiling over the difficult ground that we had fought our way up that day, the balance of probabilities about our success began to sway in my mind.

There was little conversation in the tent but there was an unspoken acceptance that we were weakening. The conversation lacked sparkle and our reactions were slowing. Our dream was slipping but we couldn't yet bring ourselves to discuss turning back.

The alarm bleeped at 4 a.m. but our sluggishness was such that it was 9 a.m. before we were back at our high point. Paul had jumared up the rope whereas my aversion to climbing the rope was such that I chose to tie in and climb while Paul belayed me. The alternative line we had chosen looked as if it would be straightforward rock climbing at sea level, but in the morning shade of a west face at over 6,000 metres it was a different proposition. It was Paul's lead. He took one glove off, touched the rock for a few seconds, commented 'No way' and put it back on again. Meanwhile I rested my helmet against the slope and worked to warm my finger, which had gone an unpleasant pasty white colour.

As ever, we were working on the basis that we should continue up unless there was a very good reason to go down. That always leaves plenty of scope for debate about what is a 'good reason', but here even our befuddled brains recognised that our problems were not going to decrease as we got higher. Try as we might to convince ourselves otherwise, we had to accept that the air higher up wasn't going to contain any more oxygen, we weren't going to move any faster and it wasn't going to get any warmer. It was clear that we were on the verge of taking on more risk than either of us was prepared to take. It was Paul who spoke first.

'What do you expect to happen if we get over this rock pitch?'

We thought the ground above had appeared easier and would draw us inexorably towards potentially difficult mixed ground below the summit. We looked at each other and the decision was made.

And so we were back to where this chapter started. Our sixth night on the face was on the ledge we had cut on night two. The rock coming through the roof had sent us a clear message: Vasuki Parbat had won.

The next day Brejish and Premsingh met us on the glacier. The snow was only intermittently frozen and exhausting to walk on. With a broad smile Premsingh offered to carry my sack. Usually I feel in reasonable shape after a climb and accept such offers only because it seems churlish not to. On this occasion I felt completely drained and couldn't hand it over quickly enough. I staggered back into base camp and lay in the tent while chai was prepared and my body could begin to recover. I had no doubt whatsoever that we had made the right decision.

Two years later, fellow British mountaineer Malcolm Bass contacted me to ask if Paul and I would mind if he and Paul Figg had a go at Vasuki Parbat. It didn't take much deliberation to give him a clear answer. Much as the line of Vasuki Parbat was inspirational, the popularity of the area and the fact that we had already had a good go left us with no great desire to return. And my objectives box file at home still bulged with possibilities.

Malcolm and Paul went on to achieve an excellent alpine-style ascent of the face followed by a descent of the north ridge. They were nominated for a Piolet d'Or, which I think they would have stood a good chance of winning if they had not dropped their camera and been unable to show any spectacular action shots to sum up the position and atmosphere of the climb. They too experienced problems with the cold, but, in the afternoon sun, managed to climb the rock wall that had stopped us. Above that they reported one hard pitch and then more straightforward ground for a further two days to the summit. As Malcolm told me about the climb I felt appropriately envious. Retreating from something you had set your heart on is never easy and there will always be unanswered questions.

With the benefit of hindsight do Paul and I regret retreating when we did? After all, the weather was perfect and we were above the most dangerous part of the face. Perhaps we should have waited for the sun to come round and warm the rock in the afternoon. Maybe if we had not wasted time and energy mistakenly traversing off left we would not have lost momentum in the first place.

We have chatted about the decision several times and what came out of those conversations was not so much a feeling of failure as a feeling that we were pleased with our performance. We had stretched ourselves fully and made a considered decision to retreat in good time for a safe (rock through the tent aside) and controlled descent. Sometimes the mountain wins. We didn't get up Vasuki Parbat, but we did our very best, were sound in our judgement, had a great time and came back safely. And these are the important things.

If we were guaranteed success in everything we tried then life would be pretty boring.

Chapter 8

Fell Running – A New, Mildly Eccentric Form of Exercise?

'I think you would love the Jura fell race.'

Noel Craine and Ali Thomas, long-standing friends of mine based in North Wales, were most insistent. I was gasping heavily, having just completed the Tigger Tor fell race on the outskirts of Sheffield. The Tigger Tor is something like fifteen kilometres with 500 metres of ascent. The Jura is twenty-eight and 2,400 metres. I stared at them incredulously. Surely they could see the state I was in?

I had started fell racing in 2006 to supplement my one evening a week of climbing, caving or other heavy-breathing exercise. It involves trying to run across often-untracked high-level terrain where the challenges comprise steep ground, bogs, rocks and frequently harsh weather conditions. I grew to quite like it because it took me to places I hadn't visited before, introduced me to a new circle of mildly eccentric friends and motivated me to try hard – something I struggle to do when running on my own. I gradually convinced myself that this was good preparation for Himalayan climbing, with the added benefit that it fitted reasonably well into family life as it wasn't too difficult to give a fairly accurate assessment of how long I was likely to be away from home and when I would be back for things like child-ferrying duties.

As a schoolboy, I once came twenty-fourth in the north Brent schools' cross-country race, but I soon discovered that I was not really a natural runner. In fact, prior to fell racing, running was something that I tended to look upon as being rather dull and boring. All that repetitive activity ... ugh! I had dabbled with five- and ten-kilometre road races, but found it difficult to maintain enough motivation to keep running.

But fell racing was different and the more I thought about it the more Noel and Ali's invitation to join them at the annual Jura race was an attractive one. I had never run twenty-eight kilometres in my life, but I viewed that as part of the challenge rather than something to put me off. There was one problem though: the race had strict entry criteria which included evidencing finishing times on at least two other 'AL' category fell races. Fell races are categorised by the Fell Running Association and AL signifies a race over twenty kilometres long with an average climb rate exceeding fifty metres per kilometre. I had never run a race like that. A closer look gave further cause for concern: ER, LK and NS were also judged to be necessary. Further delving revealed that these acronyms meant 'Experience Required', 'Local Knowledge an advantage' and 'Navigational Skills required'. I had never been to Jura so I certainly didn't have any local knowledge and I had never done anything similar so couldn't say I had the experience required, either. But having safely found my way around misty Scottish hills I felt I probably passed one of the three.

I listed my concerns to Noel but his response was just to laugh and suggest I failed on all counts as we had once spent a wild and dark winter evening going in exactly the wrong direction on the Cairngorm plateau after I had mistakenly assumed that the red end of the compass needle pointed to the south. (*Surely* compasses made in the northern hemisphere should have the red end pointing towards the equator? After all, it's hotter there – more red – than at the pole.)

I dutifully posted my application but wasn't very confident that I would be accepted. On the section that asked for evidence of previous comparable experience I listed a few Himalayan multi-day routes and kept my fingers crossed. Remarkably, I was accepted. I can only assume the organisers judged that I probably wouldn't cause them any problems and that it might be amusing to marvel at my efforts.

Come the end of May, Jon Coe and I met at Jon Morgan's house in Bradwell and headed north. I knew Jon Morgan from the climbing scene but had never met Jon Coe, a Sheffield-based runner, before. It quickly became clear that I was travelling with talented company. Tips poured forth as I wondered increasingly if it was a good idea. At length we arrived at the tiny village of Tayvallich on the Kintyre peninsula. Here there was a very fine cafe packed with fell runners waiting for the fast RIB ferry that was to be our transport to Jura. There is quite a big crossover between the climbing and fell running scenes, so I recognised a few faces. The main thing I noticed was that without exception everyone looked distressingly lean, mean and fit. Noel and Ali were there tucking into tea and cakes and greeted me with their customary enthusiasm.

'Welcome to elite fell running,' they announced in unison.

I suddenly felt very out of place. Whatever was I doing?

I sat quietly contemplating and trying not to be seasick as the throbby boat roared across to Jura in an hour or so. My first impression was one of wonder that there were so many people camped on the lawned area in front of the only pub on the island. It was immediately clear that the 200-plus entrants with their hundred or so family members and supporters dominated the area. The race is a major event on Jura each year and the number of people attending significantly outnumbers the 200 or so residents. We squeezed our tent in amongst the masses, enjoyed a beer in the pub and settled down for the night. The weather was absolutely glorious and I had already decided I loved both the place and this curious event that awaited me.

The morning could not have been more different. The mist, or clag as they say in Scotland, was down to a hundred metres and there was a steady drizzle. I had brought along an OS map, but Jon Coe, presumably recognising my inexperience at such events, had kindly copied a detailed map for me. On it he had marked checkpoints, compass bearings and lines showing the best route to follow to achieve the very fastest result. I thanked him gratefully while thinking to myself that just finishing would satisfy me. Ahead there were eight checkpoints that had to be reached by certain times if I was to avoid being asked to drop out. My first dilemma was whether to wear my varifocal glasses, which were great for close-up and distance vision but not at all good in the rain, or to go for my contact lenses which would be great in the rain but, being single-distance focus, would preclude my reading the map without moving one to one side. Jon was helpful as ever:

'Don't worry. There will always be people to follow.'

I wasn't so sure about that but chose contact lenses and dutifully presented my kit for the necessary pre-race inspection.

'Plenty there for a night out,' commented the kit checker as he cheerfully signed me off as ready to start. It would appear that my efforts to shave the weight down compared poorly to the average.

Back at the tent the two Jons were undergoing their final preparations and applying copious amounts of Vaseline to toes and bum.

'Essential,' they explained. 'After a few hours it can get really uncomfortable if you don't.'

This was news to me but I took off my shoes and socks, smeared Vaseline over my feet and headed towards the start.

'Did you do your bum?' asked Jon. 'I find that the most important bit.'

It was true that I had forgotten, but the 10.30 a.m. start time was fast approaching and, rather than get back into the tent, I took the tub of Vaseline, reversed into a nearby bush and dropped my trousers. Almost immediately I was interrupted by a young girl's voice.

'Daddy! Look!'

It appeared that the narrow road from the pub to a jetty ran behind my bush and I hadn't noticed. I am generally quite difficult to embarrass but being already out of my comfort zone I could feel my face redden and it was a rather flustered version of my former self that quickly completed the job in hand and arrived at the start line. The organiser said a few words, a bagpipe player burst into action and suddenly we were off.

It was immediately clear that something was wrong. My feet were slipping around all over the place. I had chosen to wear fairly loose-fitting shoes and applying liberal quantities of Vaseline to my feet was not having the desired effect. What a cock-up. With fewer than a hundred metres completed, I stopped and stepped out of the field wondering if I should return to the tent and address the problem.

'Look Daddy! There's that man again.'

The voice was enough to make me decide to continue. Stepping back into the field I judged that I was about three quarters of the way down. If I could maintain that position I would be well pleased. The route followed a Land Rover track for half a mile or so and then struck out across the moor beside a forestry plantation. It was clearly boggy in front and I kept an eye on the runners ahead to help me choose the best way through.

Some way ahead was a lady wearing a pair of tight black leggings. Suddenly she sank in, so that I could only just make out a small triangle of light between the tops of her thighs. A couple of other runners stopped to help her out of the bog but the sight stuck in my mind. This was clearly not going to be a 'normal' fell race. And I have to admit that I felt quite excited at the prospect. Soon though we were in the clag and life become a bit more difficult. The field had spread out and I was having trouble keeping the runner in front in sight. I knew the first checkpoint was on the highest piece of ground hereabouts but the best way to find it seemed to be to follow those in front and hope they got it right. Gaining height via a grassy ramp, I emerged on a broad rocky area and was surprised when a group of runners approached from my right. Amongst them was Donna Claridge, who I knew vaguely and certainly knew to be a much better runner than me. This was all becoming very interesting. Clearly this NS rating was relevant and there was a lot more to this fell racing business than speed alone.

Checkpoint one loomed out of the clag and a glance at my watch showed I had been on the go for fifty-six minutes and was four minutes inside the cut-off time. So far so good. The way forward was over grass and intermittent rock. Up to now I had been struggling to keep up and a steady stream of runners had been passing me. Now the tables seemed to be turned and despite my squidgy feet I found myself able to use gravity to my advantage and began to pass people. I was moving up the field and beginning to enjoy myself. I recall chatting to Donna and, as someone who had done the race before, asking her how long we were likely to take if we kept up the same pace.

I forget her answer but soon the poor visibility caused the runners to bunch up even more and our group merged with another. All continued well as we passed the remains of an iron gate and started to climb towards the next checkpoint. But suddenly the entire group stopped. Maps were produced and it was immediately clear that uncertainty prevailed.

'Shit!' It struck me that I had just been following other people and had no real idea where we were.

I pushed a contact lens to one side and peered at my map. Jon had marked the old gate and I could see that we needed to be going more or less due north from it, but as I had no idea of our current position this wasn't very useful. From the conversation around me it was clear that several people in our group had done the race a number of times before and if I was to stand a chance of continuing, rather than escaping to the road by heading in an easterly direction, I was in their hands.

' … done it about fifteen times now … ' I heard one person say as he headed off confidently.

Others followed him but the group was splitting with about half holding back. Making a quick decision Donna and I stepped in beside Mr Experienced before he disappeared into the clag. As we hung in behind him I looked back and was concerned to see the remainder of the group moving off in a markedly different direction. Soon we were scrabbling up untracked heather and there was a general admission that we had no idea where we were. Time was ticking by and I was becoming concerned that we would be timed out when a runner emerged from the clag, coming downhill from our left. It transpired that we had somehow completely missed checkpoint two and had hit the route between checkpoints two and three.

'I just made it,' he announced gleefully before bounding off and disappearing quickly.

A glance at my watch showed that the cut-off time for checkpoint two was fifteen minutes earlier. Agh! The marshals were very understanding but there was no doubt about it, we had missed the cut-off time. Our group of four or five stood around dejectedly. This was a new experience for me and I wasn't quite sure what to do.

'We are out of the race but can't we just carry on anyway?' I enquired to no one in particular.

It was Mr Experienced who responded.

'As president of the FRA I can't really do that. It's very much against the rules.'

I felt slightly sheepish. In retrospect I realise what a silly suggestion it was. The organisers go to tremendous lengths to put on races like this and if runners don't obey the rules the potential for lost runners and false alerts to rescue services is high.

Donna and I walked the walk of shame together. It was a surprisingly long way across difficult tussocks interspersed with serious bog. Just after we reached the finishing line at Craighouse the leading runner came into sight. I recognised him as Ian Holmes, a legend on the fell racing scene, and I couldn't believe how fresh and bouncy he appeared. It was truly sobering to ponder that he had run over all three paps, plus an outlier at the far end, in the time that it had taken Donna and me to fail to reach the first pap and walk out to the road. As other runners began to finish, with the two Jons well up the field, I observed that the fell racing scene seemed to have a good combination of mild eccentricity and extreme achievement. And it seemed ideal for achieving a level of fitness that would serve me well in the Himalaya. I could feel myself getting increasingly interested.

As the evening progressed my failure to summit the paps nagged me. The beers went down well and it struck me that the slowest finishers had taken around seven hours. If I started at 5 a.m. then, all being well, I could run the course in the morning and be down in time to catch the 1 p.m. ferry back to Tayvallich. The Jons, being sub-4.5-hour finishers, felt this was easily achievable and with their encouragement ringing in my ears I set the alarm for 4.30 a.m. and settled down for the night.

The clag had thinned by the morning and another fifty-six-minute run to checkpoint one saw my confidence rising. Noting my time I carried straight on to checkpoint two. The top was clear this time and it was obvious where to go, but even with four minutes in hand, I still couldn't reach it inside the cut-off time. I sat down to eat a chocolate bar and contemplate. This was all looking a bit more challenging than I had expected. I managed the distance from checkpoints two to three in time but then the huge rise to checkpoint four on Beinn a'Chaolais, the first pap, again saw me slower than was needed to avoid being timed out. This wasn't going at all well and my spirits were only slightly lifted when I covered the ground over Beinn an Oir and Beinn Shiantaidh, the second and third paps, well within the cut-off times. By this time I was getting a bit concerned about missing the ferry and headed direct for the road, missing out the final outlier, Corra Bheinn, which is included in the race course.

I made the ferry but was very quiet on the drive home. The experience had given me a lot to think about.

Chapter 9

Jura Success – A Passion is Born

First thing on the morning of 1 March I printed off my Jura application and popped it in the post. I might be refused an entry based on (in)competence but I wasn't going to fail due to missing the rush for places. The theory had been that I would use the year after my 2009 failure to do more fell running but, as so often seems to be the case, the competing demands of work, family and mountaineering meant that my running plateaued at entering the occasional race and just sort of doing my best. As I completed the entry form it was still at the forefront of my mind that, in my early morning round the year before, I had been unable to do many of the stages quickly enough to avoid being timed out.

I had, though, done some training of a sort: I had read Richard Askwith's book *Feet in the Clouds*. Tales of the history of the sport, stories of fell racing legends and an understanding of the Bob Graham Round had inspired me such that I was mentally more in tune with what was going on than I had been the year before.

I leant the book to John English, an old climbing friend from early days in London, and he too was inspired by what he had read, such that he was keen to experience the event with the thought of entering in years to come. He also held a private pilot's licence, owned a light plane and was keen to fly to the airstrip near the point where the race route joined the road at Three Arch Bridge. A quick glance at pilots' blogs revealed that the Jura airstrip was held in high regard, with many pilots going out of their way to avoid it. One reported a trench crossing the grass strip at one point and another recalled 'Oban advising us that it is not advisable to land due to high grass'. This all seemed to suggest that landing could be interesting, but John is not one to be put off by such things and it was agreed that we would fly up together.

There was room for three in the plane and the third person was to be Jane Hartog. I had known Jane off and on for many years, but had recently got to know her better by frequently meeting her towards the back of the field in fell races. She is the sort of runner that is not incredibly fast but just seems to go on forever.

John kept his plane at East Midlands Airport and it seemed incongruous to be taxiing down the runway between Ryanair passenger jets. They looked frighteningly big from the cockpit of a small single-propeller plane. John was clearly in his element, speaking pilot language with the control tower and manoeuvring confidently around the acres of tarmac.

East Midlands to Jura is about three hours' flying time so, having had a short day at work and taken off at about 5 p.m., we were approaching the landing strip by 8 p.m. and were soon bouncing through long grass in what looked like a field. The fabled ditch appeared all too soon. Why there is a ditch across the 'runway' I have no idea but I did know that it had been John's intention to land one side of it or the other. Now we were about to hit it quite fast. The plane seemed very flimsy and I couldn't imagine a good outcome. It seemed that the undercarriage would buckle followed by … I wasn't quite sure what really.

But sometimes it is good to be wrong. To my amazement we simply bounced and came to a slow and apparently controlled halt. It struck me that this appeared at least as challenging as some of the more noteworthy Himalayan airstrips. John, though, seemed completely relaxed and simply taxied to a halt in a sheltered spot, after which we hitched a lift to the pub. Three and a half hours after leaving East Midlands Airport and we were enjoying a pub meal on Jura. The weather was beautiful. It felt almost unethical.

Noel and Ali were there, along with lots of others that I recognised from the year before, and it was clear that Jura had become a regular annual event for many runners. It was great to see so many familiar faces and if all went well this year I could imagine it becoming a regular event for me too. As I snuggled down in my sleeping bag I wondered what the next day would hold.

The first thing it held was a change in the weather. The clear skies of the evening before had been replaced with a grey landscape, with the paps hidden in the clag. Oh dear. I had a nasty feeling that I might replicate the previous year's efforts.

Someone had told me that eating lots of porridge before the race would be a good idea. Jane was not a fan but John and I had brought copious quantities that we tucked into until my stomach was taut like a drum and it was clear that I had eaten too much. Meanwhile Jane was looking nervous and struggling to eat any of the large Tupperware container of coleslaw-type stuff she had brought along. I too felt a touch nervous although I have no idea why. At the very worst I would be timed out again. In the toilets I realised that I was not the only one feeling this way. At the urinals was a mega-fit-looking chap and as we stood there together he passed the time of day.

'Not sure that I will run today.'

He was fully kitted out and even had his race number pinned to his vest. I looked sideways at him, slightly mystified. The race was due to start in ten minutes and he had travelled all the way to Jura, got ready, registered and was good to go.

'Not feeling quite right,' he said.

I wouldn't recognise him and have no idea if he did run but I remember the encounter vividly. He looked fit, there didn't appear to be anything wrong and yet he was nervous. In a way it gave me and my taut stomach a little boost. I can't say that I felt my best, but the Vaseline had been discreetly and sparingly applied, and I was certainly going to give it a go.

At 10.30 a.m. sharp we were off. This time I was ready for the crotch-deep bog and chose a wiser line, overtaking a few people in the process. Then it was up into the clag, keeping those in front in sight as much as I could. Reaching the first checkpoint in the same fifty-six minutes as my previous effort meant that I would have to speed up if I was not to be timed out. This time, however, I at least knew that dead north from the rusty old gate would lead directly to the next checkpoint. The clag was down and runners bunched into groups again, but I kept an eye on the compass and was pleased to see an intermittent track with lots of stud marks, suggesting I was going the right way. Rather to my surprise the group I was with arrived in good time. It's odd how much faster I go when in a race compared to out on my own. Must be the competitive spirit I suppose.

The way to checkpoint three lacked any trace of a track for some distance and it was a new experience for me to see people either side of me running on compass bearings. As I couldn't see the map clearly without removing my contact lenses I took the middle road between them, which seemed to work well as when we dropped out of the clag I could see we were heading in just the right direction. And as I had managed the distance from checkpoint two to three inside the cut-off time on my own I was pretty confident.

The real challenge would be whether I would be able to make the big climb to the first pap in the time allowed. You would think that doing lots of mountaineering would make me relatively fast on the ascents but that is absolutely not the case. True to form I was faster than those around me on the descent to Gleann Astaile but soon dropped back again on the climb to the first pap, Beinn a'Chaolais. It was a real struggle to keep going but, just before the summit, my mental state was given a boost when I passed someone who had been well ahead and was now obviously tiring badly. It's odd how someone else's problems can boost confidence and how moving up the field, albeit by only one place, can induce such positive feelings. Looking down I could see that there were quite a few runners behind me and could just make out Jane among them. Redoubling my efforts, I joined a small group of runners and crossed the summit. I didn't think to look at my watch but was clearly within the cut-off as none of the marshals suggested otherwise. Yay! The rest of the course over the paps I had done on my own within time the previous year. The weather was improving and I felt much happier. All I had to do was keep going and not burn out completely. And the rougher ground now was much more to my liking.

Our little group carried on together over Beinn an Oir, the highest pap, and on to the rocky summit of Beinn Shiantaidh, the third pap. The skies were clear and I could see John above us taking the opportunity to get an aerial view of the action. I knew it was very important to take the right line down the scree slopes below the summit of Beinn Shiantaidh and was pretty confident that I knew the way from my endeavours the previous year. The clag was down again but I felt good on the rough ground and even managed to pass the occasional person. Usually they were carefully picking their way down steep or rocky sections but nevertheless, overtaking was very much a new experience for me and I must admit I quite liked it. I pulled away from the group, overtook a few others and gained the traversing track towards Corra Bheinn with no problems. As I ran I realised that I was enjoying myself and feeling good.

The clag lifted and down below I could see runners clawing their way back up the hillside having dropped too low and missed the traversing path. They seemed to be really fast as they overtook me on the rise to Corra Bheinn and a couple of them I recognised as 'proper' fell runners. I could not believe how well it all seemed to be going.

Corra Bheinn was new territory. Up over the summit, down a long but gentle slope, across the Corran River and I was at the road at Three Arch Bridge. I glanced at my watch: just over five hours. My target had been seven hours and now I was in with a chance of finishing in under six. Road running is far from my forte and even with the inspirational Jura landscape spurring me on I made a sorry sight. People kept overtaking me and I overtook no one, but I finished in five hours and forty-nine minutes; I was so pleased. Jane came in at just under seven hours. She too had that look of an elated Jura finisher.

In the pub later we shared a table with a chap who was clearly well over sixty. We got chatting and it turned out that he had completed the race many times and was in fact in the group that I had been part of over the paps. With his hood up I had barely recognised him and could hardly believe that he was the same man who had danced so nimbly over the rough ground and surged ahead uphill. At the age of fifty-four I had already decided that Jura was a great fitness milestone to aim for each year but I don't think I will ever be in the record books. A glance at the results indicated that there were over ten 'V60' (over sixty) finishers, with the fastest completing the course in a remarkable four hours and twenty-three minutes.

In 2014 a new course record was set by Hector Haines in a mind-boggling three hours and six minutes. Go up to Jura, walk the course and think about that. It is absolutely amazing.

Chapter 10

Sulamar – The Hottest Bath Ever

As I get older, my list of objectives seems to grow longer. I suppose that's a good thing. If it got shorter I might run out and have to think about changing my hobby. For years, as I pored over possibilities, the thought lurked that one day my children would be grown up, I would no longer work in a tax office and I would have more time. Then, in theory, I would really be able to start working through my list. Alternatively, and this thought kept repeating uncomfortably, I might end up leaving it too late and spend my twilight years thinking about all the climbs I could have done if I had not spent so much time in the tax office. It's all very difficult, this business of getting the most out of life.

In 2009 east Tibet was still off limits and my never-ending search for the perfect objective was moving towards the Tien Shan range straddling the borders of Kazakhstan, Kyrgyzstan and China. Many years previously, a Russian climber had given me a faded colour transparency of an inspiring buttress on a 6,900-metre mountain in the area called Military Topographers' Peak. That photograph had lodged deeply in my memory but I always held back from visiting, put off by the height and south-facing aspect. Nevertheless I kicked myself when I saw reports that a Russian team had climbed it, albeit using siege tactics, in 2006. The Russian ascent reawakened my interest, although ultimately it was the Scottish mountaineer Bruce Normand who set the scene for my visit to the Chinese Tien Shan.

Bruce is a roving genius physicist who was spending an increasing amount of time in China and in 2011 took up a position at Renmin University of China. In 2008 he had teamed up with Guy McKinnon and Paul Knott to lead the first team to visit the north side of the Xuelian massif in the

Chinese Tien Shan. This is well to the north-east of Military Topographers' Peak and was a real coup. His photographs opened my eyes to a wealth of spectacular 6,000-metre objectives and email exchanges with him further awakened my interest and led me to understand the ways through the protective bureaucracy.

It didn't take long for Paul Ramsden and me to conclude that, as much as it was a pity that Bruce had got there first, you can't win them all and the area was ripe for a visit. Finding people to make up a team is never difficult and for the Tien Shan the ever-buoyant Mike Morrison was keen, as was his main climbing partner Rob Smith.

Mike and I first met back on the southern sandstone outcrops in the early 1970s. In those teenage days I would extract maximum value from the north London disco scene on a Saturday night and then be up to catch the 6 a.m. train to go climbing on the Sunday. Mike was replicating such activity in south London and it would be two weary but motivated climbers who would finally exit the train at the small Kent station of Groombridge just in time for the 10 a.m. opening of the local meeting point of 'Terry's Festerhaunt'. The Festerhaunt was an aptly named relaxation spot incorporating a cafe and a small but well-stocked gear shop. The proprietors were Terry and Julie Tullis. Terry was a real enthusiast for the southern sandstone outcrops and had been one of the most talented climbers of the area before an accident left a rotavator blade embedded in his leg. Julie went on to make her name in the big mountains before tragically dying on the descent of K2 in 1986. I clearly remember reading the terrible news during a flight back from the Russian Caucasus.

There is a bit of a north London/south London divide, so Mike (and John Stevenson, who was also from south London) and I made unlikely climbing partners. But we formed a strong team and, once I had become the proud owner of an ageing minivan, spent every weekend for several years climbing on cliffs throughout Britain. Hard work and an increasing enthusiasm for skiing meant that Mike had not been on a greater range trip since 2002, but Bruce's photographs and the unexplored nature of the Chinese Tien Shan made an irresistible combination.

Mike's partner for the trip, Rob, was a builder in Somerset who, Mike explained, lived with his family in a yurt. He sounded an interesting character although his living arrangements were not entirely voluntary. Incompetence on the part of his solicitor had caused the bank to withdraw their offer to

1 Andy Cave cocooned in his bivvy bag on our attempt on the west face of Mount Grosvenor, China, in 2003.

2 Kajaqiao (*left*) and Manamcho (6,447 and 6,264 metres respectively) in the Nyainqentangla East range of east Tibet.

3 Hiring porters in Tibet on the 2005 Kajaqiao expedition.

4 In 2007 during our Manamcho expedition we became the first Westerners to see this lake and these unclimbed peaks.

5 Looking across to Manamcho, Tom Nakamura's 'Matterhorn of the Nyainqentangla', from Pt 5,935. Steve Burns in the foreground. **Photo:** Ian Cartwright.

6 The west face of Vasuki Parbat (6,792 metres).

7 Leading out on the traverse on day four of our attempt on Vasuki Parbat. **Photo:** Paul Ramsden.

8 Paul Ramsden testing the comfort level of a bivvy – our fourth – on Vasuki Parbat.

9 Successfully completing the Isle of Jura fell race in 2010 after my failure in 2009. **Photo:** John English.

10 Me failing dismally to duck under the planks in the Xiate hot springs on our Sulamar expedition in 2010.

11 Not to be recommended: my view having fallen in a crevasse while acclimatising for Sulamar.

12 Paul at the site of our hanging bivvy on Sulamar – the cornice is only twenty-five metres above!

13 Sulamar, day two: a storm, benightment and no bivvy in sight – a bad combination.

14 Paul on the beautiful summit ridge of Sulamar (5,380 metres).

15 Dave Turnbull, CEO of the British Mountaineering Council, and the Nepali border defence on our walk in to Mugu Chuli in 2011.

16 Dave Turnbull climbing on day one on Mugu Chuli.

17 Looking across to Mugu Chuli (6,310 metres) from our acclimatisation camp.

18 Dave Turnbull climbing on the upper slopes of Mugu Chuli.

19 Topping out closer to home on one of our dawn raids on the Nottingham Castle cliffs. **Photo:** Paul Ramsden.

lend funds to make his barn habitable and so he was forced to live in the garden until the situation improved. He was a big, instantly likeable chap whose laugh could be heard well before his arrival.

It was in autumn 2009 while we were in the early stages of planning that Bruce contacted us with details of his second extremely successful trip to the area. One of the routes he had just done, on the north face of Xuelian West with the Americans Kyle Dempster and Jed Brown, looked absolutely brilliant and had us cursing that we had not got there first. Nevertheless a wonderful, panoramic photograph taken by Jed highlighted the beautiful scenery and wealth of spectacular objectives. In particular we were drawn to the peaks of Xuelian East (6,380 metres) and Sulamar (5,380 metres). Both sported eye-catching buttress lines that looked to give spectacular climbs that led directly to summits. And they were in a culturally interesting part of the world that none of us had been to before. It looked very much as if we had found our objective for 2010.

Then, suddenly, in early 2010 email and telephone contact to China was blocked. Urumqi, our intended point of entry, had been the scene of riots in 2009 and the authorities responded by clamping down on communications. This was an additional bureaucratic challenge. As usual, no explanation was given and intending visitors had to get around the difficulty as best they could. Luckily there were people we could to turn to. John Otto in Beijing, who Paul and I had met on a trip to Sichuan province in 2002, pointed us in the direction of Taher. Taher was an agent in the old Silk Road town of Kashgar who, by dint of ridiculous amounts of travel, was managing to operate his business by picking up emails in other provinces. Sometimes we don't realise how easy we have it in the West.

Taher had never been to the area we wanted to visit but proved to be young and resourceful, even doing a reconnaissance to the roadhead to make sure that everything would work smoothly. He emailed me on his return to the world of electronic communication.

'It was raining hard all the time. Miserable. Couldn't go beyond the roadhead. But all looks fine.'

If the trip was to go ahead we had little option but to move to the next stage, pay him a deposit and keep our fingers crossed … for both easy bureaucracy and good weather.

Mike Morrison offered to sort out our visas. Little did he know that he was volunteering to tackle the bureaucratic crux of the trip. The Chinese visa-processing centre in London was clearly not used to issuing visas for the extreme west of China. According to the embassy website, the centre was set up to 'provide a better service' to those applying for visas. Quite how it does that, when it simply accepts applications, refers them to the embassy and then relays its response three days later, is rather beyond me. But they do charge a healthy administration fee for whatever it is they do.

Mike failed twice to collect visas. It seemed our applications were first refused because we had not produced evidence that we had return air tickets. The administration fee for telling us that was £142, not to mention two visits to the centre. At the next attempt the refusal was because we had no evidence that we had hotel reservations for every night we intended to spend in China. Mike pointed out that we were camping but it made no difference. That was another £142 and another two visits.

Mike was sounding pessimistic. 'I just don't think this is going to work. It's as if they don't want us to go.'

That was certainly the impression given by the officials he had spoken with. Rather than helping to overcome problems and encourage tourism, one had gone as far as to ask why we could possibly want to visit such a dull and uninteresting part of China.

Frantic emails to Taher resulted in bookings being made and hotel reservations we never intended to keep being emailed to us. There was time for just one more attempt and we wanted to make sure our documentation was in order. The trouble was that everything was in Chinese and the only people I knew who might be able to translate were those at my local Chinese takeaway. I duly headed in that direction and joined the queue of customers. The man in front of me ordered crispy duck with pancake and I ordered translation services. It all felt a bit odd but the serving staff were very interested and those behind me seemed more intrigued than upset. It transpired that the list of bookings was incomplete and there were a couple of nights unaccounted for. But there was nothing we could do about that beyond dream up plausible explanations.

And so on his fifth visit to the processing centre Mike dropped off the now-thick wad of papers. Three days later we returned together for the crux visit. If we didn't get the visas there wasn't enough time to try again. We were so pessimistic about our chances that we had even gone so far as to arrange permits for a fallback trip to the Kyrgyzstan side of the range.

Mike was an expert by now. 'We queue at this window to pay,' he explained.

'If the charge is £142 they'll give us a visa rejection slip at the next window. So we want them to ask us for more than £142.'

The queue seemed to take an eternity to move and then, heart in mouth, we were standing at the screen and the official on the far side of the glass was picking up a thick wad of papers. I steeled myself to launch into a complex explanation as to why our paperwork wasn't quite in order.

'That will be £261,' he announced.

I could feel myself shaking. I could have kissed him. Fortunately he was behind a glass partition.

Part of the attraction of climbing in the Chinese Tien Shan was that none of us had ever been. In fact, somewhat to my embarrassment, I had to acknowledge that I knew little about the area and had hardly heard of Urumqi, a city of around two and a half million people, the capital of Xinjiang province and our point of entry into China.

A little research whetted my appetite. It certainly seemed a city of extremes: a temperature range from an average of –7.4 °C in January to 30 °C in July, famous in the *Guinness World Records* for being the furthest city from the sea in the world, and ranked in the top ten most polluted cities on earth. Somehow it didn't all quite add up to the name 'Urumqi', which the Chinese bestowed upon the town in 1954 and which translates as 'beautiful pasture'.

Incentives for Han Chinese people to settle here have been extremely successful and the 2000 census showed approximately seventy-five per cent of the population as Han Chinese, with the second biggest group, the Uyghurs, only making up about thirteen per cent. The influx of Han Chinese was not exactly popular with the Uyghurs and in July 2009 conflicts resulted in a reported total of nearly 200 dead. It was the aftermath of this that had led the Chinese government to shut down communications and make it so difficult for us to organise the trip.

Taher was a Uyghur and so we were to see the area from his ethnic minority point of view. This meant getting used to the fact that the Uyghurs operate on a different time zone to the rest of the country. For the Han Chinese there is only one time zone covering the whole of China. The Uyghurs operate on what they refer to as 'local time', which is two hours different from Chinese time. Can you imagine working on a time that is out of synch with the official time that the infrastructure operates by? We couldn't quite believe it, and even by the end we needed to check whether or not people were talking in Chinese or 'local' time.

As Taher had promised, mountain foodstuffs and gas were readily available. It seems a long time since it was necessary to freight such supplies from Britain; every expedition used to start with bureaucratic battles with customs officials. Mind you, one side of me looks back nostalgically on the wondrous sights seen in the customs warehouses of Pakistan and India. Never will I forget the family in Delhi that had imported a huge, luxurious white rug. One customs official made them unroll it completely on the dusty warehouse floor. No sooner was it completely unrolled than a forklift truck shot out from behind a pile of boxes and ran straight over it. The family screamed and shouted in an appropriately unimpressed manner which in turn distracted the driver such that he stuck the prong of his truck straight through a box full of expanded polystyrene. I dread to think what fragile item the box contained. With such memories in mind it all seemed a little tame to fly in with our twenty-kilogram allowances, knowing that we could simply purchase our supplies in Urumqi.

But that is not to say that the Urumqi experience was lacking in memorable moments. The Carrefour store and the outdoor shops selling top-quality equipment at Western prices were something of a surprise, as was the sheer boldness of the sole skyscraper dweller who had the audacity to build his own balcony attached like a wart on the smooth side of the towering building.

More surprises were in store. The town of Yining is 800 kilometres from Urumqi, close to the Kazakhstan border. Taher had hired a minibus for the journey and, having readied ourselves for two days of bumping along semi-metalled roads, it was something of a shock to find ourselves whizzing smoothly along on a modern motorway with freshly painted light blue crash barriers.

Naively we had expected the traditional way of life to be far more dominant and were slightly taken aback at the cultural contrast between the immense amount of modern infrastructure that was being built and the traditional yurts of Central Asian nomads that existed side by side. At one point we cut through a range of low hills where the road was still under construction. A huge viaduct was being built with supporting pillars perhaps 150 metres high and the latest high-tech equipment was in use.

'Fifteen dollars a day,' announced Taher, answering Mike's question about the pay of the ant-like workers covering the scaffolding. As on the Grosvenor trip seven years earlier it didn't take much to understand how the combination of cheap labour and advanced engineering was fuelling the

Chinese dream.

Confusingly, Taher called Yining by its Uyghur name of Ghulja, while many people also referred to it as Ili. Even the most straightforward things in China can be confusing. Anyway, whatever name one used, it was a pleasant place. The popular street eating, with all manner of interesting food cooked on street carts, was amongst the best I have ever experienced and the place – at least superficially – enjoyed a relaxed and happy atmosphere.

I felt less relaxed and happy after slipping in the bath at our hotel. Ignoring the bath mat (for old people, surely), I slipped and bashed my ribs so heavily against the side that I lay on the floor for some time and was in pain for most of the trip. Remarkably dangerous things, baths. The others seemed to find this very funny.

'A proper old man,' laughed Paul on regular occasions.

We wondered why Taher had not stayed at the same hotel as us and were later told that Uyghurs were not allowed to stay in hotels that were approved for foreigners. Conversely, foreigners were only allowed to stay in approved hotels. Later in the trip our Uyghur guide entertained us lavishly in his house but explained that it would not be safe for him to allow us to stay.

'Too many people with too many eyes,' he explained.

Being approved for foreigners is a big thing in China as it allows the charging of Western prices. Aside from the tiny number of foreign tourists (we saw none), only well-off Chinese or those on official business stay at such hotels.

The climate around Yining is less arid than Urumqi and on leaving the town we drove through lush agricultural land, across the fast-flowing Ili River and on towards the town of Zhaosu and our first, distant view of the Xuelian massif. We were amused to see speed cameras on the road, so much a feature in overcrowded England but rather unexpected in the sparsely populated parts of Xinjiang close to the Kazakhstan border. Around lunchtime we passed a large tourist sign sporting a huge photograph of the Xuelian range and prominently featuring the buttress we were interested in on Sulamar.

'Nearly there,' announced Taher. 'Just need to register at the police station.'

Twenty kilometres of dirt track beyond the police station the road ended where several low buildings were built into the bank.

'Shat Hot Springs – nearly there,' announced Taher. I had never before considered that 'Xiate' might be pronounced 'shat'; it seemed an unfortunate name for a hot spring.

The low buildings housed the springs and Taher explained that they were graded by temperature from right to left with the coolest being on the right. The looks of the few locals about made us wary. Was it just that they don't exactly see many white-skinned types around these parts or could they be suspecting that the springs might prompt a reaction worth hanging around for? Either way we resisted our normal temptation to check out the extreme end first and headed towards the right-hand building. The decor was just as I like such things: nothing flashy, just a stone hut with a small changing area and a water-filled hole divided into four by two planks of wood. There was no steam and initial impressions were that the water couldn't possibly be very hot. Soon though four naked bodies were discovering that to insert more than a toe for any length of time was impressively challenging. The cries of scalded white men prompted much merriment outside while inside much willpower was displayed in an effort to avoid complete humiliation. The self-imposed challenge was to immerse sufficiently to duck under the wooden planks which divided the pool into four quadrants. No one succeeded. Rob came closest, Paul and I turned impressively pink and Mike failed to put in more than a toe. We emerged with maximum respect for those 'enjoying' the baths further up the heat scale.

Despite it being a drizzly afternoon, Sulamar was intermittently visible at the head of the valley. First impressions were good, with the prominent buttress that had attracted our attention catching the afternoon sun. We were introduced to Abdhul, our 'guide', and discovered a set of sprightly looking horses waiting for us. Having loaded them up one soon bolted back towards the start (understandable considering the load it was being made to carry), but that aside, progress was steady and by early afternoon on our second day we had reached the delightful summer grazing meadows of Igraldi, which we understood to mean 'male horse' in the local language. By now the weather was not looking so good. Storm clouds were gathering, rumbles of thunder could be heard and the two or three herding families living here were gathering clothes that had been drying in the sun.

Ahead, the track rose towards the 3,800-metre Muzart Pass with our intended base camp on the far side. Soon the rain began; a stream crossing delayed us and we were left trailing as the horses disappeared into slate-grey clouds. Caught out by the weather, we had all left our overtrousers in the loads on the horses. Rob had left his jacket as well and was feeling increasingly cold as the rain turned to sleet and the wind strengthened. It was clearly much further than we had expected and I started to have a strong this-could-all-go-badly-wrong feeling.

One of our horsemen passed us going down with a couple of our horses. He shouted something unintelligible and rode off into the mist, leaving us wondering what the hell was going on. At length we came across some of our bags lying in slush on a steep moraine bank falling into a lake. Visibility was down to five metres or so and there was no sign of Taher, Abdhul, our cook, the other horseman or the horses.

'Hellooooo ... ?'

It felt rather silly standing there shouting weakly into the grey murk, but miraculously Abdhul appeared out of the gloom. He was shivering violently and clearly showing signs of hypothermia. But he did manage to explain that two of the horses had fallen into the lake and swum across to the far side while the others had dumped their loads and returned to the valley. Base camp, he assured us, was only five minutes' difficult walking round the lake.

Anticipating a hot drink and cooked food we carried as much as we could and stumbled onwards. But what greeted us at the base camp was not what we had hoped for. I had never seen local people in such a bad way. They were standing in a half-erected tent, darkness was approaching, nothing was really happening and it was painfully obvious that some were already suffering from hypothermia. Frantic activity followed. Loads were ferried, the cook tent erected, stove started and some semblance of normality achieved.

'Where are our sleeping tents?' asked Paul who had been looking through the loads.

Taher looked blank. It wasn't just a hypothermic blank look, it was a genuine 'I haven't got a clue' look. A horrible realisation came over me. I had thought that Taher was supplying sleeping tents whereas he clearly thought we were bringing our own. As the 'leader' who had arranged everything with him I felt rather embarrassed about not double-checking this. Oh *shit* ... !

Rob was too cold to comment and Mike looked glum, but Paul seemed remarkably unconcerned.

'Not to worry. We will hardly be at base camp anyway,' he pointed out.

But that line of thinking didn't solve the immediate problem. With our mountain tents not being waterproof it was a toss-up between using them or settling down in the mud in the hastily erected cook tent. I chose to sleep in a mountain tent while Paul, Mike, Rob, our cook, the remaining horse owner and his assistant settled down in the mud. Abdhul and Taher slept in the one base camp tent that they had brought. It was sleeting, windy and wild outside and I felt sorry for the two horses that had swum the lake. But from what I could see they were wandering contentedly about munching the slush-covered grass. Sometimes, animals put us humans to shame.

The next day was absolutely beautiful. We could sort ourselves out, dry our equipment and appreciate our surroundings. Abdhul explained that the meadows where we were camped were named Shpalak, meaning 'healthy spring', and had been an important overnight spot when the Xiate Trail was in its heyday. The situation was truly magnificent. Below us, just five minutes away, was the huge mass of the Muzart Glacier and, across it, the stunning west face of Xuelian West – the peak climbed by Kyle, Jed and Bruce. My immediate reaction was that we had missed out on the true plum of the range.

It was time to acclimatise and take stock. As ever, we aimed to climb to within about a thousand metres of our intended summit, spend a couple of nights there and then descend to base camp for a day's rest before tackling our main objective.

We duly climbed a mountain of around 5,400 metres (Khanjaylak I – first climbed by Bruce Normand in 2008 with Guy McKinnon and Paul Knott) and then descended to a good bivouac spot at 5,200 metres. The weather was glorious – so hot that Paul felt it necessary to remove his leggings and hang around in his underpants. I felt too lethargic to move and lay sweating gently while reading my book. On the evening of the second day the sky was still clear and so we ate all our remaining food, saving just a muesli bar each for breakfast. With an early start we expected to be eating well at base camp early the following afternoon.

Snow flurries in the night were of no great concern but by morning a couple of inches had settled. We dithered slightly about the potential for avalanches on the descent, but judged conditions safe enough and so headed down into the mist. But the conditions soon became unpleasant. It had started snowing heavily and the snow conditions on the glacier were appalling. Even wearing snowshoes we were soon sinking in badly. I particularly remember that my fully extended ski poles could nearly always be pushed in right up to the handle. This made it impossible to probe for crevasses and induced a niggling feeling of discomfort. These were snow conditions as bad as any I had come across. To add to the rapidly accumulating problems the mist was down, making for white-out conditions. We proceeded hesitantly for perhaps fifteen minutes until Paul, a dark blur ahead of me, suddenly disappeared. I jumped back into the snow and steeled myself for a force that never fully came. He had fallen into a crevasse but, remarkably, managed to stop himself on a projecting snow platform just below the surface. We continued even more cautiously but, gradually, I felt I was losing my bearings. Up ahead, Paul was persevering in the heavy snow and whiteness.

'Are you sure you know where you are going?' I asked him.

'Not really.'

I am relaxed about my navigational limitations but Paul doesn't like to admit to being unsure. This was a major admission for him.

Wandering aimlessly on a crevassed glacier seemed a pointlessly dangerous exercise so we pitched the tent and sat there staring at each other. The temperature was hovering around freezing, it was damp and our remaining food had been eaten that morning. This was, after all, only an acclimatisation outing and we expected to be back down at base camp that evening. Every now and then one of us would peer out of the door.

'Hope we are not pitched on top of a crevasse,' I commented unhelpfully.

We sat there, slightly unsettled by my uncalled-for comment, and gradually began to feel the damp and cold. Eventually Paul spoke the question that was impossible to answer but most on our minds.

'Wonder how long before it clears?'

We peered into the whiteness. After perhaps an hour I was starting to think about getting into my sleeping bag when a slight thinning of the mist revealed a rock wall and we were able to get our bearings.

Off we went again on the deep, unconsolidated snow, over ground we knew was riddled with crevasses. Neither of us felt comfortable. We switched positions. Probing carefully, I wasn't in front for more than twenty metres before I felt the snow around me beginning to collapse. I tried to jump back but to no avail. The snow around and beneath me appeared to be bottomless hailstones and I could feel it giving way and sucking me down. With a sense of resigned acceptance I surrendered to an experience akin to being sucked down a giant plughole.

My body was pulled forwards and my face forced hard into the snow. Snow was jammed into my mouth and nose and down the open neck of my clothing and then I fell into blackness. There was no jerking halt – I just kind of floated down. It didn't strike me fully at the time, but Paul was obviously being pulled across the surface. Later he described being dragged through the soft snow like a giant snowplough, only coming to a stop when a veritable dam of snow had built up in front of him.

I came to a gentle halt. My senses first registered that I was hanging in complete darkness. The next sensation was one of extreme discomfort as water poured down my unzipped neck and my specially chosen lightweight harness cut harshly into my thighs. I could feel my body temperature rapidly dropping; urgent action was essential to avoid a bad outcome. Removing my sunglasses shed new light on the situation: I was hanging completely free and our single seven-millimetre rope had cut deeply into overhanging eaves adorned with huge icicles that poured with water. I was rotating slowly and could see that I was ten metres below a surprisingly small entry hole through which weak rays of daylight filtered. A metre or two below my feet was a fragile twenty-centimetre-wide ice bridge where a huge icicle had somehow frozen across the crevasse. Either side of this I could make out glistening, gradually converging ice walls plunging into blackness. I dangled forlornly, rucksack pulling me backwards and snowshoes and ski poles feeling an ineffectual encumbrance. All in all, it did not seem to be a great position to be in.

'Slack!' I screamed as loudly as I could.

I thought that if I could get into a position where I was at least half supported by the icicle bridge I might be able to escape the water and be in an easier position to sort myself out. But immediately after I had shouted I feared I had made a terrible mistake and Paul might lower me all the way into the blackness.

Perhaps fortunately, there was no response whatsoever and I instinctively knew that my shouts were being completely absorbed by the snow and ice. Braced ten metres or so back from my entry hole, Paul had no chance whatsoever of hearing me. It was entirely up to me to do something.

At the point where I was dangling the crevasse was perhaps two metres wide and I could just about touch the far side. Above me the wall on my side overhung gently. I had last practised prusiking out of crevasses on the Kent sandstone in 1970 and this was not the ideal spot to test my memory. In any event there seemed little point in ascending a rope that ended in an icicle-adorned horizontal overhang pouring with water.

My first priority had to be to get out of the water. I was getting increasingly wet. The hood of my down jacket had wrapped itself around my neck and the wet clamminess of the fabric was pressing uncomfortably against my skin.

The far side of the crevasse was just about vertical and I was pretty confident I could climb it if only I could remove my snowshoes and somehow get into a position where I could use my axes and crampons – both of which were attached to the back of my rucksack.

As a first move I wriggled my wrists out of the ski pole wrist loops and carefully made sure that I clipped them into my harness. The light was such that it was difficult to see clearly, and if I dropped any crucial equipment that would be the end of any climbing aspirations for this trip. Next, I swung my rucksack round in front of me, removed my axes, and after some tricky swinging manoeuvres, managed to get one of them well placed in the wall. At least I could now clip into a secure placement, get out of the main flow of water and not be completely reliant on Paul, who I guessed must be hanging on to the rope for dear life and wondering what the hell was going on down below.

My footwear posed more of a problem. Removing my snowshoes was difficult but the more serious challenge was my crampons, which I had foolishly tied on to my sack with a length of thin black cord. In the gloom of the crevasse it was difficult to pick out the knot. The situation was not eased by my contact lenses, which allowed excellent distance vision but made close-up work extremely blurred. I contemplated getting my head torch out but decided that the risk of dropping things was too high. Instead I removed one contact lens to give me some close-up focus and, with increasingly numb fingers, picked at what I could now see of the knot. It was with a sense of relief that I finally managed to remove my crampons and clip them safely into my harness. Further contortions followed as I tied them to myself to prevent them being dropped while I secured them to my boots. Eventually, after what seemed an age, I was ready to climb and screamed up to Paul.

'Take in … '

As expected there was no response, just the sound of water pouring from the icicles. Communication was impossible. I started to climb but the ice was so hard that I had real trouble getting secure axe placements. Fortunately Paul sensed the slack rope and took in until finally, with the help of a very tight rope, I was able to thrash inelegantly out of my entry hole.

Gasping on the surface I felt distinctly like an exhausted seal emerging from a blowhole. Paul was kind enough to comment that I looked like one too. Falling in crevasses, I decided, is not to be recommended.

The trouble with getting out of a crevasse on the same side as your partner is that you still have to cross it. After a rest, I proceeded to do so with extreme caution and much crawling. Despite the soft snow we both replaced our snowshoes with crampons and held axes at the ready. Anything but risk a repeat of my earlier contortions.

By nightfall we had managed to descend to the main Muzart Glacier. The snow had been falling amazingly fast, so much so that what had been snow-free moraine on the way up now avalanched frighteningly. What had taken a few hours on the way up took a whole day to descend.

The following morning it was still snowing, with an even metre of accumulation. Progress was painstakingly slow. Paul was moving strongly but I was exhausted. Midway through the day I shat myself and as we pitched the tent and ate our last boiled sweets we were still only halfway back.

On the afternoon of our third day of descending we arrived at base camp having been without food for two days. Our acclimatisation exercise had proved a little more testing than usual.

Our plan had been to walk up to the head of the Muzart Glacier to tackle Xuelian East, but the prospect of a twenty-five-kilometre wade on a crevassed glacier was unappealing. Instead we decided to aim for our reserve objective, the north face of Sulamar. Sulamar is a 5,380-metre peak which had attracted our attention in a panoramic photograph of the range and dominated our walk in to base camp. From what we had seen the face sported an eye-catching and steep buttress line leading directly to a summit that had been visited just once before, by Bruce Normand's team two years earlier.

The more we contemplated our revised objective, the more enthused we became. The fact that none of the photographs we had seen or the views we had obtained showed the bottom section of the face was merely an extra uncertainty to add to the usual raft of unknowns that go with greater-range climbing. There was, though, one huge uncertainty: which valley was the foot of the face actually in? Our rudimentary map had disintegrated when the horses fell into the lake and the answer was by no means obvious.

It was with a sense of exploratory excitement that we left base camp, retraced our steps along the walk in, confused the Kazakh herdsmen at Igraldi by wandering through their summer meadows wearing full mountaineering gear, and headed in the direction that we hoped would lead to the north face of Sulamar.

Soon we were fording difficult watercourses and thrashing through lush, green vegetation. It was with some elation that, late that afternoon, we exited as almost certainly the first mountaineers to ascend this long and delightful ablation valley, and were able to see that not only were we in the right valley but there were no insuperable obstacles to reaching the foot of the face.

Pitching our little tent on snow at the foot of the face, we ate our crunchy fish heads (being unable to read Chinese we never know what's in food tins!) and noodles and scanned the full face for the first time. There looked to be some extremely steep ice on the first half and difficult mixed ground towards the top. But the main thing that struck us was how big the face was for a 5,380-metre peak. The height from bergschrund to summit was about 1,600 metres.

'Four a.m. alarm?' suggested Paul. 'Local time?'

Local time or Chinese time aside, a clear night gave a good frost and we were pleased to be at the first challenge, a steep band of snow-dusted rock, by daybreak. The difficulties and problems started immediately. The first pitch was tricky mixed ground and for reasons I still can't explain both of my crampons started to come off at the same time. Paul watched with an air of detached despair as the minutes ticked by while I perched, stork-like, on little steps cut in the ice and secured each crampon in turn. I was beginning to feel a bit of an expert at attaching crampons in tricky spots but, concerned about a repeat performance, I tied a safety cord to each one. They never loosened again but I did regularly trip over the cords.

The rock was interesting or appalling, depending on one's take on such things. It varied from slate-grey shale to shattered marble – both equally unhelpful for finding secure protection. With the benefit of hindsight it would probably have been easier to link together surprisingly crisp snow patches, but having committed ourselves to rock, we persevered with time-consuming technical looseness, finally gaining what had looked to be an ice field rather later than we would have liked.

The 'ice field' was in fact rock slabs covered in powder snow. It demanded care and was not at all the fast ground that we had hoped for. Above, ice beckoned in the form of two unusual and very steep ice cones. How these cones had formed prompted a fair bit of discussion. The left-hand one was near vertical for a good hundred metres, whereas the right-hand one was perhaps seventy-five degrees. We concluded that they were almost certainly an unusual result of particularly severe spindrift avalanches and we would do well to get above them before the regular afternoon electrical storms began.

It was not long before we had failed in our race against time and our theory had been proved correct. The deluge, when it arrived, was huge. The 900 metres of face above us emptied vast quantities of fresh snow down the shallow gullies above each ice cone. I was belayed near the top of the right-hand one, just to one side of the flow, and the noise was akin to standing next to a speeding express train. The air was full of choking, wind-blasted snow. Paul had just pulled out of sight and I could only hang there, well muffled on my belay, and wonder how he was doing.

Nothing happened for a long time. Eventually the rope started to be taken in and I could only assume that I was expected to climb. It transpired that he had managed to cross the main flow before it came down and was belayed on the far side – a situation that meant that I had to climb directly through the maelstrom. The experience was distinctly memorable and not one that I would care to repeat.

A brief attempt at further upward progress failed in incessant spindrift and we focused instead on digging out a sitting bivouac shelf from the impressively loose and fractured rock. Later, as we sat, the clouds parted momentarily and it was reassuring to see that we were now level with the unclimbed peaks on the opposite side of the valley.

A grey dawn prompted gentle grumbling. Paul's back was aching and my ribs were still hurting from my incident in the hotel bath. On the bright side, the spindrift had stopped, upward progress was possible and challenging climbing is a great cure for aches and pains. The section that stopped us the previous day was quickly dispensed with and, in improving weather, we made good progress up a pleasant snow crest, across a delicate traverse and up a shallow couloir with great climbing up steep icy steps. Way above us we could see a prominent overhanging rock wall that we knew marked the top of the face.

Paul and I tend to adopt a relaxed nine-to-five approach to mountaineering. We enjoy savouring our limited time in the mountains and have no desire to rush up and down as quickly as possible. Usually, we start keeping an eye open for reasonable bivouac sites from mid-afternoon onwards. Here though, there seemed good reasons to make an exception to the rule. Above us it was pretty obvious that steep, uncompromising ground continued all the way to the top and comfortable bivouac sites were non-existent.

Furthermore, it seemed just possible to get to the summit ridge before nightfall and we guessed there would be a good spot there to pitch the tent. The temptation was too much; we made the decision to climb into the night if necessary.

Having made this decision it was perhaps inevitable that the daily electrical storm should be earlier and more intense than usual. Clouds gathered, visibility reduced and the ground was illuminated by wild flashes of blue followed instantly by ear-splitting cracks of thunder. The wind seemed to gust from all directions and the face was awash with spindrift. Regretting that we hadn't dug ourselves in earlier, we persevered. But it was hopeless; the combination of darkness, cloud and snow made route finding impossible. There was nothing for it but to bivouac as best we could.

The chosen site from limited options was a small ice step under a slanting overhang. It was protected from the worst of the spindrift but inconvenient in every other possible way. After two hours we had fashioned an unattractively outward-sloping bucket seat and Paul had ripped his down jacket on jagged rocks. The conditions remained wild, and in an effort to keep crucial equipment dry and facilitate a quick exit if need be, we decided to don all our clothes, keep our boots on and not get into our sleeping bags.

Positioning ourselves with the tent fabric over our heads as best we could, we set about tying ourselves snugly into the belay loops that Paul's mother-in-law had expertly sewn through the corners.

'She will be happy to know that her efforts are being put to good use,' commented Paul.

It was probably the last positive observation of the night. After less than an hour my wriggling was attracting adverse comment.

'What are you doing? Can't you sit still?'

I suppose Paul was right that a little fidgeting was going on. At the time of his asking I was experimenting with a new position that involved a semi-inverted hang with my head down and knees and elbows against the slope. This went some way towards relieving pressure from my leg loops and restoring circulation in my legs but did not satisfactorily resolve the general discomfort problem. Much to Paul's annoyance I spent the rest of the night in a never-ending quest for a comfortable position.

Daybreak revealed that we had been hanging a mere twenty-five metres from an easy exit through the summit cornice. If we could have seen where we were going it wouldn't have taken more than twenty minutes to gain a spot where we could have escaped the face and easily fashioned a ledge for the tent.

But the difficulties were not over. Instead of a straightforward ridge to the summit we were faced with a long and crenellated snow crest that was roasting hot on one side and bottomless powder on the other. Initial impressions were that it looked horrendous and, although nothing was said at the time, we both admitted afterwards that we wondered how feasible it might be. After a slow, exhausting and precarious couple of hours we came across a flat area, and despite it being only midday convinced ourselves of the reasonableness of stopping and enjoying an idyllic, relaxing afternoon brewing, reading and generally soaking up the view. In a predawn start the next day it was amazing how much easier it all seemed, and an enjoyable traverse in spectacular positions led to the summit.

Traversing a mountain has an aesthetic appeal about it and we had decided that, in the event of success, our preferred descent route would be the unclimbed south ridge. Realistically the only other option would have been descending the route Bruce Normand and Guy McKinnon had followed in 2008, which would involve descending the full length of the glacier that sported the crevasse that had so occupied me earlier in the trip. That was something I was extremely keen to avoid.

It is often said that the descent is the most dangerous part of mountaineering and I have to admit that it is my least favourite part of any mountain adventure. Abseiling in the big mountains inevitably leads to reliance being placed on a single piece of gear, whereas descending slopes and glaciers opens the doors to avalanche and crevasse danger. Both are a big move away from the relative security of technical climbing where one person is belayed at all times and the leader will almost always have placed additional protection.

We had had a good view of the south ridge from walking up the Muzart Glacier and had seen what looked to be a reasonable descent from the south end. From the summit, the upper section could be seen to be straightforward and after thirty minutes or so of summit relaxation we were off, moving easily together. But again the snow was soft and deep and the enervating ground began to take its toll. A short rise proved ridiculously exhausting and the prospect of another, longer slope leading up to the final prominence on the ridge was enough to prompt a re-assessment. Snow slopes to the west looked to give a less tiring possibility.

'Straightforward.'

'Just a walk down to the glacier.'

'Much easier than continuing along the ridge.'

Persuasive observations flowed thick and fast and soon we were descending easy ground, confident in the belief that we would be off the mountain that night. Considering our combined experience of over fifty years in the mountains, we shouldn't have been surprised by what happened. But we were. After descending about 600 metres it became clear that our smooth, easy slope ran out into enormous ice cliffs that were completely invisible from above. And to add to the challenge bad-weather clouds had reduced visibility to an intermittent white-out. Retracing our steps up to the ridge was dismissed as out of the question, and with our mountaineering acumen brought back sharply into focus, a bivouac seemed the sensible option.

Morning was slightly better. Although the sky was grey and bleak we could at least see the Muzart Glacier below. Unfortunately we could also see the true scale of our predicament. The ice cliffs stretched right across the slope and dropped into a series of rocky, avalanche-swept gullies of the most unpleasant kind. In places the cliffs overhung and looked to exceed the length of our fifty-metre ropes.

All in all it was very distressing. We downclimbed, made a short abseil to a lower platform, traversed backwards and forwards, and eventually chose a spot for a completely free forty-metre abseil. This would lead to ground that we hoped to be able to traverse to an obviously safe spur from where it looked possible to walk down to the main glacier.

It was one of the most frightening abseils I have ever done. In the absence of any other possibilities we constructed an Abalakov thread. Named after the Russian climber Vitali Abalakov, this way of abseiling has transformed descents on ice. A tubular ice screw is used to bore two interlocking holes in the ice and a piece of tape is then threaded in one hole and out of the other to make an abseil sling. The strength obviously relies on the consistency of the ice and the dimensions of the thread but in general they are amazingly strong.

I had never done a free abseil on seven-millimetre ropes before, or done one with my new superlight belay device. It all made me a bit unsure how much friction there would be. Wrapping the rope below me around my leg for a bit of extra friction, I jiggled around to get the knot over the edge to minimise the horrific possibility of the rope jamming, and eased myself nervously over. The rope hung completely free and it was immediately obvious that the whole cliff was ripe for collapse. Huge flakes of ice appeared poised in a sort of overhanging ice honeycomb structure. I let the rope through the belay plate quickly to accelerate my descent. Unfortunately, the friction of the rope around my leg, together with the weight of my sack, was enough to start turning me upside down and Paul marvelled as I fought to extract my leg from the system while spinning gently in an inverted position. Being someone who feels sick and dizzy at the slightest fairground-ride-type movement, I was not feeling my best by the time we pulled the ropes and contemplated our new position.

From above it had looked as if successful completion of this single memorable abseil would more or less see us safely down. Now, it was clear that we would have to traverse very steep and crumbling marble covered with a dusting of powder snow. And with an obviously unstable ice cliff above us speed was very much of the essence. Coiling a rope as fast as I could I hooked it over my head and set off after Paul, who was moving like a man possessed. It was soon obvious that in my haste to get going I had not coiled the rope at all well. Fighting numerous dropped coils, ongoing queasiness and difficult ground it was a great relief when I finally gained the spur and moved out of reach of any falling ice cliffs.

It was a pretty good feeling to finally walk down easy snow and relax in complete safety with a brew at the side of the glacier. From here we could see that the descent we had originally planned would have been relatively straightforward.

'It's important to make mistakes,' I commented.

'One day we might learn from them.'

We looked at each other and burst out laughing.

Back at base camp, Adbhul, our 'guide', had celebratory beers to hand. In his enthusiasm for them Paul cricked his neck and further activity had to be put on hold for a day.

Chapter 11

The Xiate Trail – Trade Routes Can Be Challenging Too

On the walk in to Sulamar, the odd carefully constructed section of trail had hinted that the route had once seen much heavier use than it does today. A bit of research had revealed that the trail dates back to the Tang Dynasty (*c.* AD 700) and had gone through various ups and downs over the years. It runs for about 150 kilometres from Xiate in the north to Aksu in the south, compared to about 2,000 kilometres by the lowland route. With these distances in mind it is perhaps unsurprising that many were prepared to risk the dangers of the higher path and the trail was an important trade route connecting the two centres of population. But the challenges of keeping it open were very real, and in its heyday up to seventy families lived at the side of the glacier section and were employed to maintain the trail. In the mid-twentieth century, the building of motorable roads on the lowland route signalled a decline in the usage of the high trail and, from what I have read, it was last used regularly in the 1940s when the Uyghur armies used it to launch surprise attacks on Chinese troops based at Aksu.

In the 1980s the significance of this historic trail was increasingly appreciated and in 1989 a Japanese team was reported as the first to travel the route in modern times. The second team to make it all the way was reported to be a Chinese team in 2001, although the leader of their party was swept away while trying to cross the fierce river emanating from the snout of the Muzart Glacier. Since that time it has been reported that 'many had tried but few made it through'. This fearsome reputation had been reinforced by news we received at the beginning of the trip that three trekkers had been drowned on the trail just before our arrival. Curiously though, Abdhul reported that two trekkers had passed through base camp while we were climbing, having come all the way from the Aksu side and successfully waded the Muzart River in the early morning when the upper slopes were frozen and the water level relatively low. Intrigued, we were keen to explore the southern section of the trail, not only because it sounded interesting, but because it would provide access to the Chulebos peaks, an area of unclimbed 6,000-metre summits stretching towards the Kazakhstan border.

From our base camp there was clear evidence of the trail descending towards the chaotic rubble covering the glacier. Having no idea where the trail went next, we followed discontinuous streaks of bare ice down the centre of the glacier until, at the head of an icefall section, the terrain became so broken that awkward climbing and balancing along knife-edges of ice separating open crevasses was necessary. Even bearing in mind the changing conditions caused by global warming, this just didn't seem right. We sat down and peered around. Progress in any direction looked difficult.

Although it had been gloriously sunny when we left base camp, mist filled the valleys. We had assumed this would burn off as the day progressed but by now it was nearly lunchtime and down by the snout of the glacier it was a grey and murky day with visibility of only a hundred metres or so.

Paul was in a positive mood.

'I reckon it's up there,' he announced, pointing to the top of a horrific-looking moraine.

He was right. Over the years the moraine had collapsed in several areas but it transpired that over most of its length a delightful grassy ablation valley housed a still-recognisable track. At one point we even came across what appeared to be old horse or mule droppings, although with access difficult from both ends quite how such animals got there was a mystery.

At the Aksu end of the ablation valley high above a major icefall in the Muzart Glacier stood the readily identifiable remains of an old toll booth with thick walls and completely blocking the way. Nearby were the remains of what appeared to be the accommodation used by those charged with keeping the route open. The only way to have avoided tolls looked to be by braving the icefall we had experienced earlier. That seemed out of the question, so I can but assume that those in control had a pretty free hand in what they charged.

A steep track zigzagged up from the lower end of the icefall. Huge smooth walls of rock hemmed in the broken ice and it was impossible to gain the track from the Aksu side without climbing a few hundred metres of icefall.

We had one axe between us, which was just about adequate. It was difficult to imagine this section being very different when the trail was in regular use and I didn't envy those once charged with keeping the trail open to traffic.

The Muzart River flowing from the snout of the glacier was an angry mass of boiling grey water which appeared impossible to cross. Fortunately, we didn't need to worry, as we were on the north side and the Chulebos valley that we wanted to explore was not far downstream on the same side.

Our permit only covered us for access to the north side of the range, so it felt slightly naughty to be beyond the end of the glacier on the south side. The odd piece of rubbish and, surprisingly, gas cylinders suggested visitors to this area, presumably from the plains to the south. It was just as I started to feel the need to be wary that Paul stopped ahead of me and stared quizzically at the ground.

'Take a look at this.'

He pointed at an indistinct track in the sandy deposits between the rocks.

'Tyre tracks.'

There was no doubt about it. A vehicle with huge tyres had been this way. We stared in disbelief, thinking of the force of the Muzart River, the crossings that were apparently necessary downstream and the drownings we knew had occurred.

'Must have been an outrageous vehicle.'

There was no sign of any reason for such a vehicle to have come this way and we could only conclude that it might have been an army truck driver who had been bored and experimented with how far he could drive towards the glacier. Nevertheless, with the permit situation in mind we didn't want to risk any awkward encounters and proceeded cautiously, wondering what other surprises might lay in store.

We did not have long to wait. Perhaps ten minutes later a huge square shape loomed out of the mist. I grabbed Paul's arm and gesticulated wildly. We could hear no sound above the roar of the Muzart River. What could it be? There was no way to avoid it if we were to carry out our explorations as planned.

As we ventured forward cautiously the mists parted to reveal an ancient stone fort overlooking the plain at the junction of the Chulebos and Muzart valleys. It was perfectly positioned to guard access to the trail and was the ultimate symbol of the historic significance of this route. Although long-abandoned, the stature of the structure was clear and it didn't take a lot of imagination to appreciate that the size and two-metre-thick walls would have made for an intimidating and impregnable fortress.

Now though, the place was derelict and quiet. With the mist clearing at last we could see that there were no other signs of human habitation in the area. What we could see was the churning, coal-black mass of the Chulebos River joining up with the Muzart River to flow on south down the Muzart gorge. How any vehicle had managed to cross such a forceful body of water prompted a lot of discussion between us. There was no doubt about it: it must have been a very large and impressive vehicle. And, we noted simultaneously, if we could somehow gain use of one in the future it could provide easy access to the mountaineering potential from the south.

Turning easily up the broad start to the Chulebos valley we felt reasonably certain that no Westerners or mountaineers had ever been this way before. It was an exhilarating feeling knowing that a whole massif of untouched 6,000-metre peaks lay ahead and we would most likely be the first to view them from close quarters.

Camping on a flat patch of alluvial sand we refreshed ourselves by swimming in a small lake of ice-cold meltwater and soaked in the spectacular view of untouched mountains to the south. Above us the first of the Chulebos peaks could be seen up a side valley. No stunning lines were visible, but we looked forward expectantly to what sights the following day would bring.

It brought a seemingly never-ending slog up the moraine covering the Chulebos Glacier. The broken surface and unstable rocks made for slow going. As the hours passed it became increasingly clear that the glacier was huge – a good thirty kilometres long – and time constraints meant that we would only be able to cover the first third. It was also becoming clear that as much as the Chulebos peaks make up a long ridge over 6,000 metres, the north side that we could see was snowy and did not appear to offer any eye-catching lines. Recognising that our tortuous progress was unlikely to open any new doors we ended by climbing up in to a delightful ablation valley behind a huge side moraine on the north side to soak up a final panoramic view before starting the trek back. If the Chulebos peaks had not particularly inspired us, the whole business of exploring definitely had.

We arrived back at base camp just after the horses had arrived and sat drinking tea as the animals were loaded. I pondered silently before breaking the silence.

'I could get into this exploring business when I'm too old for mountaineering.'

Paul looked at me warily.

'How long away is that then?'

I thought of the future. Objectives beckoned in east Tibet (lots), India, Bhutan, Pakistan … and then Pat Littlejohn and Steve Sustad were always hinting that I should join them on rock climbing trips to Ethiopia. I felt that perhaps I was back where I had started. There just seemed to be more objectives than time available.

'Not yet,' I heard myself saying.

Chapter 12

Alpine Club – The Establishment Beckons

I remember the telephone call vividly. I was sat at my desk drinking coffee, lounging in a suitably relaxed manner and wondering what to do about a bizarre tax case, when the phone rang.

'Hi, Tut Braithwaite here. The committee want to know whether, if you were offered the position, you would take on the presidency of the Alpine Club?'

Tut was the current president and was nearing the end of his three-year term. His approach was not the first time this suggestion had been put to me, but I was wary. The Alpine Club is the oldest mountaineering club in the world and a prestigious organisation. Since its formation as a gentlemen's climbing club in 1857, its members have achieved a fantastic series of first ascents ranging from the Matterhorn to Everest. The latter, climbed in 1953, was a momentous achievement and the numerous members who were involved played a leading role in the club for many years. Typically these people and their successors were very senior people in their professions and ran the club in a tightly controlled and financially efficient manner, such that by the time of Tut's call to me, the club owned assets totalling several million pounds, including a substantial property in London, a valuable library and various heritage assets and investments.

It felt an honour to be asked, but the prospect of being president was daunting. I had served as vice president before and had witnessed first-hand how demanding the role could be. I particularly recalled one occasion when the president was absent and I was called upon to chair the monthly committee meeting. As a young manager in my twenties I was used to chairing meetings of junior tax office officials. This was a completely different challenge. One senior committee member stood up and launched into a long, passionate delivery about something that I had not prepared for and was totally unfamiliar with. Several times I tried to focus him or draw him to a close but I clearly lacked the authority or wasn't firm enough – probably both. Eventually he sat down, by which time I had completely lost track of the point he was trying to make. I still vividly remember the long silent void from which the honorary secretary finally saved me by stepping in to move the meeting forward. With the benefit of hindsight it was a valuable learning experience, but at the time it was an embarrassing nightmare that left me recognising that I would have to up my game significantly if I was ever to successfully lead an organisation like the Alpine Club.

By the time of Tut's call the scene was changing. The 'old guard', as they were affectionately known, were ageing and the focus of greater-range mountaineers had moved from big, organised expeditions using fixed ropes and high-altitude porters to small teams climbing in one push with no support. This way of climbing had become known as 'alpine style' as it was the style of climbing prevalent in the European Alps. And it was exactly the kind of mountaineering that I enjoyed.

Against this background I was very aware that the club faced major challenges. The age profile was a concern and I knew a lot of leading mountaineers viewed the club as 'old school' and had no desire to join. A quick scan through some key statistics emphasised the problem. The Mount Everest Foundation is the main grant-giving body for British mountaineering expeditions and yet less than fifty per cent of expedition leaders applying for grants were AC members. And of the nominees for the Piolets d'Or, the prestigious awards for the 'best mountaineering ascents of the year', only one of the last five British nominations was an AC member. These figures suggested to me that, despite all the hard work I knew was going on, the AC clearly wasn't for everyone.

I felt rather sad about that. As a well-resourced club catering purely for keen mountaineers in a country with no alpine mountains, I wanted it to draw like-minded people together and be an accessible focal point for British mountaineering. And to encourage the majority of leading young and active 'alpine style' mountaineers to join, I felt it was important to have an active president who young mountaineers could relate to.

So how should I respond to Tut's question? When asked previously, young children, a full-time job, writing and lecturing commitments and my urge to go mountaineering had always made me feel that it wasn't possible for me to do justice to the role. But now my children were sixteen and eighteen, my confidence in leadership roles and chairing meetings had increased and, much as I was still concerned about how I might fit everything in, I thought the time might be right. At the age of fifty-five I didn't exactly fit the bill of being 'young', but I would only get older and at least I was still actively climbing new lines in the Himalaya.

I told Tut I would let him have an answer soon and headed home to seek Nicki's views. She was supportive and so the next step was to talk to my tax office boss. He too made positive noises and agreed to my suggestion that I work more flexibly so that I could fully take on the responsibilities. The decision was made. I phoned Tut and gave him a positive answer. He seemed pleased, and the next stage appeared to be straightforward approval at the annual general meeting.

It was then with some surprise that, a few weeks later, I received a phone call from another member asking if I would make way for long-standing member Henry Day, who was keen to be president. I'm afraid the call had exactly the opposite effect to that intended. Having finally decided that I was prepared to take on the role, I had sought informal feedback and concluded more strongly than ever that the club needed an active mountaineer at the helm. I liked Henry and knew he had achieved some great mountaineering ascents, but he was sixty-eight and no longer an active leading mountaineer. I simply did not feel that he was the right kind of person to lead the club at what I saw as a crucial time.

The end result was ironic really. Having initially been so hesitant about taking on the role, I ended up having to go head to head with Henry and put forward a case to a difficult annual general meeting that I was the best man for the job. The names of the proposers and seconders perhaps summed up what a key moment for the club some members felt it to be. On one side, representing the 'old guard', was retired Colonel Henry Day, proposed by consultant neurologist Dr Charles Clarke and seconded by his honour Judge Michael Baker QC. On the other was Mick Fowler, proposed by Tut Braithwaite and seconded by Joe Brown. Apparently it was the club's first contested presidency in its 150-year history and it caused quite a stir in some quarters. The AGM was busier than most and a memorable experience. Only those present could vote and one member even went as far as to stridently criticise the committee for seeking the views of the membership at large and making them known to the meeting. It all struck me as very bizarre.

I won – but winning the election was only the start. As I took up the reins it soon became clear that the structure of the club was such that the president was consulted far more frequently than I had expected or thought necessary. I was fortunate to be supported by John Town, a very able honorary secretary. But even so it was obvious that the time and effort required to fully appreciate the issues and then embark on the restructuring programme I felt was necessary to build a pyramid of responsibility and better co-ordinate the huge amount of volunteer effort was going to be immense. Tax office work would occupy me during the day and Alpine Club matters during the evening. As I strained to satisfy family, organise my own expeditions and keep to writing and lecturing commitments, my juggling talents were soon stretched to the limit.

Initially, I didn't have a smartphone and would get home to find minor issues had generated so many emails that it took me ages to resolve them in the evening. Acquiring a smartphone helped in that I was able to receive emails at work and act promptly to nip problems in the bud. But civil service cutbacks meant that I no longer had my nice private office with high-back chair and curved mahogany desk. Instead I was ensconced in a corner of an open-plan office and visible to all. I felt uncomfortable spending too much time tapping away on my phone and until I started to get more on top of things my colleagues must have wondered why I spent so much time away from my desk. Some must have noticed that I spent a lot of time in the toilet.

In addition to the day-to-day issues there was the need to modernise the club's image and come up with initiatives to persuade more leading mountaineers to join. This required seeking lots of input from others and I could see that, during the three years of my presidency, many sleepless bivouacs would be spent discussing ideas and Alpine Club issues with my unfortunate climbing partners. Little did I know that, in the year that I took up post, my Himalayan climbing partner would be the most senior climbing administrator in the UK and an ideal man to both educate me in the world of climbing politics and to bounce ideas off.

Chapter 13

Mugu Chuli – The Bureaucrats Go Climbing

In 2011 Paul decided to study for a Master of Science qualification to help his work as a self-employed health and safety adviser. Rather understandably he felt that rounding off an income-free year with a Himalayan trip might not pave the way towards marital bliss. A different partner was required.

The climbing partner issue is always a tricky one. I was keen for a 6,000-metre-plus challenge, and for multi-day technical climbs on such mountains it is pretty obvious that both climbers need to have complete trust in each other. However my track record with new partners is not good. I'm not quite sure why really. It's not that I feel nervous or awkward or anything like that, but there have been several occasions over the years when first climbs with new partners have not gone well.

I particularly remember my first route with Paul. We had gone for a winter weekend in Scotland and had chosen to climb *Route II Direct,* a line that finds its way up the steep Carn Dearg Buttress on Ben Nevis. I had done it years earlier and confidently marched up to the start and uncoiled the ropes. Paul clearly expected me to move swiftly and competently and was noticeably taken aback as it became obvious that I was feeling less and less comfortable. Eventually I had to admit that I couldn't make progress and seemed to have followed the wrong line.

'I think perhaps we should be over to the right. I'll climb down and across.'

At this point I slipped and fell a short distance, ending up hanging against the iced slabs and trying not to look too embarrassed.

'I'll just lower a bit to an easier-looking line.'

I could see Paul wondering how the hell he had ended up climbing with this chap and how he was supposed to descend the blank slabs I had just lowered down.

But that was early days. Since then we have forged a great partnership on greater-range climbs and are well used to situations where one or the other is struggling, lost, cold, frightened, gone the wrong way or whatever.

The partner issue was at the front of my mind when a fortuitous email arrived from Dave Turnbull, chief executive officer at the BMC.

'Potentially interested in Nepal,' it said.

Word had obviously travelled fast. I stared at the screen and contemplated. Since my taking over the presidency of the Alpine Club quite a few emails had flowed back and forth between us.

I thought back. Dave had shown a glimmer of interest in greater-range mountaineering on a climbing trip to Cornwall a few years previously. I knew that he shared my taste for 'away from it all' adventurous climbing. I recalled a very fine winter weekend on the Isle of Skye where we managed to make the first ascent of *Madness Gully* on Trotternish (a long-standing objective of mine) and enjoy a pleasant evening as the only customers of a fine French host in The Flodigarry Hotel. I wasn't aware of Dave having an Alpine career as such – even less a Himalayan one – but we got on well and I knew him to be a solid, competent and reliable climber on both rock and ice. I also knew that, as he was a family man, keen climber and long-standing CEO of the BMC, our lives were full of much the same time-juggling challenges. We would certainly have lots of non-climbing common ground to discuss. The more I thought about it the more I felt he would be a great partner.

So confident was I of his qualities that I never bothered to quiz him closely about exactly what he had done. It was only after we returned from the Himalaya that I read Dave's own potted history of his mountain experience:

> *My only Himalayan experience up to that point was doing the Everest trek from Jiri the year I left school. After that I'd dabbled with the Alps, but generally opted for adventurous rock climbing in the tropics and desert regions rather than snowy peaks. I put this down to an experience in 1990 when Frank Ramsay and I shared a three-day epic on Mont Gruetta. This was to be our 'warm-up' route for the Eiger, but after being hit by a TV-sized block, falling into a crevasse, and skewering my shin with a crampon, we binned the idea and scuttled off home.*

But by that time we had already proved what my sixth sense had told me.

I stared at the email again and picked up the phone. Within minutes Dave had committed himself to a holiday being strapped on to a steep unclimbed face in a remote part of west Nepal.

East Tibet was off limits again and it was becoming pretty clear that I had been lulled into a false sense of optimism by reaching the Nyainqentangla East range in 2005 and 2007. Fortunately, the objective issue was resolved when a rummage through my file reminded me of a possibility in west Nepal that Ed Douglas had drawn my attention to a couple of years previously.

'Came across this face which might interest you,' said the accompanying email.

It showed a very steep face on a spectacular peak with just one obvious line of weakness.

Ed's email continued: 'Not sure how you might get down.'

That worry could wait. The route was eye-catching, on an unclimbed face and in a remote, interesting area of Nepal I had not visited before. Apparently without a local name, the peak had been christened Mugu Chuli. An objective had been found.

For one reason or another none of the usual suspects were available to join us. Dave came to the rescue.

'Graham Desroy has been very keen on Nepal lately. He might be interested.'

I was aware of Graham, or 'Streaky', as a well-known character on the climbing scene for something like thirty years, and had heard stories about his taste for lurid Hawaiian shirts and bandanas – but had never actually met him. Although about the same age as me, he had focused on his rock climbing and managed to keep to a much higher standard than I had. In the last few years though he had become increasingly keen on Himalayan climbing and Nepal in particular. This would be his second trip to Nepal this year.

We had some email exchanges and Graham teamed up with fellow North Wales climber Jon Ratcliffe, who again I knew by name only. Jon, still in his thirties, was the youngster of the team and this would be his first trip to the Himalaya. He too was a talented rock climber and knew Dave well.

We met for the first time outside Terminal 4 at Heathrow. Graham was instantly recognisable by his distinctive features and brightly coloured shirt.

Both Graham and Jon (and Dave for that matter) sported lean and mean physiques that prompted me to peer self-consciously at the little paunch that I tend to develop between expeditions. The thought of getting rid of it is a major incentive for me to make annual trips to stretching climbs on 6,000-metre peaks.

'It's like going to a health farm for four weeks each year,' I explain to incredulous tax colleagues who quiz me about why I put myself through the hardship of multi-day climbs in sub-zero conditions.

On returning I always make a special point of proudly tapping my reduced paunch. I also make an annual promise to myself to keep it that way. Somehow though, it never happens.

Mugu Chuli stands at an altitude of 6,310 metres on the Nepal/Tibet border. Well off the tourist trail, the history of exploration in this part of the Himalaya is not extensive. Members of the Osaka Alpine Club visited the area in 1998, but it was probably a Spanish team who were the first Westerners to get a good view of it in 2008. They christened it Mugu Chuli, decreed it 'outstanding' and returned for an attempt in 2009. They were not successful, but a British team led by Julian Freeman-Attwood visited the area the same year, after which Ed Douglas kindly sent me his email. A Japanese team also visited in 2009 when attempting Kojichuwa Chuli, the highest peak in the area. They failed on their objective but returned in 2010 and succeeded in making its first ascent via the long west ridge. And at the time of my researching that was it: a very small number of foreign visitors and just one ascent in the area.

The more I visit such areas the more I appreciate the rewards of remote adventure and the excitement of visiting new places. And partially to maximise the time spent in the mountains, the more I do my best to minimise the time spent in centres of population such as Kathmandu.

When I visited Kathmandu back in 1995 it was all new to me and I was fascinated by the bustling tourist throngs, the smoking funeral pyres, and the tourist traps of Boudhanath stupa and Durbar Square. On that first visit I had been with Pat Littlejohn, Mike Morrison and Chris Watts en route to the north-east buttress of Tawoche. I particularly remember meeting up with Alison Hargreaves, who was starting out on her 'solo the world's three highest summits in one year' venture. I had never really given much thought to such ventures before and was rather taken aback to realise that the easiest way to secure permission to climb Everest was to buy a place on an expedition which had already booked a place and was being organised by someone else. We met in a Kathmandu bar, and although I didn't know her very well, rapidly it became clear that she knew us – Pat in particular – much better than the team that she was to spend the next couple of months with. I couldn't help but notice that the other team members were chatting happily as friends do while Alison looked very much the outsider. I recalled her telling us that she would get Everest done and then return to the UK to see her young children for a few days before heading off to Pakistan to solo K2, the second highest mountain in the world. And then straight after that she would be off to get Kangchenjunga, the third highest, in the post-monsoon period. Was she really doing it for enjoyment we wondered? And, if she were successful, what would she do afterwards? It all seemed a world apart from our small group of four friends who were just out to have a good time on our chosen climb.

Pat and I enjoyed a great climb on Tawoche and, not long after returning to England, Alison's success in soloing Everest without oxygen was trumpeted across the British newspapers. Both the national press and the climbing magazines were alive with gossip. Is a solo achievement less noteworthy if there are already steps in the snow? What about using fixed ropes? Should the soloist avoid such artificial aids to achieve a truly unsupported ascent? And what about other people – does their presence on the mountain reduce the degree of commitment and therefore the achievement? Is the only true unsupported solo ascent a naked one? But even Reinhold Messner wore clothes when he soloed Everest in the monsoon season with no one else on the mountain and no one in support except for his girlfriend at base camp. And no one would ever suggest his solo ascent was compromised in any way. It's all very complicated, this ethics business.

A few weeks after Tawoche, Pat and I were copying each other's slides and generally wallowing in retrospective pleasure. But the newspaper headlines had drastically changed. Now they were all about Alison's death on K2 and the debate was over whether she had been an irresponsible mother to take on the risk inherent in climbing K2.

Back on that first visit to Kathmandu I had been excited to be there and spent hours exploring the back streets in search of new sights. This time, a combination of overfamiliarity, extreme commercialisation and limited holiday made me keen to restrict my stay. And so, the evening after we flew into Kathmandu airport, the members of the British Mugu Chuli expedition were settling down for a sixteen-hour public bus ride to the town of Nepalgunj. Somehow we had ended up on the back row of seats. This was bad planning as the road to Nepalgunj is not the best and Nepali buses tend to have a lot of bus projecting behind the rear wheels. This means that every now and then those on the back row are catapulted forcefully into the ceiling. The window seats, taken by Graham and me, had the added challenge of ceiling fans to smash into, whereas Jon and Dave on the middle seats found that it was simply impossible not to slip forwards on to the floor.

This was the first time I had travelled outside the tourist areas of Nepal and the contrast between them and the rest of the country was immediately apparent. For a start we were the only white-skinned people on the bus. Occasionally we would stop for breaks at ramshackle eating places, but there was none of the glitz and Western food of Kathmandu here.

For us limited-holiday types an unavoidable concern when visiting remote places is that things never go quite according to plan. Delays caused by porters refusing to continue or vehicles being halted by landslides can usually be sorted out in a day or two. Here though, the next leg was by light plane to an airstrip five or so days' walk from Mugu Chuli. Nepalgunj Airport had a small but modern-looking LCD display detailing outgoing flights, helpfully recording three departures to Rara, our intended destination. But the morning mist hung around and by the time of the last scheduled departure no planes had taken off. I am not a great fan of hanging around waiting for planes. It's a kind of impotent feeling. Frustration builds, other options are out of the question, and there is absolutely nothing that can be done except hope the delay is a short one. Expedition folklore is littered with stories of aspiring mountaineers who never actually made it to base camp. I hoped we wouldn't join them. Luckily, by mid-afternoon we had loaded up and were ready to take off. Our pilot, we couldn't help but notice, sported a delightfully inappropriate T-shirt featuring rows of skulls wearing old-fashioned Biggles-style aerohelmets.

At first sight the airstrip in Rara appeared stuck to the side of the mountain. Disturbingly it was just possible to pick out a crashed plane carcass to one side. By the time of our return journey, our plane too would be resting forlornly at the side of the runway, its buckled propeller sitting sadly next to the little tent which appeared to be the pilot's living accommodation while repairs were arranged ...

As an incentive to encourage more tourism, some of the bureaucracy traditionally associated with Himalayan climbing was no longer necessary in west Nepal. For peaks below 6,500 metres the mandatory liaison officer requirement had been lifted and, beyond securing the necessary permits and reporting to the authorities in Kathmandu, we were more or less free to do as we wished. We decided it seemed sensible to employ a cook/security guard/interpreter and an assistant, but being keen to keep the costs as low as possible we shunned all other assistance and proceeded on a 'do it yourself' basis. This is the approach I have always adopted, although I have to admit I sometimes wonder whether it might be worth the extra cash to agree an inclusive price with an agent and take it from there. But as both Prem our cook and Purbah our kitchen boy had been all the way to base camp with the British team in 2009, we felt pretty confident of a smoothly executed, good-value expedition.

The muleteers who arrived first thing the following morning looked a surly couple of lads and it soon became clear that our cook's efforts at negotiation were not going well. Everything else in the area seemed very cheap but mules were apparently the exception. Unhappy faces greeted the realisation that it was going to cost in the region of £1,500 to take our equipment to base camp and back. I shouted, Graham put on his stern face and we stressed that if they insisted on charging so much other parties would be put off and ultimately it would be them that would suffer. It must have been something like two hours after negotiations began when all appeared to be amicably agreed and we were ready to go. It was then that Prem relayed that a little 'problem' had arisen and it became clear that our stern looks and vague threats to future income had clearly had no impact whatsoever.

'What do you mean we need to pay extra for their food?'

I recalled this issue arising on a trip to Peru back in 1998. On that occasion the cost of donkey food had become a major issue. Cash had eventually been handed over after which I never saw the donkeys eat anything other than the lush grass growing freely alongside the track. I was determined not to be ripped off like that again so Prem was instructed to refuse any additional payment. The argument raged but as luck would have it the mules gave timeous support to our case by starting to eat cardboard boxes.

'Look,' I gesticulated angrily. 'They eat anything. No way are we paying extra for their food.'

And so it was left, the arrangement being that for £1,500 they would get our equipment to base camp and back. Beyond that matters were vague. The expectation was that it would take five days. We said we would consider a bonus if they made it in less but there was no agreement about what would happen if it took longer. As we finally left one of the loads fell off immediately. It struck me that maybe we should somehow have tried to be more precise in the event of incompetence preventing successful completion of the job.

Nevertheless, it was great to be underway at last and the first day ended with us in high spirits, camped on the field of a tiny school in the hamlet of Lumsa. The headmaster proudly showed Dave and me around his little school. I knew that the area was in receipt of international food aid, but everyone that we had met thus far appeared well fed and it had not truly dawned on me how impoverished the region was. Tess, my daughter, had recently returned from a six-month teaching placement on a remote island in the Vanuatu group and, perhaps with that in mind, I was particularly interested in the facilities. Taking after her father's penchant for the interesting and unusual, Tess had asked to be placed in the most remote and culturally interesting placement possible. She ended up teaching in a small island school that had never had any volunteer teachers before and stayed with a family that only spoke the local language, Bislama. Nevertheless the classrooms had plaster on the walls and rudimentary teaching aids were on hand. Here in Lumsa the two or three classrooms were in a low, single-storey building overlooking the river. The situation was idyllic but the walls were bare stone, the furniture was wooden benches and the only visible teaching aids were a blackboard and chalk. In the headmaster's study a few alphabet charts adorned the walls, but the overall impression was of an establishment that could only provide a very basic level of learning. We asked about placements for foreign students willing to help out but the headmaster just laughed. It would be a harsh posting but, for better or for worse, it appeared that help of this kind didn't stretch as far as Lumsa.

The night on the school field was all very comfortable but by 10 a.m. the following morning there was no sign of our muleteers and from the gesticulations of an increasing crowd of locals it was clear that a problem had arisen. It transpired that our muleteers had started out along the track to check out a landslide which the locals suggested might be impossible for the mules to cross fully laden. Why it took so long to decide what to do I will never know, but, perhaps inevitably, the end result was further payments to everyone even vaguely associated with a very limited amount of load ferrying. In fact by lunchtime the four of us had borne the brunt of the effort required and were in no doubt that unloading ten mules, ferrying their loads across tricky terrain and reloading them is very tiring and time-consuming.

But it was to get worse. Prem valiantly scouted ahead and soon rushed back in an agitated fashion. It seemed that the way ahead was blocked by a landslide that would be impassable for the mules and the only way forward was to cross the river on a narrow suspension bridge and follow a small path on the far side. With the benefit of hindsight this was a ridiculous decision. The track was narrow, the hillside steep and the way forward uncertain. The muleteers must have only had to glance at the intended way forward to know that they didn't stand a hope in hell of making progress this way, but they persevered for a couple of hours before it became obvious that the track was absolutely unsuitable for mules. At this point Prem and I wasted more time by running on for thirty minutes or so just to prove what we already knew in our hearts. We would have to turn back. Finally we ended up recrossing the suspension bridge and camping on the track just as it got pitch black.

I could feel stress levels rising. After two days we were a little over a tenth of the way to base camp. We only had thirty days away from Britain so unless we could somehow speed up the mule travel we wouldn't stand a chance of getting to base camp, let alone climbing the mountain that we had set our hearts on for the last year. We counted out our piles of Nepali rupees and dithered over whether we should ditch the mules and try and employ porters, who could cross landslides, instead. We decided to stick with the mules for one more day. I couldn't help wondering what the next day would bring and slept intermittently. Such concerns tend to result in more sleepless nights than bivouacs on the mountain.

Prem's 'impassable' landslides turned out to be relatively straightforward and were crossed with only one short carry. But there was a strong hint that further challenges were to follow when an old man relayed to us that it had been the worst monsoon he could remember. I had already had an inkling of this when the view from our flight to Kathmandu showed huge fresh sediment fans spewing out from the Himalayan valleys and flooding the plains. It was clear that thousands of man-hours would be necessary to repair the mule tracks and restore normality. And by mid-afternoon news was reaching us that a landslide ahead would necessitate a major detour away from the main track and up through the village of Mangri, which stood on a grassy alp overlooking the main valley.

Agitated screaming in a native tongue was mixed with shouts of increasing concern from Jon Ratcliffe.

'Watch out! What are you doing? The black one's in that garden. And the white one is under that house!'

I ran frantically into Mangri's carefully tended vegetable gardens shouting my best Nepali mule commands. But the more I focused on bringing one animal under control the more the others would roam off to munch nurtured garden produce. The locals were not happy and the situation was beginning to feel dangerously out of control.

In an effort to speed things up Jon and I had taken it upon ourselves to take over mule driving. It wasn't as if we wanted to be doing this but our two muleteers were proving to be enthusiastic drinkers who had stopped for yet another drink and were nowhere to be seen. On the open tracks leading up to Mangri, Jon and I had controlled things relatively smoothly but the narrow alleyways and distractions of the village were proving a challenge.

Jon was a star at it and his Nepali mule-controlling shout brought admiring looks from the locals. My performance was less convincing. The local children seemed to find this very funny and the adults less so. In fact, adult agitation was beginning to run high before a local man took over and guided our sorry train through the village and out of harm's way.

By Mangri the devout Hinduism of the lower valley had more or less given way to Buddhism, and stupas, mani walls and fluttering prayer flags were much in evidence. The world through which we travelled gave the appearance of not having changed for generations. Subsistence farming dominated with electricity and generators in short supply and not a games console in sight. Children came out in force and gave every impression of never having seen a white man before. It struck me that we were five or six days' walk from the nearest road and these kids could quite possibly never have seen a motorised vehicle. After all, they lived in a well-populated valley with apparently thriving communities, well connected by mule tracks and had no obvious reason to trek for a week to reach a roadhead. I can hardly imagine what the local children must have thought when, in 1998, the Osaka Alpine Club had apparently landed close to Mangri in a huge Russian helicopter.

It was with a great sense of relief that the landslide problems receded after we rejoined the main mule path beyond Mangri. By the time we stopped for the night, by a suspension bridge over the river, we were beginning to get positive messages suggesting that all might be well, at least up as far as the village of Mugu, the last settlement before the Namja La pass leading into Tibet. Above Mugu, the bridges had apparently been washed away. But that would be a challenge for a later day.

Much to my surprise day four of our walk-in was interrupted by a police check post and permit check. At first I didn't recognise it as a police post. We hadn't passed any buildings for hours and the 'police station' didn't advertise its presence as such. The police officers were not in uniform and appeared to be deeply engrossed in Dashain celebrations. Dancing, coloured face paint and half-drunk bottles of alcohol were much in evidence.

To my surprise, Prem appeared to be offering to show our permit. The police seemed much more interested in inviting us to join them in their festivities. If Prem hadn't mentioned anything I very much got the impression that we could have exchanged pleasantries and continued on our way. In the event, we were soon sat at a table drinking from generously filled glasses of a strong but unidentifiable local liqueur. At least Dave, Graham and Jon were. I had been struck down with the horrible feeling that I hadn't seen our permit for some time and had no idea where it might be.

While the others were encouraged to drink and eat to excess I began unpacking the mules and searching frantically. One of the joys of getting older is more frequently forgetting where I have put things for safe keeping. Where had I put the permit? It was important, so I would probably have put it in a 'special' safe place. Paperwork was located, passports, money ... but no permit. Eventually I checked the paperwork in my waist belt yet again and there, crumpled between research papers, was the all-important permit. I had no recollection at all of putting it there.

By now the police had persuaded the others to join in with their dancing. Somehow the quick glance afforded to our permit seemed not to do justice to my thirty minutes of increasingly panicky searching. We left the police check with smiling faces, cheery goodbyes and a wobbly step.

The settlement of Mugu charmed us with its unusual medieval-style buildings, adorned with weighty accumulations of firewood. This accumulation had clearly gone beyond practicality and we were told it had become something of a competition that was now putting the structural stability of many houses at risk. Meanwhile the structure of the community was rather obviously at risk from excessive alcohol consumption. Virtually all of the men we came across appeared to be drunk, and, judging by the number of Chinese beer bottles, it would seem that most of the alcohol here had come across the border from Tibet. True to form our muleteers enjoyed an evening drinking session before livening proceedings by having a loud and impressive fight in the middle of the night. The result was one very swollen cheek, one apparently broken thumb, a very frosty relationship and yet more delays.

Being the last village before the border, the Nepalis clearly felt that extra security was necessary as a defence against Chinese invasion. A solitary guard equipped with a gun resembling a blunderbuss stood rigidly to attention. Dave posed next to him for photographs as he stood proudly with his weapon while keeping a keen eye open for any waves of tanks that might descend menacingly from the Namja La.

In fact the prospect was not quite as ridiculous as it must sound. To my amazement, a vehicle track of sorts snaked up the valley towards the border. Although the Tibetan plateau north of the border is at an altitude of about 5,000 metres, it is generally very flat and relatively easy to build roads across. Indeed, if cost was no problem and permits could be easily arranged it would be quicker and easier to approach Mugu from the Tibetan side. The local people we spoke to were enthusiastic at the prospect of better communication with China, although I couldn't help but wonder whether this was influenced mainly by hopes of more reliable alcohol deliveries. Anyway, for whatever reason, it transpired that the improved track only stretched for a kilometre or two and nothing at all had happened for a couple of years.

Seven days after leaving Rara airport the peaks lining the Kojichuwa Khola valley finally came into view. Mugu Chuli was immediately recognisable from Ed's photo and looked every bit as exciting as we could have hoped. And from a beautiful base camp site at about 4,400 metres, only 400 metres lower than Mont Blanc, we could not fail to notice that it was not the only fine-looking unclimbed 6,000-metre peak hereabouts.

The delays with the landslides meant we had only twelve days before the mules returned. With this timescale very much in mind Dave and I set off immediately to incur some altitude headaches. Here, as the terrain immediately west of Mugu Chuli is rolling hills rising to just over 5,400 metres, we were able to acclimatise by making a couple of walking forays over hilly summits and soaking in marvellous views of the mountains and the Tibetan plateau. We endured three nights at a 5,100-metre camp before decreeing ourselves acclimatised and ready to attempt the wonderful-looking direct line up the west face that we had first seen in Ed's photo. Taking into account a day sorting everything out at base camp we now had just seven climbing days until the mules arrived. With the face one day away from base camp that left just six to climb the mountain and get down. And our best estimate was that it might take seven.

The squeaky, white ice could not have been better. The heavy monsoon must have sent thousands of tonnes of spindrift cascading into the narrow lower couloir of our chosen line and compacted it to give perfect climbing conditions. Dave, enjoying his first climb in the Himalaya, expressed surprise. This was a million miles away from the Himalayan snow plodding so often portrayed in the press. Clear skies dominated the horizon and spindrift was minimal. Desperate-looking pitches succumbed with relative ease and as the sun dipped in the sky we were only a couple of rope lengths below the easier-looking central section.

'Where do you think?' Dave looked at me quizzically as I suggested a bivouac on a steep patch of snow to one side. Soon a new experience for him was being savoured. Having cut two narrow ledges, I snuggled down on one in a bivouac sack and Dave on the other in the tent fabric. The weather was perfect, our one-portion-sized dehydrated food between two was almost pleasant and, after a couple of rehydrating brews, we settled down for a good night's sleep.

Next morning dawned fine. Steep, thin ice and spectacular ice streaks led up to more open ice fields and by the end of our second day we were about halfway up the face. We were going a little slower than planned but all in all it couldn't have been much better. It was at this point that I was to demonstrate that nearly thirty years of greater-range experience doesn't make one immune to the most elementary mistakes. The decision to be made was how best to bivouac when faced with a uniform fifty-degree ice slope and intermittent waves of spindrift. I should have insisted that we cut a bum ledge and sat together shielded from the spindrift by the tent fabric. But the temptation of a lying-down bivouac was too much and so I suggested a nose-to-tail ledge. As this was Dave's first Himalayan bivouac in such conditions he was happy to defer to my judgement. But the bivouac sack I was using was new to me and so claustrophobic that I was wary of suffocating if I zipped myself completely in. And so, after a night of increasing spindrift and much squirming, so much snow got into my sleeping bag that it became distinctly damp for the top twenty centimetres or so. Noting that this had happened when there wasn't a cloud in the sky did make me feel particularly silly. In the morning, Dave – relatively snug and dry – marvelled quietly as I sheepishly packed my bedraggled sleeping bag away.

'Just a little dampness. It will be fine,' I mumbled unconvincingly.

Our third day on the face started easily but soon steepened into rock walls thinly covered with ice. The climbing was not too difficult but with the ice too thin to take screws it required concentration and a steady head. As dusk began to threaten we were in a similar bivouac predicament to the previous night. The slope beneath the headwall was smooth and icy and this time there was no hesitation in going for a cut-bum-ledge-and-sit-in-tent-fabric bivouac.

It was only when I unpacked my sleeping bag that I fully realised the effect of the night before. My flippant comment that morning had almost convinced me that my bag was only a bit damp but now the whole thing resembled a frozen football. I unravelled it to the sound of cracking ice and tried my best to remain cheerful and get in. The upper part, I noted, was heavy with blocks of ice.

I tend not to find sitting bivouacs very comfortable at the best of times but usually I am at least able to snuggle down and enjoy being warm. This time I could not bring myself to wrap the upper section around me and was soon shivering badly. Meanwhile Dave had pulled his hat over his eyes, inserted enormous earplugs and was snoring gently.

I spent some time contemplating the coldness of late October night-time temperatures and wondering whether to cut the ice lumps out of my sleeping bag and throw them away. It wouldn't do my sleeping bag much good but they must have weighed at least a kilogram and weren't exactly keeping me warm. I dithered, made a midnight brew, shivered more, and was incredibly grateful that my down jacket had somehow recovered from the dampness. As it happened the jacket was a prototype that I was testing for Berghaus and it was filled with snazzy new water-resistant down. I didn't know that at the time and was just very pleased – if a little mystified – as to why it had recovered so well. Even so, my shivering must have been impressive as at one point I managed to vibrate Dave into a state of semi-consciousness during which he agreed to share his sleeping bag with me if matters should get any worse over the days ahead. Regardless of how the situation had arisen it did seem silly to have one climber using up all his energy shivering while the other snored blissfully. Ultimately I decided to leave the lumps and hang the upper section of the bag out of my rucksack the next day where it would hopefully dry a little in the anticipated afternoon sun.

The previous day had also seen communication difficulties. Dave had been suffering from increasing throat problems that meant that he could only shout in a sort of strangulated cry. And I couldn't hear; firstly because I increasingly can't hear very well and secondly because the cold was such that I spent most of the day with all three hoods up. 'Pardon?' had become the most used word on the mountain.

It was as I emerged from my shivering bivouac that Dave moved very close and whispered in my ear. Initially I found this slightly disconcerting. However, it soon became clear that although he was in good condition in every other way, his throat problem had worsened and whispering at close quarters was now the only way he could communicate. Climbing signals would have to be in sign language from now on. At least that meant we understood the limitations and wouldn't bother saying 'pardon' every few minutes.

Dave continued to whisper quietly as we each enjoyed our usual Snickers bar for breakfast. Soon though his throat problem was such that silence prevailed and he was reduced to a quiet thumbs-up signal to indicate that he was ready to start the difficult-looking traverse to the summit ice fields. We had feared this might be time-consuming powder snow on rock but it turned out to be superb mixed ground in a fantastic position. Each pitch was intricate and absorbing with thin ice providing little secure protection and the easiest way not obvious. We persevered slowly while away to the south we could enjoy the backdrop of the lush mountain valleys of western Nepal, and to the north the skyline was dominated by the arid brown plain of the Tibetan plateau. Along the crest of the Himalaya we could see the conical unclimbed 5,800-metre summit that we knew Graham and Jon would be climbing at that very moment. I hung from the belay and admired the view. It really did feel a privilege to be here. Dave quietly signalled that he too appreciated our position.

The end of the traverse marked the end of the technical difficulties. A few pitches of easier mixed climbing, a series of lung-gasping rope lengths up the final slopes and, just before nightfall, we breached the summit crest to find a perfect wind-scoured flat area for the tent. The summit itself was just a hundred metres or so away and could wait for the morning. It was the first time we had managed to pitch the tent since the foot of the face and we both collapsed thankfully into its protective embrace.

'Wherever did that come from?'

Dave had unpacked a pillow. I recognised it immediately as one that he had used to wedge himself into the driving seat of his car on a previous trip to Cornwall. But whatever was it doing here? I had not seen it on earlier bivouacs and had never seen a pillow used on a Himalayan alpine-style bivouac before. As someone who prides himself on cutting back on every ounce I could hardly believe that I was seeing one now. Dave signalled satisfaction and looked so smug that I took the opportunity to ask him if he had enjoyed his climb and gleefully videoed the resultant croaking and whispering. As I lay my head down on my pillow of rope and boots, Dave snuggled down with his feathery monstrosity and spent some time levelling his sleeping mat by wedging bits of clothing under it.

'Important to be comfortable,' he managed to whisper before falling asleep within seconds.

The spot was wonderfully sheltered and I lay there listening to his slow, heavy breathing. My drying efforts had slightly improved my ice-lump problem and I had managed to get completely inside my sleeping bag and was definitely shivering less than the night before. Mind you, if things had been worse the chances of being able to wake Dave looked slim and the chances of successfully sharing his sleeping bag even less so.

The weather had so far remained absolutely perfect – not a cloud in the sky, and I looked forward to standing on the unclimbed summit early in the morning. A slight concern was that the face had taken a day longer than planned, but I wasn't going to let that interrupt the sense of elation I felt at having reached the summit ridge. With a bit of luck we would be able to catch up later and still arrive in base camp the same day as the mules.

We were somewhat taken aback to unzip the tent and find threatening clouds scudding across an increasingly grey sky. The summit was gained quickly via a pleasing snow ridge, but a biting wind meant lingering was out of the question and thoughts of the descent began to dominate.

Ed Douglas's 'not sure how you might get down' comment had provoked much discussion in Britain. Abseiling back down the route lacked aesthetic appeal and we always knew that it might not be safe because the lower couloir would be exposed to avalanches in bad weather. There was an option of descending into Tibet and then crossing back into Nepal, but the distances involved were such that enthusiasm for that was distinctly lacking. Ultimately, we had told the others that our plan was to traverse the frontier ridge over an unnamed 6,200-metre snow peak and descend the Nepali side from the low point between Mugu Chuli and Kojichuwa Chuli. But this would involve venturing on to the summit snowfields on the Tibetan side, and good visibility would be required for safe progress. The fast-approaching clouds looked likely to rob us of that just when we needed it most.

Graham had brought along a walkie-talkie set and as much as I make an exceptional effort to keep the weight down, it seemed churlish not to use it. In fact, by the time we were at our summit bivouac I was ready to admit that I enjoyed our regular daily chats with the others. Somehow they made everything seem a bit friendlier. In our evening contact from the top of the face we had confirmed that we were sticking to our original plan for the descent. At least, we thought we had confirmed that. In fact, we had unknowingly demonstrated a problem inherent in unclear communication. The signal had been poor but I recall the exchange from our end more or less verbatim:

'All good here,' Dave had croaked. 'It looks easiest for us to start off on the Tibetan side and join the crest at the first col.'

'OK. Enjoy.'

It was to be the last contact we had before arriving back at base camp. But Graham and Jon had formed the impression that we might go for the long-distance option of descending into Tibet, crossing back into Nepal and eventually joining the main valley back to Mugu. Standing on the summit in rapidly deteriorating weather, Dave and I were not to know that. We shook hands in an appropriately British way, managed a brief hug (quite challenging in blustery conditions on a sharp ridge) and headed off back towards our bivouac site and what we hoped would be a gentle contouring descent to the col that separated Mugu Chuli from the snow peak we would have to cross to get to our descent. We estimated that in good weather gaining the top of the descent route should be a long but straightforward day from the summit.

Soon things were not going well. The wind was strengthening, visibility was worsening and the ground was proving much steeper than anticipated. However, beyond concluding that images taken from Google Earth can be very misleading, there was not much that we could do except press on. At length, when we were both traversing horizontally on the front points of our crampons, it became clear that there was a large ice cliff beneath us. Abseiling over vertical cliffs tends to be a one-way affair and, after my experience on Sulamar, I was particularly wary. I was relieved when the mist cleared slightly at just the right moment and we could see that a couple of abseils would take us to what appeared be a reasonably straightforward, if steep, traverse to the col.

By the time we arrived the weather was doing its worst. The wind howled and it was difficult to tell whether the waves of snow that hit us were falling from the sky or being blown up by the wind. Bearing in mind the perfect weather of the previous ten days, I suspected it was the former. To add to the problems, Dave's throat infection was getting worse and it was obvious that he was not feeling at all well.

'I'd be off work if I felt like this at home,' he mouthed in a barely audible whisper.

It is always difficult to know exactly how one's partner is feeling but I was encouraged that he managed a weak smile as he spoke.

Regardless of how either of us felt, visibility was zero and it wasn't at all clear exactly which direction we should take. There seemed no option but to pitch the tent, hole up and hope for better weather the next day.

A niggling concern was growing in my mind. We were perhaps one third of the way along the frontier traverse and it was the end of day six. The mules would arrive the next day and yet, even if the weather suddenly became perfect, it would take at least two days for us to get down. We tried to contact the others on the radio at the agreed time but there was no reception. And that added to the niggling concern. We wondered what they would make of there being no contact.

The next morning steady snowfall added to the challenge and by evening we had managed perhaps two hours of wading. A memorably undignified crawl through deep snow had very much slowed progress on one section. Along the way we used the semi-clear spells to take photographs with our digital cameras in the hope that they would help us avoid crevasses in reduced visibility. They proved laughably inadequate and ultimately, in knee-deep snow and a white-out, we had to acknowledge that for the second night in a row the only safe option was to stop, pitch the tent and wait until we could see something.

The mules would now be at base camp ready to leave and we were still holed up at around 6,000 metres. This was not looking good. We lay in the tent wondering what Graham and Jon would do. We felt guilty causing them so much worry and inconvenience, but didn't think they would leave without us. At the last walkie-talkie contact they knew we were at least one day behind schedule. And, although we had not been able to get in touch with them since, they could see the weather was bad, so it seemed reasonable for them to suspect that we could have lost another day. But what if the bad weather continued? At what point would they conclude that the alarm should be raised? We lay there thinking, as the squalls blew so hard that the fabric of our little tent was pressed flat against our bodies. I wondered vaguely whether we might be better off digging a snow hole.

'How long do Himalayan storms tend to last?' enquired Dave.

There was no easy answer to this question. Having suggested the climb to Dave, I felt rather responsible for the position we were now in. I was also uncomfortably aware that the storm would be dumping lots of snow which would make progress along the ridge slow and tiring and the descent slopes avalanche prone.

'Well ... er ... it varies. Hopefully it will be OK tomorrow.'

My response can't have been very reassuring. We lay in our sleeping bags and passed the time discussing common interests of the Alpine Club and the BMC. By now the committee had accepted my restructuring proposals and my personal time investment had dropped to perhaps a couple of hours a night. A previously time-consuming suggestion that the Alpine Club should negotiate a new relationship with the BMC had dropped off the radar, but there were still plenty of common interests to discuss. Insurance was one issue that exercised both of us. Nepal in particular had seen an increasing number of fraudulent rescue claims and insurance companies were reluctant to offer cover. We discussed options, drew up action plans, righted the wrongs of the world ... and eventually came back to discussing our own predicament.

We had plenty of gas left and so hydration was not a problem, but our food was down to one Snickers between the two of us. Lying there hydrating and gradually weakening for days on end was not a very attractive proposition. The quickest way to lose height was to descend into Tibet. Before the clouds had rolled in we had seen that relatively easy-angled glaciers flowed a long way north to the Tibetan plateau about 1,100 metres below us. So much snow had fallen that the much discussed descent possibility of going down the Tibetan side and then recrossing into Nepal seemed out of the question. That left the possibility of descending all the way into Tibet. I was pretty sure we could descend safely that way but it would risk an interesting diplomatic incident and, more worryingly, it would leave Graham and Jon completely in the dark with regard to our whereabouts. So how long should we carry on sitting at 6,000 metres hoping the weather would improve enough to allow us to stick to our declared descent plan?

Surfacing again for yet another brew our conversation started to drift downhill. We wondered when and how Graham and Jon might raise the alarm and what would happen then. The prospect of the publicity that was likely to surround news that the CEO of the British Mountaineering Council and the president of the Alpine Club were missing did not appeal. Aside from the extreme embarrassment factor it would be very distressing for our families. Oh dear. We discussed likely timescales and concluded that we had three days before Graham and Jon would start to get seriously concerned. Then, even if there was a telephone at Mugu, it would take at least another day to raise the alarm. In my own mind I decided that we should be prepared to stay put for one more day and then if there was no improvement head down into Tibet.

Unsettling as these thoughts were, there was nothing we could do but keep our fingers crossed that the weather would improve. I took out my book to pass the time, only to note with displeasure that it had got damp and turned into a block of ice. In the evening we again failed to make contact on the 6 p.m. radio call.

Perhaps surprisingly we both slept well. Wearing all my clothes, the ice balls in my sleeping bag were only occasionally inconvenient and I was awoken by Dave turning towards me with a big smile on his face. It was morning and the wind had dropped and cloudless skies returned. Time to spring into action. For the first time we could properly appreciate the immensity of our surroundings. We were tiny figures, insignificant in a huge expanse of glacial whiteness. Steep ice cliffs and gaping crevasses dotted the frontier ridge landscape and were an obvious risk for the unwary. Stopping and holing up when we did had been the right thing to do.

Suddenly, the atmosphere was so different. Being able to see is amazingly useful. We walked easily down a gentle, wind-scoured slope, jumped a bergschrund, felt the warmth of the sun on our faces and then sweated uncomfortably while descending south-facing slopes into Nepal. A lot of snow had fallen but by the time darkness halted progress we had made it all the way down to the glacier that we had started from. The surface was irregular rock debris covered in deep powdery snow, and with no chance of finding a place to pitch the tent, we lay down between the rocks and collapsed exhausted in our sleeping bags.

Next morning we were amazed at how quickly the grip of winter had arrived while we had been on the mountain. The upper meadows were covered with a deep layer of snow and the stream in a lush ablation valley was well on the way to being frozen. We passed our first yaks digging contentedly through the snow for a diet of frozen vegetation. I love yaks. They are such hardy animals and seemed much more at home in this environment than I felt as I staggered past. We were tired – there was no doubt about that. At one point I was in front and sat down on a rock to take a rest. I watched as Dave approached and wobbled past perhaps fifteen metres from me. He hadn't seen me and I hadn't the energy to shout; we had both been fully exercised.

At around lunchtime we met a relieved Graham and Purbah who had come up to meet us, carry our bags and deliver assorted edible goodies. Graham shared details of his and Jon's probable first ascent of a peak on the frontier ridge west of Kojichuwa Chuli. Purbah smiled contentedly and we ate and listened. Life felt good.

As is so often the situation, we need not have worried. The snow had stopped the mules arriving on time and base camp had been moved down to the main valley the day before. And we had been monitored more closely than we realised. When the weather had cleared Jon had come all the way up to below our descent route and spent the day watching us through binoculars. He had even gone as far as to leave a cache of food (that we missed) crowned by a flashing head torch to help us locate it in the dark. Now Graham and Purbah had walked up to meet us. We were incredibly grateful. It's wonderful to have good friends.

It turned into one of those occasions when everything worked. The muleteers drove their mules through the night to make up the two days we had lost, a plane miraculously arrived to replace the crashed and broken-down ones, a vehicle somehow materialised at the sleepy airstrip we were flown to and we were back in London on the Sunday in time for Dave and me to be back in our offices on Monday morning.

We had been away thirty days and had been in action every day. Our annual leave entitlement had been used to the full.

Chapter 14

Nottingham Castle 2 – A Brush with the Constabulary

The older I get, the more people ask me what I do to train for mountaineering. Training in the sense advocated by 'trainers' and gyms and the like is something I have never really fancied. Many years ago, in pre-children days, I used to spend every weekend in the UK climbing. And that was, if you want to look at it that way, my training for mountaineering.

As the years have moved on, my obsession with climbing has broadened slightly and my 'training' exploits tend to be more varied, less frequent and more carefully chosen. They include most things that involve playing outdoors: caving, fell racing, biking, kayaking and of course rock climbing. These activities usually take place in the Peak District after work, but opportunities closer to home are always welcome. In this respect, the reinforcement-rod-ridden crack that Paul and I had climbed on Nottingham Castle cliff had stayed firmly implanted in my memory. At the time we were convinced that it would be a one-off climb that took advantage of a lull in the vegetated nature of the place. But we had underestimated the passionate and ongoing enthusiasm that Nottingham City Council was to display for removing vegetation. And so, during regular lunchtime clear-the-head strolls from my office, I was able to monitor an ongoing and thorough cleaning process and feel a sense of excitement building as more climbing possibilities were revealed.

The time came when a glaringly obvious crack line on the left side of the steep central section of the cliff had been thoroughly cleaned and I could feel a growing urge to try and climb it. There were sections that looked as if they might prove too difficult for me, but at least the crack was continuous and might offer some protection at the most difficult points.

After the obligatory 5.30 a.m. Sunday start we crossed the spiky railings and Paul set off enthusiastically. At fifteen metres a small ledge beckoned, on which the workmen had kindly left a curious threaded rod sticking out of the rock. It was only six millimetres or so in diameter and a little too far to one side to make an ideal belay, but Paul tied himself to it all the same. My pitch then involved a tricky traverse into a wide crack of the most sandy and once-vegetated kind. The kind workmen had removed the vegetation but pigeons had already taken up residence and appeared well established. Insecurely fighting my way up through pigeon shit and general sandiness, I was surprised to come across an angle peg – presumably dating from Doug Scott's exploits back in the 1970s. I briefly considered removing it and sending it to him as a memento, but the insecurity level was such that I decided to use it as a runner instead. Ten metres or so higher I pulled on to a tree stump protruding from the crack where the angle eased. The workmen had gone to great pains to reduce root damage by killing off any substantial trees, but fortunately there had not been enough time for decay to set in. The stump felt pleasingly secure as I attached myself to it and stood looking out across the rooftops to the building where I worked.

We were now at the level where camouflaged fibreglass shell replaced rock. Climbing that would be a bit like climbing a thin shield of detached ice, with an embarrassing fall into an alarmed castle tunnel as the penalty for poor judgement or incompetence. Grateful for the opportunity to avoid this, Paul thrashed up short, overhanging walls and ivy to battle finally through dense vegetation and emerge on to the castle balcony.

A man was leaning against a secluded section of the castle wall and smoking a cigarette. He appeared unsure about Paul's sudden appearance and held back until both of us arrived at the terrace. He looked sufficiently scruffy for us to wonder whether he had slept there and we had just woken him up.

'Good morning,' announced Paul cheerfully.

The man drew uncomfortably on his cigarette and walked towards us.

'What you're doing is dangerous behaviour.'

'What leads you to say that? We are enjoying ourselves,' Paul replied.

He pointed towards a sign on the inside edge of the terrace wall.

Dangerous Behaviour Will Lead to Prosecution.

'It's not dangerous. Look, we have all the right equipment.'

The man peered curiously at our ropes, nuts and camming devices. He seemed to find our chalk bags particularly interesting.

'He is president of the Alpine Club,' announced Paul, pointing to me.

I wasn't very sure that this was a good way forward. But the man's gaze had already turned to me.

'The first British ascencionist of Everest climbed here,' I announced grandly.

'I don't give a **** about that. I am going to call the police.'

This was an interesting development. It still wasn't clear to me that he wasn't just dossing round the back of the castle. Now he was certainly acting as if he was a security guard. Whoever he was, it had become clear that any hope of a calm and considered outcome was ill placed. We decided it was time to leave.

At this point the man leapt forward to try and physically obstruct us.

'You ****ers are not going anywhere,' he shouted.

Paul seemed to know his rights in this kind of situation and responded along the lines that physically preventing us from leaving could be regarded as assault and could render *him* liable to prosecution. The man stopped and looked bemused. Unhelpfully I stoked the fire further:

'And you will risk prosecution for wasting police time.'

'You won't ****ing get away with this!' he screamed.

It still wasn't 7 a.m. but it was turning into quite a memorable Sunday morning.

A stand-off ensued. Paul and I discussed whether to force our way past him and try to exit the grounds via our previously used abseil position. Paul was quite keen whereas I urged caution, wondering what this increasingly out-of-control man might do to our rope (and hence us!) if we abseiled in front of him. I also thought that any police that he managed to summon were very likely to arrive in time to catch us and might view an abseil descent as us trying to run away from the scene.

The man was already on the phone by now and we could hear him shouting how urgent it was that police officers attended immediately as there was 'an incident'.

By the time two officers arrived our awkward trio stood in silence by the big iron gates of the castle's main entrance.

'And what is the problem here?' a policeman asked.

I stepped forward: 'This man can't accept that we have been enjoying a climb. He seems to think that we have been trying to break into the castle.'

The police officers took a moment to take in our bright orange helmets and jangling array of climbing gear.

'Not exactly what we would wear if we were trying to break in,' suggested Paul.

'They climbed over the bloody wall,' ranted the guard. (We had by now accepted that he must be some kind of guard.)

A few questions followed, during which it transpired that the police lady was from Paul's home town of Pudsey. The guard was shouting in a curiously incoherent manner by this time and insisted that the policeman join him in a circuit of the walls to check for evidence of a break-in. Meanwhile Paul and the police lady were engaged in much pleasant reminiscing about Yorkshire childhoods.

Unsurprisingly no evidence of a break-in was found. In a final fling of defiance though the guard pressed for our camera cards to be confiscated. A sort of compromise was reached in that we would allow our pockets to be searched for anything incriminating. And on finding nothing of interest beyond mud and pigeon shit there seemed little more to be done.

'It would be better if you sought written permission before climbing here again,' commented the policeman.

I vaguely wondered how the challenge of securing a permit from the bureaucrats in the council might compare with getting a permit to climb from the Chinese authorities. Nottingham Castle cliff and the Himalaya certainly have more in common than the casual observer might think.

A few weeks later a new sign appeared at the base of the castle rock:

Anyone caught climbing will be reported to the police.

It seemed a remarkably weak sign; being reported to the police had been very pleasant.

Chapter 15

The Prow of Shiva – Are We Good Enough to Do It?

The terse finality in the email was no surprise by now. 'Beijing says no.'

Years of rejection have forced me to become adept at preparing reserve plans. And this year the reserve objective was sufficiently inspiring for us to wonder if it ought to be our main objective anyway.

It had all come about after a small photograph in the 2011 *American Alpine Journal* had shown a spectacularly steep buttress on a mountain called Shiva in the Indian Himalaya. The photograph had been taken by an Italian mountaineer called Bruno Moretti, who had led one of only two mountaineering expeditions to have visited the Tarundi valley immediately to the east of Shiva. His objective was Shiv Shanker, or Sersank, 6,050 metres, at the head of the valley and, although his team did not get to the main summit, they reached a forepeak and got a fantastic view of what their report described as the 'magic east pillar of Shiva'. As is so common in the small world of Himalayan mountaineers, Bruno was incredibly helpful. He confirmed our suspicions that none of the peaks around the valley had been climbed from this side and provided much advice and numerous additional photographs that I stared at with a mixture of excitement and apprehension.

For such a rarely visited mountain it was a great coincidence that the same edition of the journal included a report from a Russian mountaineer who was part of the only team ever to have visited the valley to the immediate west of Shiva. Andrey Muryshev had attempted the north-west ridge and he too was incredibly helpful, providing fantastic photographs showing the buttress in profile from the west.

Soon, with remarkably little hassle, permits for Shiva were secured, tickets bought and bureaucratic hurdles overcome. And, as an added bonus, a dodgy operation to fix Paul's back problem appeared to have been a resounding success. Pre-expedition excitement was building. And then, a month before departure, we received an email and more photographs from Andrey. The email did not make for optimistic reading:

> *Frankly I cannot imagine how you will do it. Do you mean the north-west buttress? It is c.700 metres of climbing after the col and it is north-west side in October – all the rock will be frozen. From the other hand, the ice will be scarce as the buttress is very steep. So it will be very hard dry tooling and very hard protection. I saw your route on Siguniang – it is much easier. Frankly I cannot imagine how you will do it.*

That sounded bad, particularly from someone who was clearly aware of the detail of the climb that Paul and I did on Siguniang in 2002 and was pretty obviously clued-up in terms of assessing mountaineering difficulties. From the accompanying photographs it was clear that points of the compass had become rather confused; Andrey's 'north-west buttress' was the same as Bruno's 'east pillar' and was our intended line. And Bruno had already suggested that as much as the line looked stunning, the rock was likely to be terrible. Oh dear.

All in all it didn't paint that positive a picture. But the photos Andrey and Bruno had provided spoke for themselves. Shiva is an isolated 6,000-metre peak in the Pangi district of the Indian Himalaya. Bruno felt the line was the best in the area and Andrey's email ended by saying he thought it was inspiring. That was good enough for us. I did wonder if we were up to it, but loose rock, difficult climbing or whatever: we had to give it a go.

The Pangi district borders Kashmir and the troubles there had impeded access for the last twenty years or so. By 2012 the political situation had improved; roads were being blasted ever further into the Himalaya and mountains such as Shiva had become accessible in thirty-day trips from the UK. To further ease matters, direct flights from London to Delhi were available at much the same price as indirect ones along with, most attractively, a forty-six-kilogram baggage allowance. Times had certainly changed since my early trips to India where multiple flight changes were needed to keep the cost down and the first couple of days would be spent enduring bureaucratic misery retrieving freighted equipment from the Delhi customs warehouse. With all our equipment fitting easily in our hold baggage and with it now being possible to buy mountain gas cylinders in India rather than freight them from the UK, life was certainly a lot easier than it used to be.

Steve Burns and Ian Cartwright again made up our tried-and-tested four-man team, and in late September 2012 we were in Delhi marvelling at people braving the sweaty heat on the new competition-standard climbing wall at the Indian Mountaineering Foundation (IMF) building. It was Steve and Ian's first time in India and they sat through the briefing procedure with a sense of extreme bemusement.

'Your liaison officer, Rinku, will look after your needs on the mountain,' announced the briefing officer.

'What's all this about? What needs?' whispered Steve.

Clearly I had not briefed Steve sufficiently well about the usual course of events at these briefing meetings. I couldn't help but remember the time back in 1993 when the first week of our four-week trip was spent negotiating permit issues with bureaucrats. A few curious briefing statements were small fry compared to the problems we faced then. And although we had only just met Rinku, we knew that he worked together with the agent we had employed to help us in India and he knew full well that we were paying him to get us to base camp and back with the minimum of fuss. And, of course, make sure that we didn't do anything that we ought not to do – whatever that might be.

I must say that I used to always wonder why mountaineering expeditions to mountains like Shiva have to have liaison officers, whereas trekkers visiting the same area have no need for such close attention. Of course, asking tends to prompt responses along the lines that 'it was all taught to us by the British' and, thinking about it, there has been the odd incident that has led to understandable concerns about what mountaineering trips might get up to. The classic one was back in the 1960s when it was reported that the American CIA tried to use top mountaineers to place a nuclear-powered listening device on the summit of Nanda Devi. The device was designed to intercept signals from Chinese missile test-launches in Xinjiang province but was a lost in an avalanche and, so far as is known, has never been found. We had no nuclear-powered tracking devices with us but I have to admit that after incidents like that, I can understand why the Indian authorities might like to monitor exactly what mountaineering expeditions get up to.

There was one other duty to fulfil before leaving Delhi. I had agreed to give a mountaineering lecture at the IMF building. The audience size was underwhelming, but it was illuminating to be told that the thirty or so people present represented just about everyone in Delhi's population of sixteen million that had an interest in technical mountaineering. It would seem that there is no tremendous pressure on India's unclimbed technical gems from the indigenous population.

It is a twelve- to sixteen-hour bus journey from Delhi to the 'honeymoon town' (as our liaison officer called it) of Manali in the Himalayan foothills. Ever keen to save time, the plan had been to catch the evening bus after flying into Delhi that afternoon. But the delay caused by my lecture meant that we were late and had to arrange a private vehicle instead. That was fine, but why all such vehicles have to have 'Tourist' emblazoned across the front does mystify me. I'm not quite sure why but I always interpret 'Tourist' as something of a derogatory term. Perhaps 'Mountaineers' would be better? Or maybe not. On reflection, perhaps nothing at all would be best.

This was my first trip to India where we negotiated an all-in price with an agent in advance. Previously I had taken the view that the agent's cut was such that I would prefer to arrange everything ourselves. Perhaps I am getting old, but I quickly started to change my view after the normally hassle-packed problems were overcome with apparent ease and it became increasingly clear that Westerners tackling the problems themselves inevitably end up paying over the odds such that there ends up being little difference in the overall cost.

A relative of Rinku's ran a hotel in Manali and this made for a comfortable night before starting off for the 4,000-metre Rohtang La pass. For better or for worse construction work was well underway to complete a road tunnel under the pass. When finished, it would make a huge difference to the villages to the north as the pass is closed over the winter months and sizeable towns such as Udaipur are more or less cut off. By 2015, if all went according to plan, these settlements would have an all-weather link to the lowlands south of the Himalaya. No longer would 'tourists' and 'mountaineers' face the challenge of dodging rockfalls caused by bulldozers pushing debris down on to vehicles coming up the hairpins below. I found this behaviour rather amusing, although my views would no doubt be different if I was ever on the receiving end. Paul, as a professional health and safety adviser, simply marvelled at the action. 'It's OK. I am not at work,' he frequently announced.

Sometimes I wonder whether driving is the most dangerous part of a Himalayan mountaineering trip. Here our driver was clearly proud of his vehicle, a Force minibus, which looked a bit like a Ford Transit but could climb hills that seemed ten times as steep.

'What the fuck's going on?'

Paul is normally calm and serene in driving situations but, being in a position in the back well away from the doors, I could sympathise with the urgency in his voice. We were beyond the little village of Saichu and nearing the end of the road. The freshly bulldozed track that we were following was deteriorating badly but Rinku had been telling us about forthcoming elections and how those in power were making every effort to get the electorate on their side by pushing roads and electricity lines further and further towards remote communities. With such thoughts in mind we had every confidence that the track we were following would enable us to drive to the next village, Twan, which Bruno had told us was the last settlement in the valley. With luck, that would shorten our walk-in to just one day. Spirits were riding high at the prospect. But soon the zigzags became so acute and the surface so poor that concerns were becoming evident – at least in all but our driver, who ploughed on regardless with a distressingly manic grin on his face. At a particularly steep bend the wheels spun, the engine stalled and it quickly became clear that the handbrake wasn't strong enough to hold the vehicle. As we rolled gently backwards towards a huge drop Paul could be forgiven for swearing from the back; I rested my hand firmly on the door handle as the now rather severe-looking driver struggled to get the engine started again.

But, as most dangerous moments do, the incident passed quickly. I suppose it had to really, one way or the other. The engine sprang back to life and a clutch-burning, wheel-spinning hill start saw us creep round the ridiculously steep bend to the next horizontal section. The track was clearly designed for four-wheel-drive jeeps rather than overloaded minibuses. Suddenly this wasn't very funny. But at least the steepest section was behind us and Twan was now visible in the distance. Nevertheless the incident left nerves frayed and nervousness levels high.

'All out,' announced Rinku decisively.

Seldom have I seen a vehicle empty so quickly. The road had ended. Just like that. Without a hint of a turning spot it had narrowed to a path just a metre or so wide which traversed a forty-degree hillside. This appeared to have escaped the attention of our driver, who was probing relentlessly forward. Rinku's shout caused him to stop and it was with considerable relief all round that his optimism faded as we abandoned ship. Doubtless thinking we were all complete lightweights, he reversed rapidly to a spot where he started a lengthy twenty- or thirty-point turn.

It had been a long day and ended with us camped on the track wondering how best to move forwards. But one of the things I have always found attractive about India is that things just seem to happen. Here, just as dusk and dreary drizzle arrived, a man with two mules appeared. I have no idea who he was or where he came from but it appeared that he owned several more mules and was happy to load them up and carry our kit into base camp.

Next morning arrived and miraculously so did the man and several mules. But it became clear there was a problem. He had a lucrative job lined up for two days' time and this wasn't long enough to get us to our intended base camp and him back to the roadhead. I felt a familiar 'here we go again' feeling come over me. But this time it was wonderfully different. We had negotiated a fixed price with our agent, and Rinku was in some kind of partnership with this agent and it was his responsibility to get us to base camp and back. I relaxed and sat back taking the view that the problem wasn't mine. I was on holiday and so the day passed with idyllic trekking through deciduous forests and grazing pastures. In that delightfully Indian way negotiations seemed to carry on throughout the day.

By evening a new problem seemed to have arisen. An area of beautiful lush grazing meadows had been reached and, despite there being several hours of daylight left, the day's walking was clearly over. That, however, was not the problem. The difficulty was that it seemed the mules 'were unable to go any further'. This new challenge was more difficult to understand. Bruno had suggested that if water levels were low enough we should easily be able to get mules all the way to base camp. They were low so what was the problem? Apparently it was the bushes. 'Too dense for the mules,' translated Rinku.

Paul and I were particularly unimpressed. It sounded like a ruse to persuade us to cough up more money or face them returning to the valley for this lucrative work that apparently existed. Despite us being relaxed and on holiday, delay was something we couldn't contemplate. A hasty reconnaissance was called for.

The valley forked, with the route we needed to follow up the Tarundi valley leading north towards the east side of Shiva. The right-hand fork, the Paphita valley, was apparently a through route, whereas the Tarundi valley had no easy pass at its head. It didn't take long to discover that neither valley seemed to have a worthwhile track and crossing the river flowing down the Tarundi valley looked particularly challenging. This left just the true right bank of the Tarundi valley and soon Paul and I were thrashing about in dense, shrub-like bushes. A track of sorts was apparent but, after I had become stuck in the dense undergrowth such that a hand from Paul was the easiest way out, we had to acknowledge that maybe the muleteer had a point. We returned crestfallen to the meadows.

'He's right. The bushes are too dense.'

Steve and Ian looked crestfallen whereas the muleteer looked smug. I couldn't help but think that we had missed something somewhere, but there was little we could do but accept that the mules could go no further.

The valley didn't look to have any impasses other than the bushes. We couldn't yet see Shiva but Bruno had told us that there was a good site for a base camp at about 4,000 metres, where both the bushes and the valley eased off. We don't bother to carry altimeters and the like but our best guess was that we were just under 3,500 metres and three or four hours of bush-whacking might see us at base camp. The decision was made that we would carry a set of loads ourselves while Rinku would try and arrange some porters to bring the rest of the gear up later.

Midway through the next morning I lay on my back contemplating that I had never tried to carry such a heavy sack through such difficult vegetation. All had started off well and the others had surged off into the distance, leaving me to wander along contentedly at my own super-slow pace soaking up the scenery and generally enjoying myself. Eventually, I had to acknowledge that I had lost the track and there was no sign of the others. The bushes grabbed at my heavy sack and soon I was having to stand on the sturdy branches of lower bushes and force my way through the low branches of trees that formed the next level up. A bush collapsed under me, I fell sideways and suddenly I was upside down in a shallow gully, pinned to the ground by my enormous sack. I shouted hopefully but there was no response. Things were not going well. Himalayan approaches are nothing if not varied, and apparently variety is the spice of life. Extricating myself from under my sack, I struggled to get it back on and continue, reminding myself over and over again that this unusual terrain was spicing up my life. Weeks later, when we walked out, I noticed a good little track through this section.

I was a sweaty, branch-scratched mess when I came across Paul on the way back down several hours later. He was perky and full of beans.

'Brilliant campsite up there. A few carries and we'll be done,' he announced cheerfully.

I mumbled something about the dangers of overexertion and the need for me to 'prepare the base camp site' while he bounded off for a second carry after having made appropriately disparaging remarks about my ability to follow tracks through undergrowth.

A little later, cliffs forced me towards the bed of the valley and here, sat amongst the water-worn rocks, I came across Steve. The weight of his sack was such that he had toppled over, damaging his hand. He too was marvelling at the Ramsden energy and appeared slightly relieved to have incurred an injury that he felt made it 'unwise' to do another carry immediately.

I relaxed as he wobbled on ahead and then followed him, scrambling up steps and over boulders in the streambed. My sack really was heavy and made it difficult to keep my balance – a situation not helped by my wearing 8,000-metre-rated mountaineering boots. This might sound a little odd, particularly with Shiva standing at a little over 6,100 metres, but a couple of years before I had taken the view that, after twenty-five years climbing in the greater ranges, it would feel silly to lose digits to frostbite now. As modern 8,000-metre boots have become increasingly snug fitting and good for technical climbing, Paul and I both had them for this trip. And to decrease the weight in my sack, I had decided to wear them for this gear-ferrying exercise. Unsurprisingly, my feet felt very warm.

Suddenly, a large boulder that I was stepping up on rolled over. A quick skip out of the way would have sufficed but, being weighed down by the sack and generally exhausted, I just sort of fell over as it landed on my foot and pinned it to the ground, demonstrating how the extra insulation in 8,000-metre boots is very good at absorbing the shock of heavy rocks.

By evening all the climbers had somehow arrived at an idyllic base camp site next to the river. Paul had managed two carries and the rest of us one each. Paul mentioned this frequently and in return I frequently I pointed out the marvellously flat site I had excavated for the tent while he had been doing his second ferry. He was actually so fast that I only finished it minutes before he arrived, but I didn't feel it necessary to point that out.

Shiva was now in view, with our intended line forming the eye-catching right-hand skyline. But I felt tired and curiously intimidated. For some reason I had not been sleeping well and if there is one thing that subdues me as I get older it is not getting a good night's sleep. I always seem to sleep badly for the first few days of a trip and put this down to excitement. On this occasion though, I felt I had hardly slept since we left the UK and was in danger of being consumed by a general sense of lethargy. That said, I couldn't fail to note that the buttress, or the prow as we quickly came to call it, looked an even better objective than we had expected. Through my sleep-deprived haze it was clear that we had come across something rather special.

'What do you reckon about the best way to approach the face?' enquired Paul, peering intently through his binoculars.

It was a good question. Normally we readily make a decision on such matters, but it was clear that the base of the route was at the head of a very broken glacier and the memory of the Chinese crevasse experience was still fresh in our minds. I too stared through the binoculars, but it was impossible to see the full approach route from base camp. Tight timescale or not, it seemed sensible to invest a couple of days in reconnaissance.

Two days later I still hadn't slept much and we weren't a lot clearer on the best approach. We had however decided that the broken part of the glacier seemed to have only a thin snow cover, and we would give that way a go to see if it would give access to not only the prow but also to a small peak on the ridge north of Shiva, which we hoped to climb as part of our acclimatisation process.

Meanwhile Steve and Ian were checking out other possible objectives in the Tarundi valley and had decided to attempt the east ridge of Shiva, which was clearly best accessed by starting up the broken glacier and then heading off to a col on the left. Paul and I were very pleased about this and commented enthusiastically about how useful it would be to be able to follow a set of tracks down from the summit.

Having grown to like evening walkie-talkie chats with the others on Mugu Chuli I had brought a set along to Shiva. This was a first for Paul, who was suspicious about the extra weight.

'We could pack another breakfast,' he commented warily, weighing the handset in one hand and a dehydrated porridge pack in the other. It took some time to persuade him that we should at least use the set to keep in touch with the others while acclimatising.

Both teams set off together to acclimatise, Steve and Ian climbing the true right bank of the glacier and Paul and me on the opposite side. Our first use of the set was that evening and the news from Steve and Ian was useful if not encouraging.

'Terrible snow over here; can hardly make progress.'

'And there's a difficult pitch to access the snow.'

'And traversing below the snout of the glacier is not much fun.'

It didn't sound very promising. Our side was far from perfect, but we had at least made reasonable progress on the badly broken ground.

By the end of the next day Paul and I had climbed the upper section of the icefall and were on the upper glacier plateau beneath the huge east face of Shiva. We could see that down below, Steve and Ian had been moving very slowly towards the col at the foot of the east ridge. A clearly visible trench leading to their little tent said it all. The snow on their side of the glacier was clearly appalling. Our side seemed more prone to freeze and thaw and, by starting early, we had been able to make good progress.

Above us an obviously difficult bergschrund gave access to the line we needed to follow to access the prow, while up to our right a previously hidden glacier looked to give access to the small peak on the ridge that we hoped would give us a good view of our intended line.

The next couple of days summed up the best of lazy acclimatisation in the Himalaya. A few hours of exertion first thing in the morning, pitch the tent, get the binoculars out, brew up, relax, admire the view, read and generally chill out in a way that I virtually never do at home. The small peak was climbed easily and did indeed give a fantastic view of the prow. Paul's powerful binoculars gave such detail that we were able to clearly pick out a possible line and bivouac positions. It felt almost unethical using them. Knowing how tricky route finding can be when one's nose is hard up against steep ground I wrote out a description and Paul, undoubtedly the better artist, drew a route topo complete with little tents at possible bivouac sites. To our relief and excitement the rock appeared to be more featured than we had expected. The clear-cut lines and golden colour suggested that in sharp contrast to the appalling rock we had come across thus far, the rock was solid granite. Nevertheless it did all look very steep and difficult and the warning contained in Andrey's email still resonated clearly.

Frankly I cannot imagine how you will do it.

We could but give it our very best try.

Having completed our acclimatisation we retraced our steps towards base camp. The icefall we had come up was a bit of a problem. Ice pillars can collapse at any time of the day and, being keen to avoid as much danger as possible, our eyes were drawn to a rocky ramp that looked to be a way of avoiding the lower half. The ramp led out from the glacier on to broken slopes and we decided to see if we could get back to base camp this way and use it to return after fattening up for a day or two. Before doing so though, we decided to cache nearly all our equipment. This meant that a steep step at the bottom of the ramp would have to be tackled with minimal equipment, but it looked very straightforward and we didn't anticipate a problem.

Soon however, I was spreadeagled on remarkably loose rock contemplating the fact that I had with me just a rope, an ice axe and a single karabiner. All the other climbing equipment had either been left at our cache or was down in base camp. What had looked easy was proving distressingly challenging. I cleared out cracks with the pick of the axe and dithered. It all felt very insecure and progress soon ground to a halt. Paul gleefully pointed out how easy it looked and how pathetic my efforts would look on camera. It took a long time before I managed to wedge the axe in a crack and leave it behind as the only vaguely reliable piece of protection on the pitch. But success was assured, Paul retrieved the axe and we gained access to the ramp which we hoped would lead safely up over the buttress flanking the glacier and easily down to base camp.

To begin with the ramp was pleasant, and we congratulated ourselves on spotting this sneaky way of avoiding the lower icefall. But soon we had contoured on to the north-facing side of the buttress and quickly began to appreciate the problems that Steve and Ian had been having. Despite having fallen over a week ago, the snow had seen no freeze and thaw. The ground comprised huge granite boulders, and by far the easiest way to make progress was to jump from one boulder to the next. Stepping on to the snow was an absolute last resort as sinking up to the waist was inevitable and made progress ludicrously slow and exhausting. Carrying virtually no equipment and going downhill we could spring comfortably between most of the boulders, but we knew that coming back up, laden for our attempt on the prow, would be much trickier. We sat and contemplated. With our crampons left at our equipment cache it was now impossible for us to climb up the lower icefall. For better or for worse we would have to get back to our cache through the snowy boulder field.

Emerging from the boulders the slopes eased and we followed separate lines down to the stream, converging not far above base camp. At this point Paul slipped and fell awkwardly. It was one of those horrible expedition moments. Being a stoical Yorkshireman, whinging is not in Paul's character, but it was obviously a painful fall. As he lay still on the boulders I could see his ears and the top of his head going red. What could I say? 'Are you alright?' seemed ludicrously inappropriate. I said nothing and waited, wondering vaguely if the redness was sunburn or just a side effect of being semi-inverted. At length he squirmed upright.

'Shit!' he announced peering at his right index finger, which was vying with head and ears for redness. It looked a funny shape. 'It'll be alright,' he added.

I breathed a sigh of relief. Having the trip grind to a halt because of an injury like this would not have been good, especially with our objective looking so exciting.

Back at base camp, Pritam our cook and Devraj the kitchen boy were proving to be probably the finest we had ever had on a trip. While we spent a day resting they made it their business to supply unlimited quantities of fine food, including baked cakes (how *do* they do that?!) and my first experience of real chocolate scones in the Himalaya. Steve and Ian had returned and the day passed in a pleasant atmosphere of relaxing, chatting, drinking unlimited quantities of tea, eating fine food and generally enjoying an idyllic base camp. As suspected, the others reported that the snow on the north-facing slopes was awful, and, of greater concern from our point of view, the ridgeline of our intended descent was not much better. Faced with such conditions they decided to transfer their attentions to the highest peak on the west side of the Tarundi valley.

Donning heavy sacks Paul and I wandered up the interminable slopes leading to the ramp and our glacier cache. Somehow we followed a better line than previously and arrived at the point overlooking the glacier more easily than expected. All that separated us from a relaxing afternoon's brewing and eating was a simple abseil down the pitch that had caused me so much difficulty a few days earlier. We rigged a sling over a spike and Paul went first while I sat in the sun marvelling at the Himalayan splendour surrounding us. The weather had been near perfect since we left the roadhead and showed no signs of changing now. Above us I could see the Prow of Shiva

20 The Prow of Shiva (6,142 metres). **Photo:** Paul Ramsden.

21 Paul Ramsden climbing on the lower section of the Prow of Shiva in 2012.

22 Paul demonstrating the *à cheval* technique to try and make progress along the crest of the lower buttress of Shiva.

23 Paul enduring spindrift on an otherwise comfortable sitting bivvy on Shiva.

24 On Shiva, with Kishtwar Kailash (6,451 metres) in the distance. **Photo:** Paul Ramsden.

25 Paul and me with our Piolet d'Or award at the ceremony in Chamonix in 2013.

26 Rob Smith experiencing the approach to Kishtwar Kailash in 2013. **Photo:** Paul Ramsden.

27 Paul in action on day four of our first ascent of Kishtwar Kailash in 2013.

28 Enjoying the untrodden summit of Kishtwar Kailash. **Photo:** Paul Ramsden.

29 Looking towards Hagshu (6,515 metres) from base camp.

30 And the view back down towards base camp from our climb on Hagshu. Paul in shade in the foreground.

31 The Hagshu base camp bear!

32 With the Slovenian team following our ascents. L–R: Marko Prezelj, Steve Burns, Luka Lindič, Paul Ramsden, Aleš Česen and me.

33 Paul and the summit ridge of Hagshu. This part of the route was shared with the Slovenians, as evidenced by their footprints.

34 The shaded north face of Gave Ding (6,571 metres), our objective in 2015.

35 Wonderful mixed climbing on Gave Ding. **Photo:** Paul Ramsden.

36 Victor Saunders choosing dinner at Sersank base camp in 2016.

37 Victor cutting off his Calvin Klein pants on Sersank.

38 The 1,100-metre north buttress of Sersank (6,050 metres). We completed our climb in an eight-day round trip from base camp.

39 A climbing reunion with Victor Saunders, almost thirty years after our first ascent of the Golden Pillar of Spantik in 1987.

basking in the golden glow of the afternoon sun. Life seemed good and I snoozed gently.

An agitated shout from below suggested all was not well.

There was little I could do but keep my fingers crossed. At length the shouting eased, the rope became slack and I abseiled down to a disgruntled Paul whose underwear leggings had been ripped from thigh to knee by a rock the rope had dislodged. Fortunately, his leg was relatively undamaged so my input consisted primarily of sarcastic comments about the pitfalls awaiting those who wear just their underwear in the big mountains.

The snow cover on the glacier had melted significantly over the three days we had been away and there was now so much bare ice that it took some time to find a flat snow patch big enough to pitch our little tent on. I was looking forward to a relaxing afternoon brewing and reading but Paul's gut was not feeling its best and I was frequently interrupted by him urgently exiting to leave little brown puddles on the ice. There was concern in the air but by morning the Ramsden body had made a pleasing recovery and we were soon trying to weave our way through the complex upper section of the icefall that separated us from the open slopes beneath the face. Several sections were unrecognisable and apparently less stable than a few days before and it was with some relief that we reached the open slopes of the upper glacier.

The sun glared on the upper slopes and drained our energy such that the final few hundred metres to a bivouac close to the bergschrund were completely exhausting. It was a joy to get the tent pitched, shade ourselves by draping our sleeping bags over the top and enter relaxation mode. The huge rock wall of the upper east face reared above us while the interconnecting snow couloirs we hoped to follow bounded it on the right and looked to be protected by a challenging bergschrund.

'Bollocks!'

I couldn't see what was happening as I was lying down relaxing, but Paul sounded uncharacteristically agitated. Sensing urgency I sat up suddenly to see him peering unhappily at his boot. The zip in the integral gaiter had broken and looked beyond repair. This was bad news. It meant it would be impossible to prevent snow getting into the boot and frostbite would be a real risk. If it couldn't be fixed we might as well descend. Paul is a bit of a whizz at DIY and his gloomy expression did not bode well. But the weather was perfect, the route looked superb and we *really* didn't want go down now unless we absolutely had to. A solution of sorts was found, using a penknife and a spare lace to tie both sides of the zip together. The upper section still worked normally, but the lower section was locked solid. Getting his boots on and off was going to be a major challenge, but for the time being at least, failure due to boot problems had been averted.

For the uninformed it often comes as a surprise that the heat is a major problem for Himalayan mountaineers below 6,000 metres or so. The couloirs that we planned to follow faced dead east and would catch the morning sun. If we didn't reach a near-horizontal snow crest at the top before 9 a.m. we would be faced with an uncomfortable day stuck on hot, disintegrating snow with the occasional rock whizzing past. That was something we were keen to avoid and so a 1 a.m. crossing of the bergschrund was deemed necessary. That meant an 11 p.m. alarm. Ugh! An inspirational climb ahead makes such starts easier than early rising for tax office days, but even so I don't exactly find them easy.

As juggling job, family et al. means I only manage one mountaineering expedition per year, it always takes a pitch or two to settle into the swing of things. Getting over the step formed where the glacier pulls away from the mountain can often be difficult, so quite why I volunteered to lead I am not sure. It certainly led to a harsh re-introduction to technical action. In the light of my head torch I struggled on a near-vertical shale wall, trying to make it safe by placing occasional ice screws in a slanting, overhanging wall of iron-hard ice that sat on top. I certainly felt fully exercised by the time I pulled out, gasping, into an ice runnel on the slope above.

Back in Britain I had envisaged that it would be straightforward to gain the crest of the buttress below the prow. In reality the angle was considerably steeper than I had expected and the combination of awful rock and powder snow made for tricky, poorly protected climbing. The amazing variation in the snow depending on the direction of the slope added further to the challenge. As we had experienced earlier, the north-facing areas were covered in remarkably steep, deep powder snow that slowed us such that the sun was well up by the time Paul led the final rope length to the crest.

'It's rubbish here. Just a collapsing knife-edge.'

His comments were not encouraging. An interval followed during which I could pick out some energetic *à cheval* activity going on. This involves having a leg either side of the ridge and 'riding' along it, supposedly like riding a horse. Mind you, when riding a horse I would hope to go forwards whereas when using the *à cheval* technique on ridges I tend to jerk up and down and sink in rather than make meaningful progress. Fortunately Paul has mastered the technique. He shuffled out of sight and, after what seemed a long time, shouted for me to climb. When I was able to see him he was standing on the knife-edge crest with the rope looped around a large ice-cream-like dollop of snow, smiling broadly. At first I assumed it was my *à cheval* activity that pleased him, but that was not the only reason for his high spirits.

'I think this could be a good spot for the tent.'

If you have never tried to pitch a tent on a knife-edge ridge this might sound like a rather odd comment. I am forever amazed at how an impossible-looking bivouac spot can be transformed into something quite comfortable. And if the snow is sufficiently deep and soft, knife-edge crests are among the very best features to work with.

The sun was hot and enervating and having reached our intended bivouac spot relatively early we had plenty of time to fashion a comfortable sleeping platform. We sliced off the crest and then, taking it in turns, stamped down and pushed away more and more snow. After thirty minutes we had a flat area the width of our little tent.

From this point the key is to get established inside the tent without collapsing the platform. Advancing years and improving equipment have led to both Paul and I carrying light inflatable sleeping mats; by first getting these inflated and inside the tent the weight of other equipment and human bodies can be spread such that, if all goes well, the soft snow beneath simply gets compressed and the end result is a remarkably secure-feeling position. On this occasion all went well, and whiling away a beautiful afternoon reading in the tent it was easy to relax, forget the huge drops on either side and trust that – if needed – our belay rope would not cut through the snow mushroom belay like a cheese wire.

Above us, the soft snow ridge looked challenging but the mixed buttress which started perhaps 150 metres up looked to offer perfect, safe climbing of the kind I scour the earth to find. By the time the sun hit us Paul had reversed the *à cheval* section and was trying to continue up the snow ridge to the start of the mixed ground. It soon became clear that even his superior riding technique was not up to the challenge of the amazingly soft and narrow crest. I took an appropriate number of photographs of him jigging up and down without moving forwards before it was decided that the face on the left might provide a better chance of success. This proved to be a steep ice slope covered in a few centimetres of sugary snow, not ideal but much more conducive to progress than the ridge crest.

By mid-afternoon we were underway on the prow proper, enjoying ice-choked cracks in perfect granite which led to a small balcony just on the east side of the crest. Below it the ground overhung steadily for at least 500 metres, while round on the cold north-west side, the way was barred by a completely smooth seventy-five-degree rock slab with an intermittent covering of verglas and powder. The only way on seemed to be up an overhanging fault line above the balcony, but that could be seen to cross the crest after perhaps ten metres and then disappear into the verglas and snow sticking to the slab. There really wasn't anywhere else obvious to go. Bolts could have solved the problem but we both feel strongly that overcoming difficulties by drilling holes is no way to tackle adventurous mountaineering challenges. As I see it, not only do bolts damage the mountain and go a long way towards guaranteeing the outcome, they send an arrogant 'if I can't do it without cheating then you won't be able to either' statement to future generations.

But if we couldn't do this pitch it could well be the end of our attempt. Our mountaineering dreams of the last year could end here.

Frankly I cannot imagine how you will do it.

I tried to push those words to the back of my mind. The overhanging start looked tricky, with loose-looking sharp flakes poised directly above the belayer. We alternate leads wherever possible, and this was Paul's lead. I watched warily as he pulled on camming devices wedged between flakes, flicked a sling over a previously hidden spike and rounded the crest on to the blank-looking slab. The rope kept slowly snaking out until he shouted for me to follow. Brilliant! The fault line clearly continued across the smooth slab in a way that was invisible from below. It was a crucial pitch and it felt great to overcome a possible impasse and get fully established on the narrow crest of the prow.

The position was developing into one of the most spectacular I have ever experienced in the Himalaya. The angle steepened but there were more cracks that looked to allow reasonable, if sparse, protection. My pitch started by laying away off the true crest of the buttress. To my left, the huge sun-kissed vertical to overhanging rock wall of the east face fell away to our approach glacier 800 metres below. To my right, the north-west face painted a cold, grey and inhospitable picture with just off-vertical slabs merging into vertical walls smeared with occasional streaks of thin ice. After thirty metres or so of weaving my way up the ice streaks and mixed ground on the northwest side the sun was getting low in the sky and the discovery of a perfect belay marked an obvious place to end the climbing day.

We had agreed to bivouac on the balcony ledge and so had left our sacks there. I really don't like being separated from my sack in the mountains, nor do I like bivouacking anywhere other than at the high point. Here though, the balcony was such a good spot that abseiling down to it did feel like the sensible thing to do – although it meant that we would start the following day by jumaring (climbing up the rope using sliding clamps) up the rope to our high point.

Jumaring is far from my favourite activity. Firstly it feels unethical, all that hanging about on ropes instead of climbing, and secondly I hate doing it. I am also notoriously incompetent at it; I always seem to end up getting my slings the wrong length and being pulled backwards by my rucksack in a way that makes progress absolutely exhausting. Having seen the steepness of the prow during our acclimatisation outing, I had decided a refresher session at base camp was sensible, particularly as, for the first time, both Paul and I had purchased small-toothed pulleys which we intended to use both as sack-hauling and jumaring devices.

Close to base camp a very large boulder with a ten-metre overhanging face had provided a good spot for a bit of practice. I had attached the toothed pulley to my harness, threaded the rope around it and attached the jumar clamp higher up the rope. After a bit of fiddling with the lengths of slings I had pronounced myself ready to go and the others had sat back to marvel at my performance. To begin with all had gone well, to the extent that Steve, Paul and Ian had started to look rather bored. Suddenly though, the clamp slipped down the rope leaving the pulley holding my weight. Steve had stretched out for his camera and Paul had not been at his most understanding.

'Only you could make that happen.'

'I didn't do anything!' I had protested, feeling both mystified and slightly embarrassed.

Returning to the fray I had made it to the top, but not without the clamp slipping a couple more times. Paul had then smoothly jumared up without any problems and we had retired for tea and cake at base camp. It bothered me that the clamp had seemed to slip for no reason, but it had only happened when it was jammed against the rock and I comforted myself with the thought that the toothed pulley seemed secure. I had firmly hoped I wouldn't be jumaring on the route anyway. Yet here I was, right out on the crest of the buttress knowing that the next day would have to start with a seventy-metre jumar.

On closer inspection the 'balcony', as we had christened it, was not quite in line with the dictionary definition of *safe platform on the side of a building (or rock face?) enclosed by a railing*. This particular 'balcony' was a block of rock four metres long and one metre wide that appeared to be somehow glued – in what appeared to be a very unsafe manner – to a completely vertical wall of rock. Along most of its length a ten-centimetre crack separated it from the wall, such that it was not at all obvious what was holding it in place. We moved gingerly, making very sure there were good belays above it. As much as the structure seemed disturbingly precarious, it was pleasingly comfortable and just long enough for us to lie down nose to tail. As the sun set we brewed, chatted happily, ate our freeze-dried meal and generally enjoyed being high in the mountains.

Weather wise, it seemed we had timed things just right. Every morning the sky was clear and the weather glorious. Usually in the afternoon it clouded over, with a gradually increasing amount of snow, and then cleared again by the evening. On this particular evening, the clouds dropped such that we could fully appreciate our position: sat on the crest of the most eye-catching feature on the highest mountain in the area. People sometimes ask me why I never go for the headline-grabbing objectives on bigger mountains. Here, on this wonderful climb in a rarely visited part of the Himalay, I had my answer. Shiva was giving me everything that I could possibly want from my mountaineering.

The temperature was perhaps –15 °C and there was only room for two thirds of my body on the balcony. Despite this, and the inherently insecure nature of the whole arrangement, I slept really well – much better than in our comfortable hotel room in Manali. For the first time on this trip I awoke feeling fully perky.

First though, we had to regain our high point. Paul went first and then it was my turn. As I put my weight on the rope the overhang above the balcony meant that I swung out into space over a huge drop. Immediately I felt insecure. I was cold and stiff, the sling attached to the jumar clamp seemed to be the wrong length and I couldn't help but recall it sliding down the rope at base camp. I hung there, unhappily fumbling to get my foot in a sling while my rucksack pulled me backwards and I rotated gently.

'Bloody jumaring,' I shouted loudly. Way above I could hear Paul cackling unsympathetically. No one seems to understand my jumaring problems.

Soon, after an immense expenditure of energy, I was round the overhang and facing a new problem. At this point the crest was very sharp and the belay was round to the north-west side. That meant that I had to make a controlled swing to get directly beneath the belay. In reality, it was more of an uncontrolled pendulum made memorable by the clamp starting to slide as I scraped across the smooth granite before coming to a gibbering halt hanging from the pulley. I so hate jumaring! By the time I reached the belay there was no doubt that I had fully warmed up.

It was a calm morning and the early morning sun was shining obliquely across the prow highlighting the features, and once I had recovered from the jumar I was able to enjoy the situation. It was Paul's lead and I snapped away contentedly as a few uncharacteristic grunts and 'watch me' calls suggested challenging ground ahead. At length it was my turn to enjoy some hard climbing up ice-choked cracks in perfect quality granite in one of the finest positions I have experienced.

'Don't pull on the belay,' announced Paul as I struggled to pass his precarious position.

I peered curiously and registered that we were secured by two ice axes hooked over a large chunk of ice frozen across a wide crack. It seemed a mildly insecure arrangement considering we were perched on the crest of the buttress with huge overhanging walls dropping away to our left. Paul noticed me peering closely at the belay.

'Best get a good runner in quick,' he commented wryly.

The only way to pass him without exerting extra pressure on the belay was via a sort of sliding bear-hug movement. Composing myself after this semi-intimate action it could be seen that the way ahead looked decidedly difficult.

'Don't like the look of your pitch,' announced Paul, peering at the desperate-looking vertical fissures above the belay.

'Frankly I can't imagine how I am going to do it,' I commented sarcastically.

The best option looked to be a wide crack up to the left that was completely choked with vertical powder snow and guarded by a blank overhang at its base. The traverse to the base yielded a secure runner that eased the tension a little but did nothing to solve the overhang problem. I was horribly aware that the crack was above a smooth, featureless sheet of rock that fell hundreds of metres to ice slopes below. The protection I had placed reduced the risk of injury from a fall but the prospect of ending up dangling over a huge overhanging wall left me particularly keen to avoid such an event. It was with some distress that I ended up with my feet inelegantly skidaddling around on the featureless granite, gasping lungfuls of thin air and trying to hook my heel over a stubbornly out-of-reach edge. Paul later commented that I made squeaking noises not unlike those of a distraught piglet. But the end result was access to the crack where I was able to wedge myself and calm my rapidly beating heart. More difficult and worrying climbing led to a patch of ice where I was able to place a solid ice screw belay and derive some satisfaction from seeing that the pitch made the Ramsden breathe heavily too.

Ahead, the route continued via memorably thin ice on steep slabs, not unlike a lean day on the harder slab routes on Ben Nevis. Snow flurries interrupted the afternoon views but by evening a ledge had been cut and again provided a lie-down bivouac with a perfect view. The clouds dropped into the valleys and the evening sun kissed us goodnight. It felt a pretty perfect spot.

The next morning I awoke refreshed and it dawned on me that I had again slept really well. Most people I speak with think that being tied on to a twenty-centimetre ledge would impede their sleep, but it is amazing what the human brain can get used to. The skies were clear, the brain uncluttered by the trials and tribulations of everyday life and I guessed that the fact that my sleeping mat had deflated was the only reason that I had woken before the alarm. A flaccid sleeping mat was a problem though. The introduction of inflatable lightweight sleeping mats has made a huge difference to sleeping on snow and ice but when punctured they become next to useless. Presumably one of our sharp pieces of equipment had nicked the mat but, whatever the cause, the shrivelled piece of fabric now provided more hilarity than comfort. Paul was kind enough to cut his closed-cell foam mat in half and I kept the flaccid inflatable, more to avoid littering the mountain than anything else.

The next day was our sixth out from base camp. A few inches of snow fell in the night and it was gradually dawning on me that a descent down the line of our approach up the east face would be unpleasant to the extent that whatever lay ahead, it was better to persevere than descend. More thinly iced slabs, followed by wonderful ice grooves and intimidatingly steep mixed pitches, finally led to a snow band beneath an overhanging wall guarding access to the summit. From our viewing through binoculars it looked as though the band led rightwards round the crest to steep snow that would avoid the final wall. But luck was against us. Snow was falling as I headed off round the corner on to the north-west side. A gap in the ramp presented a challenge that would obviously require aid and be very time consuming. I retreated forlornly to a cold Paul. There was no way we were going to get up it that evening and had to admit that an ice-choked chimney splitting the headwall looked the only option for the morning.

Squeezed under the final wall was the one ledge on the entire prow where we could half pitch the tent. Getting the poles in makes such a difference. Shielded from the heavy overnight snowfall, we enjoyed a comfortable night and were ready to tackle the chimney first thing in the morning on day seven.

First though, there was the getting-up saga. On an average steep-ground bivouac we find it takes just under two hours from the alarm going off until we are ready to start climbing. It's one of those processes that has to be gone through semi-automatically and is considerably eased if it's cold enough to be able to keep all shell clothing and our climbing harnesses on inside our sleeping bags. If that can be done it at least avoids struggling with clothes and harness in a confined space while trying to stay securely tied in. Paul's boot and my hands were particular challenges as we got higher. My hands suffer in the cold generally, but Paul's boot became stiffer as it got colder and with the front zip partially sewn up it was more and more difficult to squeeze his foot in. By this bivouac it was most definitely a two-man job that required much judicious stamping and pulling in a position not exactly conducive to such activity. At length though, by 6 a.m., just within the regulation two hours from our alarm, we were ready to go.

It was one of those glorious cloud-free mornings and after a quick video clip in the morning sun – which ended abruptly when my footholds collapsed and I slumped on to the belays – we were ready to go.

The chimney was my lead. If we couldn't do it then there would be a problem, but a quick glance suggested that there was fairly thick ice up the back and side walls. As a tight constricted chimney it was far from straight-forward, but we were nearly at the summit and there was no way I was going to retreat. Eventually, after a battle, I sat in a cosy, sheltered niche soaking up the glorious view as Paul came up and led off out of sight to gain a short ridge leading to a cornice. It fell to me to break through this and enjoy the curious sensation of being able to walk around on a flat area. A summit hug was in order.

A two-day descent of the unclimbed south-east flank completed nine wonderful days in the mountains and a climb that we already knew would give us retrospective pleasure for years to come. It was, we agreed, one of the most enjoyable climbs that we had ever done.

On return to the UK it transpired that Paul had broken three fingers when he tripped and had then climbed the whole route without complaining! And the manufacturer put out a recall for the slipping rope-ascender devices that had caused me so much grief. That made me feel a little bit better, but did nothing to cure my aversion to hanging about on ropes.

The climb ended up winning Paul and I another Piolet d'Or award at a presentation in Chamonix. The Piolets d'Or had started in 1992, with the format being that a jury would select one climb for the award each year. Contentious from the outset there was controversy over whether awards were appropriate in mountaineering and the fact that it is very difficult to make meaningful comparisons between different climbs. Some very questionable decisions by the jury fanned the flames and in 2007 the Slovenian mountaineer Marko Prezelj went as far as to reject a Piolet d'Or award on stage to express his opposition to competition in alpinism. Thereafter the format was changed somewhat, with the jury being able to award more than one Piolet and the event becoming more a celebration of alpinism than an award for one climb in particular. Personally, I feel much more comfortable with this new format where the focus is on celebrating adventurous new climbs done in good style, with the climbers showing respect for others and leaving no trace of their passing. In 2013, a record six Piolets were awarded and I found the event a uniquely excellent few days of bringing my family into the mountaineering scene and enjoying the company of like-minded mountaineers from around the world. But it cannot be denied that choosing to showcase a few climbs leads to those who climbed them being regarded as 'winners'. The debate and controversy will no doubt continue, but, as just about the only event that draws mountaineers together to celebrate in this way, I take the view that the pros outweigh the cons.

In 2013 two British teams were awarded Piolets: Paul and me for our Shiva ascent, and Sandy Allan and Rick Allen for their remarkable ascent of the Mazeno Ridge on Nanga Parbat. Sandy, Rick and I were all over fifty-five, which prompted one of the other climbers there to ask: 'Do you have any young mountaineers in the UK?' It was a comment that struck home and made me more determined than ever to dream up initiatives to draw young blood into the Alpine Club.

Chapter 16

Kishtwar Kailash – A Very Special Drive and a 12.5-Million-View Video Clip

12/8/2013 Srinagar News Report: In a direct fallout from Friday's clashes in Kishtwar, all national highways leading to Jammu are now shut. Mobile and internet services were disconnected on Monday while schools and colleges remain shut.

The Shiva experience had been so pleasurable that I didn't bother to try and engage with Chinese bureaucrats for the following year and by August 2013 the British Kishtwar Kailash expedition was as ready as it could be. There were four of us: Paul Ramsden, Mike Morrison, Rob Smith and me – the same team that had visited the Chinese Tien Shan in 2010. Our objective was the first ascent of what our map showed to be the highest peak in east Kishtwar, and excitement levels were high. The troubles in Kashmir that had caused access problems for the last twenty years appeared to have subsided and our permits were expected any day.

Then came the Indian news report.

The Indian home office put all permit applications on hold and a stressful month followed. At one point an interesting situation developed when I received an invitation to give a keynote address to an Indian government conference aimed at increasing the number of Himalayan tourists. Being as I was trying unsuccessfully to become a Himalayan tourist at the time the potential for awkwardness looked high. To add to stress levels, my father's health took a sharp turn for the worse, challenges at the tax office and the Alpine Club made for an even heavier workload than usual and Mike and Rob started asking what would happen if the longed-for permits did not materialise.

Working late into the night every evening was not going down well at home, the finances of cancelling were not at all clear and seldom have I wondered so much whether it is all worth it.

As ever – well, almost ever – somehow everything fell into place. My father's health perked up. My response to the keynote-speaker invitation was copied to a number of senior officials who seemed responsive to my pleas for assistance and the all-important invitation letter arrived four working days before departure. Steve Burns was free to spend a whole day helping gather data and complete the visa application forms, the visa-processing centre was persuaded to overlook the fact that there were no appointments available until well beyond our intended departure date and Mike Morrison was able to make two visits to London and collect our all-important 'X-mountaineering' visas the day before we left. Phew!

The briefing session at the IMF was more memorable than most as it involved being told that our friend Victor Saunders had spent a night in prison for using a satellite telephone. Civilian use of satellite phones is banned in India, apparently as fallout from the terrorist attack on the Taj Mahal Palace Hotel in Mumbai in 2008. The briefing officer explained that infringement of this rule was taken very seriously; Victor had recently been caught and so he had spent a night in the cells.

'Do you know him?' the briefing officer asked.

I had climbed a lot with Victor when we both lived in London in the 1980s and 1990s. At that time he was notoriously difficult to pin down, thus earning himself fond nicknames such as 'Slippery' and 'The Devious One'. A vivid image of him being interviewed and trying to slip out of any responsibility for making a call crossed my mind.

'Er ... yes.'

'He is very bad,' he said, waving his finger assertively.

'Yes.' I struggled hard to look serious while looking forward immensely to ribbing Victor.

Although we didn't know it at the time, the satellite phone had enabled contact after an accident, such that I ended up feeling rather bad about making light of the incident. Victor and Andy Parkin had been part of an expedition to peaks north of Leh when an avalanche struck their tent in the night. They were bowled along the glacier and Andy ended up in a deep crevasse with an injured back. After a challenging rescue operation by his climbing friends he was brought back to the surface but it was clear that a helicopter should be summoned and Andy taken to hospital as soon as possible. The incident had a happy ending and the use of the satellite phone was obviously justified – but that still didn't prevent a little altercation with the authorities.

But as we listened gleefully at the briefing session we knew nothing of all this and as soon as we were out I couldn't resist texting Victor to tell him how terribly irresponsible he was and how he was clearly not suited to the role of vice president of the Alpine Club that he had recently been put forward for. My text was met with a dignified silence.

Briefing formalities complete, the next challenge was to deliver a lecture for the IMF. Such lectures are great for building contacts and goodwill but after a sleepless night flying from London to Delhi, the weariness levels tend to be high and it was a relief to eventually collapse into a vehicle that Kaushal, our agent, had arranged to take us from Delhi to the town of Manali in the Himalayan foothills. This was not exactly the quickest route, but the problems that had caused us so much stress with the permit also meant that we had to avoid the flashpoint town of Kishtwar and so take a wonderfully indirect route via the Rohtang La pass and down the Chenab gorge.

The first part of the journey replicated that of the previous year but the last fifty kilometres down the gorge to the small town of Gulabgarh were new ground and proved to be the most exciting that any of us had ever experienced. We were perhaps halfway into this section when a bang and a loud metallic scraping noise signalled a problem.

'What the hell was that?'

Rob had not been to India before but, even if he had, his concern was understandable. Not long back our driver had stopped for us to look down at the carcass of a vehicle that had left the road the previous day.

'Six dead,' our liaison officer, Rinku, had solemnly announced as we all stared at the fresh scuff marks where it had gone over the edge.

With such thoughts fresh in mind, Rinku, who was sat on the river side of the vehicle, carefully opened his door and emerged on to the eighty-centimetre-wide strip of road between the vehicle and the huge drop into the Chenab river.

'Roof rack is stuck,' he reported.

The road was a sort of sideways 'V' cut out of a vertical rock wall. The road surface was fairly level but the height limit on the inside was less than that on the outside. Looking ahead I was seriously concerned about whether the vehicle itself would get through, let alone the roof rack. It also struck me that it had been a long time since we had seen any other vehicles and there was probably a very good reason for this to be a seldom-used piece of road. Soon Rinku was indicating strongly that the driver should move even closer to the edge. This presented the driver with a significant challenge. It should also have presented us with a decision on whether or not to abandon ship but the driver surged forward and that option appeared unavailable. We were all in this together.

At this point Paul felt it was a good time to start videoing.

'Should be excellent footage,' he announced enthusiastically as he started to try and interview Rob, who was hanging out the window in front of him.

'What do you think Rob? How far down to the river?'

Gravel dislodged by the wheels fell vertically into the boiling grey waters below. Rob appeared unable to answer. Paul continued to video enthusiastically.

'Oh my word. There's a waterfall falling on to the road in front.'

I sat trapped in the middle seat contemplating that on the return journey a couple of jeeps would enable us to drive closer to the wall and might be preferable to our Force minibus. Mind you, like the Shiva trip, the minibus was proving to be a remarkable vehicle, covering ground that a normal British minibus would have failed dismally on. But gearing and four-wheel drive and other things aside, there was little that could be done about its physical size which meant that it could only get through by hugging the extreme outer edge of the road. With some trepidation and much wondering about the crumbling edge we carefully forged towards the waterfall.

'Time for the camera to go inside,' announced our fearless cameraman.

'Agh! No!' Water poured in through the window, drenching everything.

'Window is stuck,' announced Paul as the video ground to a wet, chaotic and hilarious halt.

Little did we know at the time but Paul's three minutes of video would have over twelve and a half million views when posted on my Berghaus Facebook page.

At least all the action served to keep our driver awake. I sensed his perkiness level was dropping after fourteen hours or so behind the wheel but he looked significantly more alert after a good bit of roof rack scraping and a dousing in a waterfall.

Late in the evening, well after dark and seventeen hours or so after leaving

Manali, we arrived at the town of Gulabgarh and crashed out on the floor of a large room that was apparently part of a hotel. This was where we joined the quicker approach from Delhi that would have taken us through the town of Kishtwar. I had last been here in 1993, en route to climb a mountain called Cerro Kishtwar. In those days the troubles were more evident and I clearly recall walking across the bridge at Gulabgarh and noticing a line of rifle barrels pointing at me from a wall of sandbags on the other side. This time all was calm, but torrential rain, rubbish and turd-ridden streets did little to endear us to the place. Even the cows sheltering in the shuttered shop fronts looked miserable. The next day we were unable to find any muleteers prepared to start the walk-in in such terrible weather. The delay was not exactly welcome but at least it gave us a chance to catch up on some sleep and get everything sorted and ready for an early start the following day.

Despite our day of sorting there seemed to be a bit of trouble brewing around the ten mules that we had hired to get our equipment to base camp.

'It's because we have hired Muslim muleteers,' explained Rinku. We were slightly mystified, it not being at all clear to us what religion they were. As far as we were concerned they looked happy and ready to go and that was the important thing. But the problem soon became clear. They were owned by Muslims who had been dropping off loads carried from further down the valley and some of the local, predominantly Hindu, men wanted the work themselves and were less than happy.

This was not the first time that I had come across this kind of problem. On a trip to Pakistan in 1987 porters from five small villages had gathered looking to us for work. There were perhaps five applicants for every position and we had started our selection process by picking out the fittest looking ones. Ultimately though, we had to cave into local pressure and employ porters in strict proportion to the population of each village. As we had no idea of local village populations this was a challenging task. Here the problem was rather different: the mules were already loaded up, it was pretty clear that sharing the job was out of the question and there didn't seem to be any easy compromise that could be struck. Heated exchanges resulted, during which we could only stand around and fret as the hours ticked by. At length a fair solution was agreed. Muslim muleteers would be employed for the walk-in and Hindu muleteers would be employed on our walk out. It struck me that as we didn't know exactly where our base camp would be the Hindu muleteers would be entirely reliant on the Muslim muleteers, who had never been anywhere near the intended base camp site, for directions. There wasn't much that could be done, but I was uncomfortably aware that this arrangement had the potential to not work out well.

The walk-in shared the first part of the once well-used Umasi La crossing from Gulabgarh to Zanskar. The troubles in Kashmir had hugely reduced the number of trekkers but conversely the Machail Yatra pilgrimage every August, which started only forty years ago, saw a remarkable 350,000 pilgrims covering the first two days of trekking to the small temple at Machail. The troubles in 2013 reduced that number by about half but even so that's a huge number of people to cater for, particularly on mule tracks designed to link villages of no more than 200 inhabitants. By late September the only evidence of their passing was a very significant amount of rubbish and a laughably large number of well-used portable toilets. I sniffed warily. The track to Machail must be an outrageously busy and smelly place in August. I understood now why some might be attracted to a sign in Gulabgarh advertising helicopter transport to the pilgrimage site.

'Which tent is ours?' enquired Mike.

'Er … the one you packed?' I suggested blandly.

It was the first night of the walk-in. Bad weather could be seen moving up the valley and getting the tents pitched quickly looked to be a good idea. Soon it was clear that there was a problem. Mike and Rob had assumed that I had arranged for Kaushal to supply a base camp tent while I had assumed they would be bringing their own. Regardless of who was to blame the end result was a distinct lack of a base camp tent for Mike and Rob.

'Just like the Tien Shan,' commented Paul helpfully, recalling the previous trip the four of us had been on together. Oddly enough that was the only other time we had somehow ended up forgetting base camp tents. On that occasion though there was no doubt that the blame lay with our agent whereas on this occasion we could do nothing but blame poor communication between ourselves.

Rinku, clearly marvelling at how such experienced climbers could make such a basic mistake, stepped in to offer assistance.

'You two can use my tent and I will sleep in the cook tent.'

Being as there were three weeks or so ahead it was an incredibly generous offer. It led to me think back to early Himalayan days when I regarded liaison officers as a hindrance dedicated to obstructing progress in every possible way. How times had changed. Liaison officers tend to be much more helpful nowadays but Rinku, Pritam our cook and Devraj our kitchen boy were an exceptional team. We had met them the previous year and had specifically asked if they could join us again for Kishtwar Kailash.

Rinku's offer was typical of the man but Mike is proudly self-sufficient and had been scouring the hillside looking for alternative accommodation. Just as Rinku made his offer Mike returned to report that he had found an excellent cave that would be ideal for him and Rob.

'How will we find you for morning tea?' asked Pritam, clearly bemused by this behaviour and concerned at the prospect of Devraj wandering aimlessly predawn through the hillside forest.

Rob looked concerned but Mike was insistent. He and Rob headed off to their cave while the rest of us marvelled at their pleasingly eccentric behaviour, contemplated the amount of rubbish left by the pilgrims and caught up on events since we had waved goodbye eleven months earlier, after the Shiva trip.

Beyond Machail our route entered the Darlang Nullah, a seventy-kilometre-long valley at an altitude above 3,000 metres. It was immediately clear that we were on less-travelled terrain that had not been used by mules loaded with mountaineers' equipment for many years. The muleteers had never been this way before, the guide that we tried to employ at the last village never materialised and general uncertainty prevailed about the best route. The muleteers were understandably concerned for their animals, several sections of trail had to be built up before the mules could pass and after many tense moments it was eight days after leaving the UK before we finally left the main valley and established a base camp at about 4,000 metres, a few hours short of Kishtwar Kailash. It was a relief to arrive and be faced with just the challenge of climbing the mountain.

We had seen no one for nearly three days and our research suggested that this valley had not been visited by anyone but locals since the British climber Andy MacNae and his liaison officer descended it about twenty-five years earlier after an exploratory trip over the Muni La pass at its head. They had enjoyed a good view of the west face of Kishtwar Kailash and described the mountain as 'a very challenging objective'. Paul and I knew it to be an inspiring sight, having viewed it from Shiva the previous year, and I had also had a good view from Cerro Kishtwar in 1993. As we established our base camp the mountain dominated our view and I couldn't help but think that those two words, 'challenging' and 'inspiring', summed things up pretty well.

'Establishing a base camp' is a rather grand way of putting it. We just pitched three tents. By now Mike had succumbed to Rinku's offer so he and Rob squeezed into his tent, Paul and I were in another and Rinku, Pritam and Devraj slept in the cook tent.

The weather was indifferent but us restricted-holiday boys have to use every day to the full to stand a chance of success on a 6,400-metre peak in a thirty-day trip from the UK. With such thoughts in mind Paul and I left promptly to explore and acclimatise around Kishtwar Kailash while Mike and Rob decided to explore a side valley.

Even though the cloud was down it felt excitingly adventurous to be heading up towards the peak that had been the focus of our attention for so many months. It would have been better still if we had been able to see it and thereby choose our preferred climbing line. Instead a full day was spent clambering over moraine-covered glacier in the drizzle wondering where we were.

On our third day out from base camp we reached a col at about 5,700 metres, still without getting a good view of the mountain. The col had been spotted through clearings in the cloud and looked as if it would provide a suitable spot for acclimatising, with the possibility of ascending to a good viewpoint. It turned out to be a knife-edge crest that, once flattened, gave a comfortable camping spot but little else. Fortunately though, after over ten years of Himalayan climbing together, Paul and I are pretty well used to this acclimatising business and the fact that we spent the next two days pinned down in a small tent with just a small flattened area in front to walk about on was not a problem. We relaxed, read books, breathed in lots of thin air, discussed proposals to spend vast sums of money on the Alpine Club's property, contemplated the parking problems outside Paul's daughter's primary school and at one point even had a good view of the mountain we had come to climb. We couldn't see the face we planned to attempt but what we could see did at least convince us that our vague plan of descending the other side was a very bad one. If we were successful it was clear that we would have to descend our line of ascent.

After two nights sat in the tent we judged ourselves sufficiently acclimatised and prepared to descend to base camp. I was a little concerned about new snow in the couloir we had climbed up, but that aside, anticipated a straightforward day. So it was rather perturbing to find myself very frightened indeed after a few hours. We had decided to take a shortcut down a deep water-worn gully cutting through a huge moraine and leading down on to the main glacier. To be honest I was indifferent about it, but Paul was enthusiastic and I raised no objection. I recalled getting a glimpse of the gully on the way up and it looked to contain no great difficulties. And I reasoned that we had a rope and if necessary could always abseil over any uncomfortably steep bits.

At the bottom of the gully a huge rock was wedged such that it created a ten-metre overhanging drop. To one side was a very steep slope of grey mud and scree. Confident of my ability on such ground I launched out, digging the edges of the rigid soles of my boots hard into the slope to get a good purchase. After ten metres all was not going well. The ground was far less yielding than I had expected, my boot edges gave hardly any purchase and, worst of all, the slope narrowed to a thin diagonal ramp with a twenty-metre near-vertical drop below it. I ground to a worrying halt. I was tired and hot; to stay in my current position was wearing and it would be difficult to get back up. If I went for it then, all being well, in thirty seconds or so I would be on easy ground leading down to the glacier. I rated it seventy/thirty in favour of it all working out well. My natural tendency was to go for it but those odds made me dither badly for a moment before coming to my senses. It was obviously not worth the risk.

But getting back up posed a significant risk as well. I was perched precariously with the edges of my boots barely cutting into the slope. To return the way I had come I would need to cut steps in the slope. And that would involve using my ice axe, which was attached to the back of my sack. A careful manoeuvre followed which left me feeling so precarious that a top rope seemed a good idea.

'Can you throw down an end,' I shouted up to Paul who was watching my performance with some concern.

'It's in your sack,' he announced.

This was not helpful. It also went some way to explaining his look of concern. There was nothing for it but for me to get on with the step cutting and be very careful. It perhaps says a lot that Paul, usually an enthusiastic photographer, just looked on quietly and took no shots at all.

'Good to put your Hastings mud-cliff experience to good use,' he commented in a relieved kind of way as I finally rejoined him.

I sat there contemplating that I had very nearly 'gone for it'. It only struck me then that if I had then Paul would have had to follow me as I had the rope. We quickly arranged a straightforward abseil and walked down to base camp. I felt very silly.

Time was potentially tight but we allowed ourselves one day of resting and eating Pritam's fine dishes. Then we were ready to go. Meanwhile Mike and Rob had returned and were fattening up in preparation for visiting the unexplored upper reaches of the glacier.

It was a surprise and relief to finally see clear skies on the morning of our departure. Although we hadn't been able to have a really good look at the face, clearings in the weather had given us a good idea of where the best line might be. Our plan was to avoid icefall danger at the base of the face by climbing a couloir that led to a possible entry point above the danger. But first we had to cross the river, which posed a significant challenge. When acclimatising we had walked well up the valley and crossed on the surface of the glacier; but we reckoned it would be about three hours faster to wade the river. And for better or for worse the best crossing place looked to be very close to base camp.

Rob positioned himself for potentially memorable shots as Paul and I changed our mountain boots for our approach shoes, the plan being that we would wear them to cross the boulder-strewn river and leave them on the far side to be collected on our way down. The crossing failed to result in the shots that Rob had hoped for, but the river was deep and fast-flowing enough to make it feel distinctly insecure. I hoped that I would feel a bit more in control when we got on to the mountain.

Mind you, just getting there involved a fair degree of uncertainty. There was steep and loose ground to gain a glacier, an icefall and then a couloir of uncertain angle that led to what we hoped was the edge of the face. 'Our sneaky approach,' Paul called it, although as we couldn't see for certain that it would be possible to gain the face from the top of the couloir we were both rather aware that it could be a sneaky approach to nowhere, which could prove slightly embarrassing.

The icefall had looked straightforward through binoculars from base camp. It was a 'dry' glacier as mountaineers say, meaning that there was no snow cover, just bare ice and rock. The combination tends not to be particularly slippery and I always find a great temptation not to bother to put crampons on. Paul clearly felt the same way as he persevered on increasingly tricky ground until a three-metre scraping slide drew blood and curses.

Out came the axes and crampons, a move which was fully vindicated as the glacier we had dismissed as straightforward presented more and more difficulties, culminating in an overhanging section overcome by an acrobatic effort including a heel hook.

'We thought this bit would be easy ... ' commented Paul, gasping appropriately while wiping blood from his grazes.

After the trials of the icefall a perfect flat area beneath the couloir allowed us to catch up with reading and enjoy the evening sun. By the end of the second day the couloir had provided a memorably crumbly path to the edge of the face where we were relieved to see that our hunch was right and we could easily access the face above the dangerous-looking icefalls at its base.

It somehow feels more intimidating to step out on to a face and immediately be faced with exposure than it does to build up to the same position from the bottom. Here the climbing very soon became acutely atmospheric with smooth ice fields below us, huge monolithic walls above and no obvious way through. Our low-visibility reconnaissance had left us unclear on exactly what line we would try to follow, but from my photograph from the summit of Cerro Kishtwar in 1993 we knew that a fault line cleaved the walls, and our hope was that this would provide the key to the lower part of the face. Beyond this vague notion we were uncomfortably aware that if we were to stand a chance of success we would need to do a fair bit of sneaky route finding around wild-looking open rock faces.

Classic European north-face climbs like the Eiger tend to include sections of steep ice field that succumb to calf-wrenching teetering on the front points of crampons. The ground here was not dissimilar. As we gained height the ice became increasingly thin and the climbing increasingly precarious. By evening the ice field we had been climbing had thinned out completely and we were beneath a line of weakness splitting an intimidating band of walls stretching across the face. Pleasingly, we found a single spot to pitch our little tent on a small projecting prow. The weather remained glorious, the mountains beyond 'our' valley were increasingly coming into view and, as we snuggled down in the evening sun, it felt that we were climbing in a very special place.

'Think I might have to come down.'

Paul had already been up and tried, removed his sack and tried again, and was now sounding uncharacteristically defeated.

'Round the corner might be better,' he offered.

I hung from my ice-screw belay sucking in the cold morning air and peering around. Round the corner to the right didn't look any easier and to get there would require an abseil and a traverse that would take a couple of hours at least. I really didn't want to do that. Losing upward momentum can so easily lead to dithering and retreat. It looked to me that if we could just gain five metres above Paul's high point the difficulty would ease, for a few metres at least. Higher up I could clearly see an overhanging section of ice, but that was not the immediate problem. The section causing difficulty was a loose and thinly iced bulge in the fault line. It had looked to be standard Scottish grade V climbing before Paul had started up, but now he was actually trying to climb it I could see that it was much steeper than it looked and clearly loose and unprotected.

'Shall I have a look?'

Somehow it seemed the right thing to say. There was a long silence.

'I'll have one more go.'

As he inched higher and higher I felt a slight pang of guilt, wondering if I had indirectly encouraged him to push on against his better judgement. This was no place to fall, there was no further protection and the climbing was obviously hard. I must have been almost as relieved as he was when he finally reached a belay and shouted for me to climb.

By the time I approached the belay he was looking far more relaxed than me and his usual positive demeanour was restored.

'Hard pitch, that. Brilliant position,' he enthused as I gasped my way through inelegantly upwards. It really was distressingly difficult.

'A fine lead, Mr Ramsden.'

I didn't have the energy to say anything more.

The climbing for the rest of the day was not unlike some of the harder Scottish gullies, with steep and sometimes thinly iced grooves interspersed with a couple of wild, overhanging sections.

It was while I was leading one of these that I started to feel an uncomfortable sensation around my buttocks. Everything else seemed fine and I couldn't understand what was wrong. Soon, the level of discomfort was such that I was left with little alternative but to find a good ice axe placement, clip myself in and investigate. The discovery was a surprising one. My over-trousers were falling down, so much so that the waistline at the back was now just below the midpoint of my buttocks. This made me feel slightly silly.

And there was no one but me that I could possibly blame.

The nice people at Berghaus had given me a medium and a large pair to choose from. My legs had been a bit cold on Shiva and so this year's undergarments were a bit bulkier than usual. After much experimenting at home I had decided to abandon the size of a lifetime and go with the large overtrousers. They came with braces, but I have never been a braces fan and so left them at home. Surely, I reasoned, if there was any excess around the waist my climbing harness would hold everything together and so there was no need to clutter myself with unnecessary fiddly bits. That approach had always worked before and I'd had no reason to suspect it wouldn't this time.

But as I hung there trying not to focus excessively on the distance down to my last protection, I had to admit that it wasn't working. Quite why it had taken until midway through day four for the problem to become apparent I couldn't work out. Perhaps I was losing weight or perhaps it was my exertions on this more technical ground that had prompted them to slip so far. Whatever the cause, movement was now restricted, my buttocks were cold and sorting out the problem while hanging from an ice tool was not going to be easy. With my harness weighted I could do little but jiggle carefully and hitch them up as much as I could.

'Whatever's going on?' drifted up from below.

My explanation did not prompt an outpouring of sympathy for my predicament. Clearly this was not the kind of problem Paul's climbing partners normally experience.

I decided not to continue the exchange and did my best to rearrange things and make progress up the steep, thinly iced ground ahead. After one more trouser-pulling-up stop, I emerged above the overhangs and gained a position where I could place a good rock belay and rearrange them properly. Warm buttocks had never felt so comforting.

The millions of tons of snow that must have poured down this couloir during the monsoon had compacted the snow such that our axes twanged in securely and climbing conditions were generally very good. Much pleasure was had and, as evening approached, another solitary projecting prow allowed us to pitch the tent. Life was good. Usually on such climbs we end up bivouacked with one person wrapped in the tent and another in a bivouac sack, or sometimes we cut a bum ledge and sit side by side inside the tent fabric. On this route we had managed to get the poles in the tent every night so far. That made such a difference. We had slept well and felt positive.

Above us now the vague fault line we had been following reared up in vertical and overhanging steps for a long, long way to reach the southern end of the summit crest. That looked hard and loose and was clearly not the way to go. Even before we left the UK, close inspection of the various photographs had made it clear that the highest point was at the opposite end of what looked to be a long and difficult summit ridge. With that in mind, our intended route now lay leftwards, following ice slopes under more huge, blank walls to a shallow groove that led up the headwall to the highest point.

We were above nearly all the surrounding peaks now and new horizons were opening. To the south the Prow of Shiva was visible, while the 7,000-metre peaks of Nun and Kun reared their heads above the ridge on the far side of our base camp valley.

That evening we ended up on two separate thirty-centimetre-wide ledges hacked out of an ice patch on the headwall. Sitting there high on an unclimbed peak and marvelling at the cloudless view was one of those 'it's great to be in the mountains' moments. Paul had brought a sewing kit and in between marvelling at the view I took in the waist of my trousers by a couple of inches and we ended up discussing the final few months of my Alpine Club presidency.

Overall I felt things had gone well. Lots of people had pulled together, membership was up by over twenty per cent and the number of members under thirty had increased fourfold. But the changes had increased pressure on the office, and key committee members were very obviously overloaded. Committee meetings had been getting bogged down with heated exchanges about whether we should employ more paid assistance and, if so, how we should balance responsibilities with those of volunteers. And recently, a group that wanted to spend near on £2 million on the club's premises in London had been pressing hard to focus more effort on proposals and costings. These issues had started to dominate despite the answers seeming obvious to me. More paid resource was affordable, would relieve workload pressures, enable five-day-per-week opening and enable the committee to focus more on membership benefits. Spending £2 million on the property would enrage the significant minority that wanted a move out of London, raise all sorts of financial uncertainties and completely distract from the important work that I felt was still necessary to build the membership and provide more focus for the British mountaineering community. Paul was not on the committee and so had not been involved in the debates, but he was a patient listener and sat quietly as I rambled on. As much as it was an unusual place to be discussing such issues, I found it useful to bounce thoughts and ideas off someone whose opinions I respected. With my mind uncluttered by the ups and downs of everyday living our discussion served to strengthen my feelings and as the last rays of sun left us I snuggled down in my sleeping bag, stared across the horizon at the striking outline of Hagshu and vowed to put these issues to a vote of the committee and try to resolve them before Lindsay Griffin, my likely successor, took over.

Back in the UK the committee voted as I had hoped, Lindsay's appointment as president was approved and I felt that I had done all I could to facilitate a smooth takeover. In fact, though feelings continued to run high, members with new views joined the committee, debates continued and Lindsay was left to keep the waters calm and mediate acceptable conclusions to both property and employee issues. To add to his difficulties, a few months after he took over John Town stepped down as secretary and the treasurer, Mike Pinney, tragically died hillwalking in North Wales. I felt bad seeing the time-consuming challenges building for Lindsay, but on a personal level I must admit that I was relieved that three years of the most difficult time-juggling I had known was over.

But I digress. High on Kishtwar Kailash it seemed much warmer than at a similar altitude the previous year and Paul chose to shun the bivouac sack and sleep just in his sleeping bag. I seemed to be too excited to sleep but could hear his slow and heavy breathing through the still night air. Away to the south a thunderstorm was brewing and gradually it came our way. I lay there staring at the almost continuous lightning and wondered how close I should allow it to get before waking him and making sure we were prepared for its arrival. But then it was 4 a.m. and our alarms were beeping, so it was time to stir ourselves anyway.

The first action of a bivouac morning is to get the stove going, but on this particular morning there was a problem. I turned on the gas and nothing happened. This was bad news as we rely entirely on the stove to produce water for drinking and hydrating our freeze-dried food. Going without food for a few days is not so bad, but going without water is a different matter all together. Paul took a look at it. There was gas in the cylinder but none coming out when the valve was opened.

'Perhaps there's ice in the valve?' I commented unhelpfully.

Paul is the sort of man who likes to 'improve' any piece of equipment you can imagine, but even he didn't have anything more sensible to say. He peered at the burner unit in an appropriately quizzical manner and popped it down his trousers while we chatted away and got on with other aspects of the morning routine. Although we didn't discuss it at the time, the uppermost thought in both of our minds was what to do if we couldn't get the stove going.

All being well, I reckoned we were half a day from the summit, after which it would be perhaps two days before we reached any running water. We seemed to be reasonably well hydrated, so carrying on regardless didn't seem too irresponsible a thing to do. Paul was doing similar calculations into which he factored that he had half a bottle of drinking water. After avoiding the subject for some time we compared thoughts, noted that the pee bottle was also half full (emergencies only!) and came to an easy decision to continue regardless of the outcome of the stove problem. That's one of the great things about having a good climbing partner relationship. We both readily felt the same way, the decision was made and the issue relegated to something to be overcome as necessary.

Within half an hour though the stove had responded well to the down-the-trousers treatment, my recently sewn waistband felt pleasingly snug, happiness was fully restored and a cup of best quality Yorkshire Tea was going down very well indeed.

By the time we were ready to start climbing the thunderstorm had moved away, but a weather front was moving in. The way up the final section of headwall was not immediately obvious, but after an initial false line we gained a slanting fault that gave some fine climbing followed by a pitch of bottomless snow leading directly to the summit. And what a wonderful summit it was. As I arrived Paul was sat on a knife-edge crest with a leg on either side. The sun was shining and with good visibility we could soak up the splendid scenery. It felt a great privilege to be able to make the first ascent of a mountain like this. We loitered for thirty minutes taking photographs, experimenting with video techniques, generally revelling in the experience and contemplating that it's a wonderful feeling to dream of something for many months and then achieve that dream.

But we still had to get down. And if I needed any reminding that descents can be challenging I only had to look across the valley to Cerro Kishtwar, where I could vividly recall breaking the head off my ice hammer on the summit while placing the very first abseil peg, twenty-one years earlier.

Our preference is always to descend by a different line than that followed in ascent but here our reconnaissance had shown that the one possibility we had identified was out of the question and there was little alternative but to go down the way we had come up. And that would involve an awful lot of abseiling.

'Abalakov threads,' smiled Paul.

It is unfortunate though that whenever Abalakov is mentioned I always think of his brother, who met an unfortunate end when his Soviet-era electric bathroom heater fell into his bath and electrocuted him. Relaxed and happy one moment and no longer with us the next; what a way to go. I tried not to think about that as we focused on the descent.

All went well until midway through a very steep section. I was shifting around on a hanging belay when I dislodged my sleeping mat from the outside of my rucksack. Paul was abseiling just below me and was able to catch it but could do little else but hold it. It was an ancient piece of closed-cell foam mat that meant absolutely nothing to me. Nevertheless the right thing to do seemed to be to make a ridiculously trying stretch to retrieve it. In so doing I stretched a muscle in my neck that proved to be the most serious injury of the whole trip.

Down at base camp life was good. Mike and Rob had enjoyed their exploratory trip to the upper glacier, Pritam had prepared a Kishtwar Kailash success cake and the enduring retrospective pleasure that goes with Himalayan success was beginning to flow. The next day our perfectly timed weather window ended and snow came to base camp. The Hindu mules arrived as planned and it was time to go home.

Weeks later I was still grimacing with my pulled neck muscle and the piece of sleeping mat that I had strained so much to keep was abandoned, gathering dust in a corner of my garage.

Chapter 17

Talking About It ...

'Can you tell us about a time when you have been frightened?'

The Q&A session at the end of my holiday snap showing was proceeding as usual, but the wording of this particular question was unusual. It reminded me of the kind of questions that I ask aspiring valuers when they attend for interview. You'll know the kind of question. It goes along the lines of:

'Can you tell us about a time when you have done something wonderful that demonstrates a competence of some kind ... ?'

And then the interviewing panel sits back, looks appropriately stern and wonders whatever the poor applicant is going to say. And it is amazing what some people do say. One applicant I interviewed had stated that his hobby was 'climate recordings' and I asked him the usual question:

'Please can you tell us more about your hobby of climate recordings.'

Clearly caught unaware he explained that he charted the temperature each day. There was a silence.

'And what have you concluded?' I asked.

'Well,' he mumbled, 'I plot a temperature graph ... it, er ... varies considerably over the year.'

His arms moved up and down to indicate the significant temperature differences that he had recorded. I couldn't help but ask if his key conclusion was that it is warmer in summer than winter. He went very red. That was naughty of me, but hey: we can't be serious all the time.

Another man had listed 'photography' as his interest. He was a very large, bright and cheery Nigerian who smiled a lot and was sweating profusely. I duly asked the 'tell us more about your hobby' question and the panel waited for a response that might indicate some kind of relevant competence. Perhaps he would have shown leadership by heading up his university photography club, or teamwork by getting involved in some big photography project of some kind. But no, he leant across the table oozing an air of great confidence.

'You know, man,' he boomed through a beaming smile. 'I take great photographs of the wife and the family and that.' ... 'With a big lens,' he added as an apparent afterthought.

Interviewing can be quite fun sometimes.

Such incidents flashed through my mind as I wondered how to answer the question now that I was on the receiving end. *A time when I had been frightened ... ?* Presumably the questioner was expecting some terrifying mountain experience. Instead, I decided to talk about a rather unfortunate dog-walking incident that was fresh in my mind.

We live in rolling countryside eight miles or so south of Derby and close to the River Trent. A favourite walk of mine and our black Labrador, Bella, is along the bank of the river to the small conglomerate cliff of Anchor Church. There are a few climbs there, one or two of which I find very enjoyable, but with the introduction to the cliff in the climbing guidebook stating 'Peter Harding used to climb here in 1945–1947 ... presumably because he didn't have enough petrol to go anywhere decent', the crag has never attracted the crowds. Anyway, the walk is very pleasant, across rolling meadows from the little village of Ingleby and then dropping down to carry on through vegetation right next to the river. On this particular occasion the river was high and the vegetation abundant. Bella bounded ahead as I dawdled along texting friends. Suddenly I felt that my feet were wet. The vegetation covered standing water on the path and I hadn't noticed. But that was hardly a problem; wet shoes and socks are far from a disaster. Bella was out of sight and seeing no reason to cut the walk short I continued. Soon though the water was getting deeper and there was still no sign of her. She is generally an obedient dog but there was no response to my shouts. I continued until the water was up to my knees and then caught sight of her swimming in an area where the water was deeper and a strong current swept close to a steep bank. If she was caught in the current and swept out into the main flow of the river that could be very bad news indeed. I quickened my pace and tried to call her over to me. But the water was deeper than I expected. Soon I was up to my waist and could see that Bella was really struggling. Running forward to pull her out I was suddenly out of my depth myself and being swept out into the main stream. The Fowler swimming skills are not the best and adrenaline flowed freely. I was most definitely frightened. Flailing wildly, I managed to grab Bella and reach a tree root sticking out of the bank. This was developing into a more memorable than usual dog walk. I have always sniggered slightly at dog-walker disaster stories and fleetingly wondered how the local newspaper would report this if it should end badly. Above me the bank was very steep and thick with nettles and brambles. Bella is quite big and it took what felt like a superhuman effort to force a reluctant dog upwards and disregard my own stings and bramble scratches to escape the clutches of the water. Even then all was not well. At the top of the bank was a high barbed-wire fence with a field beyond. Around the fence the brambles were particularly dense and Bella absolutely refused to move. Getting a wet dog over my shoulders and then climbing over a barbed wire fence would not have made for pretty viewing.

The end result saw wrecked trousers and cut legs but at least both man and dog were now safely in a field and my concern moved to one of shielding my embarrassment if some more controlled walkers should pass by. I felt my pockets for Bella's lead and discovered my car keys and mobile phone. This was turning out to be a bad day. Remarkably the car key survived but my phone was distinctly unwell. Back home I responded to advice and placed it in a tray of rice. Nicki said she would genuinely eat her hat if it ever worked again. Twenty-four hours later it sprang back into life and was fine. She never did eat her hat though.

There was no follow-up question and I was left to wonder what the audience made of this fine example of when I had been frightened.

Lecturing, or 'holiday snap showing' as I tend to refer to it, has been something that I have quite enjoyed since I managed to overcome an early fear of speaking to large audiences via a coping mechanism of drinking too much beer beforehand. The audiences and the degree of organisation behind the scenes vary enormously, but I have to say that Ireland tends to come out tops for memorable lecture experiences. Three-stop trips have tended to be the norm for me: Belfast, Dublin and somewhere down south. Fortunately the tax office has an office in Belfast so I have generally been able to catch an early flight from East Midlands Airport, arrive in Belfast in time to spend a full day in the office and thereby not use up any of my precious annual leave entitlement for the Belfast lecture. Then, if Dublin can be arranged for the Friday and Killarney, Cork or wherever for the Saturday, the three lectures can be squeezed in with me only taking the Friday afternoon off work. The Irish are always tremendously accommodating, and so the theory works well. And when it doesn't, unexpected issues tend to make trips there more memorable than most.

On one visit the Belfast lecture was duly delivered, appropriate quantities of Guinness drunk and it appeared to be time for bed. At this point it became clear that no one had booked any accommodation. The organiser frantically rang around but all hotels were fully booked. It then transpired that the hotel we were drinking in was hosting a physiotherapists' conference and a young Swedish physiotherapist had a spare bed in her room. 'Would I mind?' To be honest, having got up at some unearthly hour to catch the plane, I just wanted to get my head down. It didn't seem to strike anyone that the young Swedish lady should be asked if this was OK. 'That's fine, then,' I was assured, as more Guinness was poured. I can only assume that the lady in question didn't think it was fine as I ended up dossing on a student's floor. Ah well ...

The next night I was in Dublin. The town was gearing up for England to play Ireland in the Five Nations rugby at Croker Park the following day and again all hotels were booked. Fortuitously, I was put up by the legendary Irish mountaineer Joss Lynam who regaled me with wonderful stories from 'back in the day'.

I knew the third lecture was in Killarney but had no idea exactly where.

'Con will look after you,' I was told as his telephone number was handed to me just before I boarded the train down south.

I had not met Con Moriarty but knew him by reputation as a wild and passionate Kerry mountaineer who delighted in showcasing Kerry's mountains and heritage. At the station a huge, wild-haired, bearded man rushed up to shake my hand. When I admitted that I knew little about this part of the world it took seconds for me to be bundled into his van for a tour.

After not very long at all, his phone rang.

'An explosion? OK we are on the way.'

This didn't sound good. My initial thought was that this was somehow linked to the Troubles in the north but that seemed unlikely what with hostilities dying down and us being well down in the south.

'Sorry about this. We'd better investigate.'

And with that we were off. The sight that greeted us was unique in my experience. As we rounded the entrance to a quiet, green valley a huge orange flame was erupting from the hillside. It was much higher than it was wide and looked as if someone had embedded a huge Bunsen burner in the slope.

'That'll be Pat's house,' announced Con, who appeared to know everyone and everything about the area.

By the time we arrived at the scene it was pouring with rain and the fire brigade had already arrived. An outbuilding appeared to have exploded and the heat had caused some superficial-looking damage to the main house. The plastic guttering had melted and a few tiles had been blown off one corner. A fireman was directing his hose through this hole and pumping many gallons of water into the loft space.

'Pat's away at the moment,' explained Con.

As far as I could see there was no fire in the loft and I couldn't help thinking that Pat might have something to say if he was present. The source of the problem was clearly in an outbuilding. There was just one wall left standing and the charred remains of what looked like oxygen cylinders spread around. At this point Con received another call.

'Just have to head off for a few minutes. Be back soon. You'll be fine,' he added as if there might be some lurking danger that I wasn't aware of.

The rain had turned into a torrential downpour by now and an increasingly large group of us stood sheltering under the eaves. The conversation appeared to be exclusively in the Irish language but soon the legendary Irish hospitality shone through and I was taken under someone's wing.

'It's Pat's Himalayan bottles. You should have seen them go up! Fifty metres in the air. Amazing!' enthused my new friend.

It appeared that the owner of the house was Pat Falvey, one of Ireland's leading adventurers and a Himalayan 8,000-metre man. As far as could be worked out a dehumidifier in his outbuilding had somehow ignited his supply of oxygen that he was storing for Himalayan expeditions.

At length Con returned; there was nothing more we could do at Pat's house and the tour could begin.

Con was born and raised in the remote valley of the Gap of Dunloe between the Purple Mountains and Macgillycuddy's Reeks. It was immediately clear that everything I had heard about his passion for the area and its heritage was true.

'Sorry that time is a bit short now,' Con apologised as we zoomed speedily up the narrow road towards the Gap of Dunloe.

The rain was easing slightly and despite my feeling slightly queasy from the driving, I was mesmerised by Con's non-stop commentary about the endless sights and the fascinating history behind them. I could now wholeheartedly understand what lay behind Chris Bonington writing that 'Quite simply, there is no better way to experience the Reeks than with Con Moriarty.'

But time was short, not because the lecture was due to start but because the rugby match was due to kick off. The match finished fifteen minutes before my lecture was due to begin. Ireland won, Killarney erupted, Guinness was downed by the barrel and the streets were packed and passionate as probably the sole Englishman in town strained to overcome the sound of celebrations and deliver his lecture to a more modestly sized audience than usual.

Giving presentations is always interesting but giving them in Ireland is rather special. There always seems to be something slightly eccentric and out of control happening in a delightfully cheerful way. I love Ireland. Whether it be pleasingly memorable lecture tours or fantastic adventure climbs and sea stacks, it is a place that never fails to leave a deep impression.

Chapter 18

Hagshu – The Bear, the Tension and the Climb

Back in 1989 I was dismally failing even to get started on the then-unclimbed Cerro Kishtwar in the Indian Himalaya when I spotted something of interest on the horizon. When I returned home my main concern was for another attempt at Cerro Kishtwar, but the K2-shaped profile of what I now know to be Hagshu never completely left my mind. I suppose it's a perennial problem with Himalayan climbing that the horizon is so often filled with distressingly appealing objectives.

As the years went by I was regularly reminded of that alluring peak that stands prominently on the Kishtwar/Zanskar skyline. I saw it when I returned to Cerro Kishtwar in 1993, again when climbing Shiva in 2012 and yet again from Kishtwar Kailash in 2013. By late 2013 it had risen to the top of my box file of interesting objectives, and I stepped up the background research.

Hagshu is one of those peaks surrounded by myths and folklore. The name first came to my attention in 1986 when I saw a report about four British mountaineers who had gone missing while attempting to make the first ascent. When no trace of them could be found, rumours went round that they might have been attacked and taken hostage. Eventually, after two unsuccessful search trips by friends and relatives, a local man found some signs of their passing and a third search in 1994 located various items of theirs, including a diary. The final entry was on 1 October 1986 and stated:

Recce trip to the Hagshu La, attention captured by Chiring Peak.

My guess is that they were all killed in an avalanche, but whatever it was, something calamitous apparently transpired around 2 October and their bodies have never been found.

Three years after the British team were lost, the first ascent was made via the south-east ridge by the Polish climbers Paweł Józefowicz and Dariusz Załuski, with a British team of Phil Booth, Max Halliday and Ken Hopper reaching the summit via the east face a few days later. Little did these teams know that it would be twenty-five years and many attempts before another climber would stand on the summit.

The Polish team had a particularly memorable time. After approaching from the south (Kishtwar) side and enduring long periods of bad weather, some of their team gave up and crossed the Hagshu La pass to descend into Zanskar and look round the monasteries there. The remaining two, Józefowicz and Załuski, returned to the mountain, succeeded in reaching the summit and then descended the same line to the huge plateau at the head of the Hagshu Glacier. From there they went north, descending the glacier without any prior knowledge to arrive in Zanskar. Józefowicz had suffered some frostbite damage and presumably returned home, but Załuski returned to their base camp to collect their equipment. He travelled over 400 road miles via Kargil, Srinagar and Kishtwar, walking for several more days, only to discover that it had been ransacked by bears. It wasn't the kind of trip they were likely to forget.

My research also reminded me that John Barry, the British ex-SAS mountaineer, had led four trips to the north side in the late 1980s and early 1990s. I had been very aware of these at the time and was also very aware that he kept returning. As a strong technical climber I guessed that it had to be an inspiring objective but somehow the photos that were published didn't make it look as good as I thought it ought to. I kind of wondered whether something was being covered up, but other objectives intervened and as much as Hagshu bubbled in my list of objectives, it never quite made it to the top.

That was until 2013, when a combination of seeing its fine profile from Kishtwar Kailash, a mention from Lindsay Griffin and a growing urge to visit Zanskar and Ladakh – new areas for me – prompted a decision that the time had come. Steve Burns and Ian Cartwright were keen to join Paul and me and so the British Hagshu expedition 2014 came into being. At an early stage I contacted Smiler Cuthbertson, who had been on one of John Barry's trips. His enthusiasm to join us was such that I guessed that I was right in thinking the north side of Hagshu could be rather more exciting than the published photos suggested.

And so, in January 2014, we engaged with the often stressful and notoriously complex world of Indian mountaineering permits. Fresh in my mind was our experience the previous year when the permits we needed for Kishtwar Kailash weren't issued until the day before departure. This time, for some inexplicable reason, it seemed that the special permits that had been necessary to climb Kishtwar Kailash were not necessary and our application to reserve Hagshu for the duration of our trip was approved nine months before departure. In a curious way the civil servant in me derives some sort of satisfaction from overcoming bureaucratic challenges and the absence of such hurdles on this occasion made me feel a little uncomfortable. It just seemed too easy.

That discomfort was heightened when an American climber, Seth Timpano, contacted me for some advice and decided to attempt Barnaj II, an unclimbed peak which was accessible from the same base camp as Hagshu.

'Looking forward to hanging out together at base camp,' emailed Seth.

He sounded a nice, friendly chap, but as someone who cherishes the sense of isolation and adventure in being the only climbers for miles around it took me a little time to get used to the idea of 'hanging out' with another team. The Vasuki Parbat trip, six years earlier, had been the last time there had been another party in the same valley, let alone the same site, as our base camp.

Having sorted out the permit situation well in advance and conditioned myself to enjoy the company of one other team at base camp, I was rather taken aback when, seven days before we were due to leave, news reached me that a Slovenian team of Marko Prezelj, Luka Lindič and Aleš Česen had just left Delhi bound for the exact face that we had a permit for. I was mystified. Permits are issued for one team at any given time and they didn't have enough time to climb Hagshu before our permit started. That aside, our plans were clear on the internet, I knew Marko well, had presented him with honorary membership of the Alpine Club, and couldn't believe that he was planning to step in front of us. In the small world of alpine-style Himalayan mountaineering we felt that would be ungentlemanly in the extreme.

The names of Luka and Aleš didn't immediately ring a bell, but a quick Google search revealed that they were both young, cutting-edge mountaineers. In fact, the more I researched, the more I felt slightly embarrassed that I hadn't immediately recognised their names. And this talented team were already on their way. Identifying inspiring unclimbed objectives and organising Himalayan trips takes a lot of research and energy and I couldn't help but feel uncomfortable about the whole thing. Whatever was going on?

Shortly after trading angst-ridden emails with Paul I received a phone call from my ninety-four-year-old father's carers. It seemed that he had fallen over and couldn't get up. With only days to go it was clear that I would have to arrange more care without delay. And then, as I worked long hours to get on top of things at the tax office, Nicki had a health scare with test results due just two days before departure. Amidst much relief the tests were negative, but I got as far as emailing the others to warn them that I might have to pull out at the very last minute. It's amazing how uncertainties tend to mount at the most inconvenient times and how so often I wonder why I put myself through the stress of arranging a greater-range trip every year.

Despite the fact that it looked like a fantastic mountain, concern over the plans of the Slovenian team meant that excitement levels were not as high as usual when we met at Heathrow and boarded the plane to India. My previous trips to this part of the world had all approached via the lush valleys of Kishtwar. This time we were to fly into the town of Leh in Ladakh and, as much as I had seen plenty of photographs of the starkly arid landscape, I was still taken aback to see sand dunes on the outskirts of the town. Equally surprising was the extent of the proudly advertised 'Leh Beautification Project', which appeared intent on carrying out every aspect of 'beautification' at the same time. The whole town centre doubled up as an active building site and a busy shopping area. Shoppers and mechanical diggers mixed in that barely under control way so often on display in India. Wobbly planks spanning deep trenches gave access to shops and the whole scene particularly impressed the health and safety expert side of Mr Ramsden.

Keen as ever to save time and get to base camp quickly, we left Leh immediately to drive along the 200 kilometres of surfaced road to the town of Kargil, close to the Pakistan border. The scenery was stunning, but my efforts to soak it in were regularly interrupted by stops for me to be sick. Our driver was truly appalling and appeared totally unable to drive in a straight line. The whole journey was a series of unnecessary swerves and to this day I fail to understand why we gave him a tip when my torture was over and we finally arrived in Kargil.

I had heard many rude comments about Kargil, but initial impressions were pleasing: the inappropriately named Hotel Greenland appeared comfortable and had hot water taps that ran with hot water. Perhaps it says a lot about me and the hotels I frequent, but this was a near first for me in the Indian Himalaya. I stood for a long time in the shower enjoying the experience. But away from the relative tranquillity of the hotel there were signs that all was not peaceful and relaxed. Kargil is only a few miles from the Pakistan border and was the focal point of a 1999 border skirmish between India and Pakistan. Tensions were still evident and I couldn't help but notice young children in pristine white shirts and school ties travelling to school in caged army vehicles protected by rifle-toting armed guards dressed in full camouflage gear.

In September the temperature is pleasant, perhaps 20 °C, but Rinku – once again our liaison officer – told us that winters here were ferocious and the coldest temperature ever recorded in India had been measured just down the road at the town of Dras. It surprised me to learn that the record was as low as –52 °C.

The day after we left home, Scotland had a referendum on whether or not to remain part of the United Kingdom and we were keen to learn the result. A restaurant with a television seemed a good place to find out, but it soon became clear that there was a dearth of such places here. Eventually we had to admit defeat but found a room at the hotel with a working television. The news came on and, rather to my surprise, the result was covered at some length. There were a couple of locals in the room but neither of them spoke any English and so, being unable to understand the commentary, we had to rely on numbers appearing on the screen to find out the result. Plenty of numbers crossed the screen but, almost laughably, none of them left us any the wiser. Just when it looked as if we might not learn the result there was a short clip of David Cameron, British prime minister, standing outside 10 Downing Street. His voice was all but drowned out by the commentary but we were just about able to hear that Scotland had voted to stay part of the UK. That was the result that we wanted to hear, although it did feel slightly bizarre to see the British prime minister announcing it on a fuzzy television screen in Kargil.

It was in Kargil at the Hotel Greenland that we met Jared Vilhauer, one of the American team. He was a tall and instantly likeable man who was not having the best of holidays. Having flown to Leh with the rest of his team he had been badly affected by the altitude – Leh is at an altitude of about

3,500 metres – and had to return to Delhi. After a few days' recovering he had returned to Leh and quickly continued to the lower town of Kargil where our agent had arranged for him to join us and travel to base camp a week or so behind the rest of his team.

The second day of our drive was very different to the first. A major plus for me was that we had a much better driver and so I was able to happily take in the increasingly mountainous scenery as we drove past spectacular peaks including the 7,000-metre mountains of Nun and Kun. Habitation thinned out, the tarmac finished and all became much more to my liking. After some hours of bouncing along we arrived at the remote monastery of Rangdum. An armed guard at a checkpoint outside seemed overcautious until Rinku told us that terrorists attacked it in 2000 and several monks and a German hitch-hiker had been killed. To us it seemed a most tranquil spot and an unlikely target. The news came as a sharp reminder that this is a far from peaceful part of the world.

The road continues over the 4,400-metre-high Pensi La pass and drops into the valley of Zanskar. Although I knew a fair bit about the area, it was only now that I began to fully appreciate the risk of being snowed in here. Despite around 15,000 people living in Zanskar, this road – completed in 1979 – is still the only road in and it stays at an altitude of over 4,000 metres for a long way. Our planned departure date of 15 October wasn't long before the winter snows and if there was a heavy fall we could be seriously stuck; it certainly wouldn't be a matter of hiring a few yaks to get us over a short snowed-up section. The thought crossed my mind that phoning home and tax office and explaining that I had no idea when I would be back might not go down well. We could but hope that the first big snows held off until we had left.

The village of Akshow was one of the first we came across and was notable for being small, friendly, wild and windy. The deeply lined faces of the locals spoke volumes about the harsh climate. They referred to the peak we had come to climb as 'Akshow', which did make us wonder if 'Hagshu' was a Western mutation of its local name. Our map marked it as 'Agshu', which added support to this theory. Our cook Pritam, and a 'new' kitchen boy for us, Kapil, were here already and had arranged for yaks to take us to base camp the next day. The yaks were large and hairy and had big wooden rings through their noses. The owners attached rope to these rings and tugged fiercely to control them. I was intrigued to see that yak noses are remarkably stretchy and they seemed not to mind being pulled along by them. I never cease to be amazed by yaks.

It was good to see Pritam's smiling face again, and Kapil was cheerful, positive and likeable. They had already been up to the base camp area and enthusiastically told us how they had seen a bear – a first for both of them – on their way up.

Base camp was supposedly two days' walk away. That meant that we had to pay for two days but everyone recognised that it would be done in one. My research had revealed that some years earlier a team had spent the entire day walking up the nearside of the river before deciding they couldn't cross to where they wanted to. The river did look to be a significant challenge. A couple of yaks chose to cross via a rickety bridge, but most clearly relished the refreshing challenge of deep, fast-flowing glacial water. Carrying loads of perhaps 100 kilograms plus a yak driver, the water level rose to over halfway up the loads and yet they still kept going at a steady pace, stopping for an occasional drink of the silt-laden water. I never did quite work out how they avoided being swept downstream. Impressive beasts.

The base camp site in the ablation valley on the true left bank of the Hagshu Glacier was idyllic. The American and Slovenian teams were already established in one area but Pritam had spotted a beautiful spot five minutes or so lower down and we pitched our tents there before heading up to meet the others. Compared to what I have become used to it felt a bit like arriving to greet the crowds at Snell's Field in Chamonix back in the 1970s. Jared's acclimatisation was now going well and he and his fellow Americans spoke enthusiastically about their intended climb on Barnaj.

Luka was the only one of the three Slovenians at base camp; he was suffering from a stomach upset and so had held back for a day while Marko and Aleš were out doing a reconnaissance. He confirmed that they had been aware of our plans before leaving Slovenia and explained that they had ended up here after earlier permit applications had been refused. He also told us that the IMF had cut their permit short so that there was no overlap with ours, but that they had no intention of complying with this change. We discussed the situation and he said they would decide what to do after Marko and Aleš returned.

Steve and Ian had in mind exploration of other unclimbed 6,000-metre peaks to the south of base camp, but we all decided to acclimatise together by walking up the Hagshu Glacier and seeking out a high place to spend a few nights on a 5,700-metre peak just to the north-west of Hagshu. This, we reasoned, should satisfy all our needs: Paul and I would get a good close-up view of the northern side of Hagshu and Steve and Ian would be able to enjoy a panoramic view of the peaks they were interested in.

Three days of heavy breathing saw the four of us camped in a wind scoop at about 5,500 metres. It seemed a lovely calm spot when we arrived but midway through the night I was braced against the sidewall as gusts of wind roared through. I recalled uncomfortably the last time I experienced this kind of situation, in east Tibet in 2007 when Paul had eventually asked me to climb on top of him to try and stop the wind lifting his side of the tent. This time he snored contentedly ('breathed heavily,' he would say) as I spent the night struggling manfully. By morning the wind had dropped and he was disbelieving of my night-time exertions. The skies were clear and we were treated to a wonderful panorama of the peaks and valleys of Kishtwar to the south. We could see trees down there and it was amazing to think that the valleys were lush and well populated whereas the Zanskar valley that we had approached through was harsh, dry and empty; an amazing contrast over such a short distance.

We moved the tent to a less exposed position a little higher, wandered up to the 5,700-metre summit and returned to relax and read in the tent. The Slovenians had been up here too. Their tracks were intermittently visible and we wondered what they were intending to do. What with the personal history between me and Marko, when Luka confirmed they knew of our plans *before* leaving Slovenia and that the IMF had cut short their permit, I couldn't believe that they would step in front of us and climb the north face. Paul was not so sure. We discussed the situation interminably. Permits aside, if a friend had plans on an unclimbed line we agreed we wouldn't dream of stepping in front of them. Finally, we decided that we were confident enough that they would choose another line that we would cache our equipment beneath the north face and head down to talk things through with them while enjoying a day or so of resting and eating at base camp.

On our return to base camp we somehow missed them coming up through the huge mounds of moraine on the glacier. No one at base camp seemed to know what their plans were. We tried to ask their liaison officer but it appeared that he had made a vow of silence for a fixed period of time. This seemed pleasingly eccentric, as I had rather thought that a liaison officer's job was to liaise. Initially I wondered if it was some kind of unusual religious ritual but it soon became clear that Rinku was as mystified as we were.

We later discovered that this wasn't the first time he had decided to abstain from talking and an earlier period of silence had caused some difficulty for the Slovenians. Anyway, interestingly bizarre as this behaviour was, it was of no use in communicating any useful information.

We returned to our tents where we could do nothing other than sort out our equipment, eat, drink and fret. The fact that I knew Marko well and had liked Luka during our brief meeting simply added to the feeling of discomfort I felt over the situation we found ourselves in. It weighed heavily on my mind, we spoke of little else and I slept only intermittently.

'They are on *our* line.'

This didn't sound like a good start to the day. Paul was peering through binoculars and had spotted tracks beneath the face that followed the exact line we had told Luka we intended to follow. I was really upset, whereas Paul was angry.

The last time I had climbed behind others in the Himalaya was on the north face of Changabang in 1997, and it led to several near misses as rocks and ice were knocked down by the party above us. It also left me with a general sense of exploratory dissatisfaction such that I vowed never again to climb a technical Himalayan route behind others. So the decision not to climb behind them was an easy one to make, but there were other practicalities too.

'Shit! We'll have to go back to below the north face to collect our kit.'

It was time to refocus. Building enthusiasm for something new when one's heart has been set on an objective for nine months is difficult. However, in looking at the northern end of the mountain from base camp, our eyes had been drawn to a more or less continuous edge catching the early morning sun on the north-east face. It was longer than the north face and had a very difficult-looking section at around two-thirds height. It wasn't what we wanted, but it was a wonderful opportunity for exploratory climbing leading to the north summit of Hagshu. In the space of a few hours the decision was made. The north-east face it would be, and we would start out the following morning. Although I was disappointed I felt excited to finally know exactly how things were to pan out and what we would be attempting.

I never cease to be amazed at how the body improves with acclimatisation. In one day we easily covered ground that had taken two when acclimatising. And as I pitched our little tent beneath our intended line there was still enough time for Paul to retrieve our cache of equipment. The good weather showed every sign of continuing as we settled down for the night and inspiration levels were rising. At long last, twenty-five years after I had first set eyes on it, I was about to attempt Hagshu.

The size of the avalanche cone at the base perhaps said a lot about the strength of the monsoon rains. Floods in Srinagar had been headline news in the UK, so we were not surprised to have to take on some heavy wading to finally cross the bergschrund and stand on the front points of our crampons at last.

'There we are: our bergschrund for the year crossed.' This has become an annual comment of mine, what with our full-time jobs that prevent our getting out into the mountains as much as we would like. To my embarrassment I didn't manage to get out winter climbing at all the previous winter and so not only was this my first bergschrund crossing of the year, it was also the first time that I had put on crampons since taking them off after descending Kishtwar Kailash.

From a distance, the initial slopes had looked to be soft white ice, which I hoped we would be able to climb quickly and easily. In fact they were hard ice with a dusting of hoar frost and snow. Short, sharp steep sections added interest but the challenge was more the time-consuming and exhausting business of climbing up a bullet-hard ice slope rather than any particular technical difficulty. I thought back to Changabang in the 1990s when the ice had been so hard that Steve Sustad and I couldn't even cut footholds to stand on while belaying and instead just attached our rucksacks to ice screws and sat on them. The going here was hard, but at least it wasn't as bad as that.

On a normal day like this we will start looking for somewhere to spend the night at around 3 p.m., such is our routine of stopping early and just enjoying being high in the mountains. This day, luck was with us. Just at the 'start to search in earnest' time, we found a perfect projecting prow of rock with a covering of snow just thick enough to smoothen out and pitch the tent on. We got the tent up quickly, tied it and ourselves to the mountain and settled down to get the stove on.

From this position it was clear that a sharp-topped, unclimbed peak on the other side of the Hagshu Glacier was much higher than we had realised.

The south side that we were looking at was not particularly inspiring but what we could see of the north side looked more interesting. It appeared to face a valley that I didn't think had been visited by mountaineers and, like so many others in the Himalaya, could easily contain hidden gems. Google Earth and the like might allow an insight into such places but there are still plenty of valleys that have not been visited by Westerners.

It was perhaps inevitable that a good night's sleep in our luxury bivouac should lead to a leisurely start. Thus far the way had been obvious, but now the weakness we were following reared up into a series of steep walls festooned with hanging icicles. A Scottish-style gully cleaved the lower section and appeared to end in an overhanging amphitheatre. It also acted as a funnel for the frequent spindrift avalanches caused by the wind blowing snow around on the upper part of the face. Much peering through binoculars had suggested that it might be best to try a hidden line to our right. Now we were here though, with our noses hard up against steep ground, we couldn't even work out where that line might be. The best option looked to be steep ground, right of the gully. It looked to offer hard mixed climbing and was at least out of the spindrift avalanches.

The day progressed in the way of my ideal Himalayan climbing day. Challenging pitches with much heavy breathing, relaxing sessions of belaying and a generous dose of admiring the view, all in a position that felt completely safe from objective dangers. To add to perfection there wasn't a cloud in the sky and the day ended with us coming across a totally unexpected and flat snow ledge at just the right time. The ledge was safely positioned at the base of a prominent overhanging wall and for the second night in a row our little tent was pitched perfectly. Life was very pleasing.

Being snuggled into our sleeping bags early we lay there brewing and chatting. As it is so often, the perennial problem of work/life balance was on our minds. The possibility had arisen of Paul taking a month-on month-off job in Saudi Arabia, whereas I had just committed to dropping to twenty-four hours a week in the tax office. Paul's dilemma was that he would be better off financially but if he were to continue with annual Himalayan trips he wouldn't see his wife and daughter for a three-month spell each year. The problem for me was that I had grasped the opportunity when it was offered but was concerned that it might be too soon as it prompted quite a few uncertainties around income, children, selling the family home and my ageing father. We never came to any clear conclusions but relaxed bivouacs are useful places to air thoughts when the mind is not cluttered by everyday life.

The 4 a.m. alarm heralded a cold dawn. As the years have gone by cold mornings slow me down more than they used to. Once it was me who was always ready first and champing at the bit. Now though, the erratic circulation in my fingers slows me down as I take extra care to keep them warm and stave off frostbite. This morning was particularly cold and, as Paul kicked his heels waiting, I decided that the time had come to invest in a pair of heated gloves before my next trip.

The sun was up by the time I was ready for action and the obvious way onwards was to move left into an area where snow had been blasted up under overhangs. I am always wary when I see this as it almost inevitably means that heavy waves of spindrift pour down the area when there is just the slightest snowfall. Quite how the snow then ends up stuck on the underside of overhangs I have never been sure. I suppose it's similar to the airflows that end up with the back of a car getting dirtier than the front. Anyway, the detail doesn't matter. This morning the sun shone, my fingers were toasty warm, the cloudless skies continued and there was no need to worry about spindrift.

By early afternoon we found ourselves on a snow fluting immediately beneath the summit buttress. From a distance we had seen weaknesses that led us to think we could climb the front side of this buttress, but now we were here the obvious way forward was to move right across the top of the north face and climb on its right-hand side. I made a quick foray but felt tired. The ice was glassy and brittle and the distance to cover looked significant. It seemed likely we would not have enough daylight to make it to possible bivouac sites on the far side. Thirty metres below though, the fluting eased to a short horizontal section which looked as if it might be fashioned into a useable platform on which we could pitch the tent.

I lowered and Paul abseiled and together we stood attached to an ice screw and contemplated. The crest turned to hard ice at a depth of a few centimetres and the spot was nowhere near as good as we had hoped. Paul summed it up perfectly:

'This is crap.'

But now we had no real option but to spend the night. We would have to make do. At this point though, we seemed to lose coordination. I hacked away with the optimistic intention of getting the poles in and draping the tent over the crest while Paul hacked away working towards a sitting ledge.

After a bit we took a break to marvel at our handiwork. It wasn't looking good. All we had done was chop a nick out of the crest and make a very small triangular ledge. Before the trip Paul had spent some time making a snow hammock. The idea was that it could be secured to ice screws and filled with snow to extend ledges and make them big enough to pitch a tent on. Frustrated at our lack of constructive progress, we spent some time wondering if we could somehow use this hammock to extend triangular ledges. But the idea led nowhere and time was ticking by. We cursed our dithering and contemplated that it had been several years – back in 2010 on Sulamar – since we had been caught out like this. And there we at least had the excuse that the weather had been awful and we had been making an unsuccessful break for the top of the face. Here, the weather was perfect and we could only blame ourselves for ending up with an obviously uncomfortable night ahead.

Sitting side by side works quite well on a linear ledge but not on a triangular one. After not very long my side collapsed and tetchiness prevailed. Over the years Paul and I have climbed together he has increasingly complained about my fidgeting and me about his snoring. It used to be that I fell asleep readily on such bivouacs, but the tables have definitely turned. Paul was soon 'breathing heavily' while I woke him intermittently as I experimented with numerous different hanging positions in an effort to avoid forever slipping off what remained of my side of the ledge. At length we settled down to me hanging deep inside the fabric while Paul sat awake with his head out the top soaking in the night.

'There's a lot of activity down there.'

I looked at my watch and squirmed upright. It was 3 a.m. I peered down towards base camp but without my contact lenses in didn't stand a hope in hell of seeing anything. I had brought my glasses along too but they were out of reach in the lid of my sack.

'Lights all over the place at base camp and on the south side of Barnaj too,' said Paul as I stared blankly into the night.

This at least gave us a subject to chat about and pass the time. We knew the Americans were trying the north side of Barnaj and concluded that they must have succeeded and for some reason chosen to descend the south side through the night. The base camp lights were more of a mystery and gave rise to many theories. We never guessed the truth, which was that a bear was showing great interest in our food store and resisting all attempts to frighten it off. And we got the Barnaj lights wrong, too. In fact the Americans had retreated from the north side of Barnaj and were making a determined attempt from the south which had to be done partially at night because they had so little time left before they were due to leave.

The night passed slowly but in the morning the traverse up and across towards the edge of the summit buttress looked more amenable and shorter than it had done the day before. The slopes formed the top of the north face and it was still early in the morning when the success of the Slovenians was confirmed as we joined their tracks exiting from the face to a fine camping place. We later discovered that, in sharp contrast to our 7 a.m. to 3 p.m. approach, they had climbed twenty-three hours non-stop to reach this point. Mind you, if we had pressed on rather than spent so much time cutting a small triangular ledge we too could have enjoyed a luxury camping spot.

There were now tracks to follow, which was a new Himalayan experience for the two of us. Somehow it made everything feel more familiar and less adventurous. We followed them up to steep, sunny and pleasant rock climbing on the summit buttress and then on towards the previously unclimbed north summit. Just before the north summit we were surprised to find an extensive flat area that just called out to be camped on. The view was fantastic and we were obviously gaining height well as the nearby peak of Chiring (*c.*6,000 metres) was now clearly below us and the Barnaj peaks (*c.*6,300 metres) looked about level with us. Beyond them, evermore interesting objectives reared their heads for closer study later.

Our best guess was that the ridge to the main summit would be long and time-consuming. The weather was holding good and we decided to stop, enjoy a good night's sleep (heavy breathing and fidgeting aside) and continue in the morning. The wind was light and there was no need to tie ourselves on. We wandered around unroped, felt very lucky to be able to get to such places and generally relaxed. Seldom have I enjoyed such an unexpectedly flat, sunny and extensive bivouac spot.

The north summit was just five minutes above us and it was something of a surprise to gain it the next morning and see that the way ahead looked more straightforward than we had expected. Easy walking led to the saddle between the north and main summits, near to where the British 1989 ascensionists had joined the ridge. From here a beautiful, if exhausting, few hours led along the ridge to the summit that we had been dreaming of for so many months.

For the last few years it has been a ritual for Paul and me to take summit selfies. We use these to relive summit moments and also to chart the ageing process. This self-imposed duty over, it was time to continue the traverse with the descent of the south-east ridge, the route taken by the Polish first ascensionists in 1989. We knew that there had been unsuccessful attempts to repeat this line and were uncomfortably aware that we had not been able to get a decent view of it before starting the traverse. That said, we had the Slovenian tracks to follow and we knew they had got down because we could see their tracks way below us on the glacier. We passed a comfortable-looking bivouac spot they had used just below the summit and continued along a sharper ridge until abseiling became necessary. Soon we were hanging free on big abseils, wondering exactly where the Polish team had climbed back in 1989. Wherever they went it certainly looked to be a fine effort.

Clouds were at last appearing on the horizon and after a final bivouac below the difficulties we descended the broad expanse of the upper Hagshu Glacier in a white-out by following the increasingly difficult-to-spot tracks. By that afternoon – seven days after leaving – we were back at base camp, albeit with me falling over, cutting my head and incurring the only injury of the trip 100 metres from the edge of the glacier.

Steve and Ian had arrived the day before and over tea they regaled us with their near-success on their peak. They had reached the summit ridge, and, after a tricky traverse, Steve reached a notch beneath the highest point. From here the way ahead had been blocked by a short vertical wall that they didn't have enough equipment to tackle. And so they failed by perhaps five metres to stand on the highest point. They were full of enthusiasm for both the climbing, the area in general and the panoramic view they obtained of unclimbed objectives to the north-west. They also told us about a couple of locals who had just passed through our base camp on their way to cross the Hagshu La to buy wooden shovels and say hello to friends on the Kishtwar side. The multi-day round trip involved a long section of glacier travel with minimal equipment and seemed quite an adventure to us, whereas it was clearly viewed very much as business as usual to them. New roads, easier communications and shrinking glaciers mean that the mountain passes are crossed far less frequently than they used to be, but it was heartening to know that these traditional trade routes are still seeing some use.

Next morning we lounged around immersing ourselves in the comforts of base camp. Around lunchtime Marko, Luka and Aleš appeared bearing gifts of whisky, wine and Slovenian sausage. An awkward meeting ensued as Paul and I explained how disappointed we were at what we saw as such ungentlemanly behaviour. But the alpine-style Himalayan scene is small and there was nothing to be gained by prolonging tension. I can't say that the awkwardness completely dissipated, but we shook hands, drank and ate and wished each other well as they departed the following morning.

Although our yaks were not due for a few days, Rinku and Pritam were clearly restless.

'The bear keeps visiting us and just won't go away. It's a big problem,' they explained. I had been vaguely aware of scuffling, snuffling and shouting outside during the night but nothing had been disruptive enough to stir me from my slumbers. None of us had ever seen a Himalayan brown bear, so the prospect of the bear returning was very exciting. Soon though, it became clear that Rinku and Pritam had stayed up all night for several nights to protect our tents and food and they were tiring of the situation. Now they mentioned it, they did look rather sleepy.

Rinku explained that he had applied all the standard guidelines for dealing with bears – shout, try and chase it away, light a fire and so on – but none were having the desired effect. In fact, he reported that the 'light a fire' tip seemed to have the opposite effect as the bear had immediately dug through the glowing embers in a manner which suggested it was very pleased for an opportunity to warm its paws. Other deterrents were called for and, noting its enthusiasm for rummaging in our discarded food pit, Pritam had tried to discourage it by adding vast quantities of chilli powder. The bear had happily eaten the lot without appearing at all concerned. We listened to all this sympathetically while still being hopeful that we would catch our first ever glimpse of a bear. We didn't have to wait long.

It was much bigger than I had expected and was sitting on a rock overlooking our camp. Paul stretched for his binoculars.

'Nice ears,' he announced.

I had to agree. Light-coloured tufts made the ears stand out prominently as it stared at us from a distance. As the evening progressed and the light faded it came closer and closer until eventually its close proximity was slightly uncomfortable. Trying to stop a large, strong, sharp-clawed animal doing something it wants to do could be tricky. Meanwhile Rinku and Pritam started what had become their nightly routine of trying to find new ways of discouraging it. By morning we could understand their difficulties.

'I think it best that we finish the expedition early,' announced Rinku.

Over the years I have experienced an interesting variety of Himalayan challenges aside from the climbing, but never dreamed that being hassled by a bear might be one. But as there was no particular reason to hang around we were happy to go along with Rinku's suggestion and return to our other worlds. Getting back to family and work a few days early always goes down well.

Memories of the tensions between us and the Slovenians were resurrected a few months later when we learned that they had been awarded a Piolet d'Or for their climb. We didn't feel that our climb should have been in the running but we couldn't help but notice that the jury had relied on information which incorrectly stated that it was our permit that was cut short and the award criteria included 'showing respect for members of other teams'. We couldn't help but feel uncomfortable about this. It seemed that issues surrounding Hagshu would continue to detract from the experience for us. More than anything I felt upset that the level of retrospective pleasure I normally experience after climbing such a great mountain was tarnished. In short, wonderful as the climb was, the whole Hagshu experience left a rather sad and sour taste in the mouth.

Chapter 19

Gave Ding – True Adventure

The Hagshu experience made me and Paul more determined than ever to find objectives that were remote, exploratory and adventurous. And, rather sadly, we also felt it necessary to be less forthcoming about exactly where we were going.

East Tibet was out again and my mind turned to the vast territory of north-west Nepal that I touched the surface of with Dave Turnbull on our 2011 trip to Mugu Chuli. The remoteness of the area and the very limited amount of exploration by Westerners appealed to me and I was particularly keen to visit the district of Humla in the extreme north-west. There were some indications that the odd mountaineering gem might be lurking there and by early 2015 my research channels were focusing on one particular peak: Gave Ding.

It was Julian Freeman-Attwood, a friend from Shropshire, who first mentioned it to me. Julian is the technical mountaineer's perfect friend. He loves exploring remote mountainous places and understands exactly the kind of objectives that inspire me. But he is not interested in such technical climbing himself. Perfect. Our paths cross frequently and we share enthusiastic thoughts without fear of overlap.

Julian's explorations had taken him to Humla and in 2011 he, together with Nick Colton and Ed Douglas, attempted Gave Ding via the relatively non-technical south side. Despite being unsuccessful he spoke with great enthusiasm about the scenery and ethnic pleasures of the area and I registered it as one of those places I would love to visit. But how would I find a suitably inspiring mountaineering objective? From my initial background reading on Humla, the Changla Himal, a subrange straddling the border with Tibet, sounded the most promising area. The history of mountaineering there was decidedly sparse and my research uncovered little beyond the Japanese climbing Lachama Chuli (6,721 metres) in 2007 from the Tibetan side and Changla (6,563 metres) in 2010 from the Nepali side. In 1983 a Japanese ladies' expedition had attempted Lachama Chuli from the Nepali side but failed to reach the summit despite using fixed ropes and high-altitude porters. That seemed to be about it. None of the reports I read suggested any eye-catching technical lines of the kind about which I dream.

And then in 2013 a British team inspired by Julian's trip visited the peaks of the Chandi Himal further to the north-west. Neil Warren from that team kindly supplied me with a very distant photograph looking south. It was impossible to pick out detail but it appeared to show a steep face on a prominent mountain and was enough to stir me to do some detailed Google Earth research. Sure enough, by setting Google Earth at the right time of day, the shadow of one peak's north face was longer than any other shadow in the area. That had to mean it was steeper and bigger than anything else around. I shared this with Julian.

'That's Gave Ding.'

Paul and I looked at the evidence: a new area for us, ethnically interesting, remote, adventurous, eye-catching, unclimbed, a valley never previously visited by Westerners ... the search was over and the appropriately vaguely named British Far West Nepal Expedition came into being.

Steve Burns and Ian Cartwright were keen to join us and we could but keep our fingers crossed that our gut feeling was right and we had made a good decision. If we had got it wrong we would be opening the door to a huge amount of effort for nothing. The far north-west of Nepal is not the easiest of spots to get to, which is great for keeping the crowds away but does add a whole raft of uncertainties to any trip.

In 2015 those uncertainties were to start rather earlier than we had expected. In April Nepal experienced its worst earthquake for many years, with over 8,500 people killed and terrible devastation in some areas. Many remote settlements were particularly badly affected and the village of Langtang was completely wiped out by a landslide triggered by the earthquake. Even five months later, as we left the UK, the foreign office was still advising travellers to be very cautious. That said, Mahesh, the agent we had employed to help us overcome bureaucracy in Kathmandu, was keen for us to stick with our plans and we understood that north-west Nepal had been little affected.

Paul had started the month-on, month-off job in Saudi Arabia and the plan was for him to fly direct from there while the other three of us came from London. Unknown to us we both had long changeovers at Delhi at the same time and were simultaneously trying to sleep behind rows of seats perhaps 100 metres apart at the airport. And we both took an intense dislike to Radio Delhi Airport, which blasted loudly through the speakers and seemed to exist for no other purpose than to disturb snoozing travellers. Ironically the broadcast was interrupted every now and then by an announcement about how Delhi was now a 'quiet' airport as flight departure announcements had been discontinued.

Although it made sense, I was not very comfortable about having to rely on our flights arriving in Kathmandu at more or less the same time. I couldn't help but recall the last time we tried this in 2001, on our first Himalayan trip together. Our plan had been to climb a mountain called Kyashar in the Khumbu area of Nepal and, with me being short of leave, we decided that Paul would fly out a day early and sort out the bureaucracy in Kathmandu. I would then arrive and we would transfer seamlessly on to a flight to Lukla. All went well until my flight was approaching Kathmandu. New in those days was a nice little LCD screen charting the flight. 'Five minutes to arrival,' it announced.

Seat belts clunked and a general atmosphere of getting ready to land prevailed. After ten minutes we were still airborne. Without any announcement the time to landing indicator now read over two hours. All very mystifying. Some time later the crew clearly felt they ought to give an explanation.

'Due to bad weather we are returning to Dhaka.'

The announcement had been a long time coming, was brief and to the point, and was not welcome. But I remembered when a Pakistani plane crashed trying to make a bad-weather landing at Kathmandu in 1992. Several mountaineers that I knew had been killed, and in comparison to that, a return to Dhaka didn't seem too much of a problem. But it did mean that Paul was in Kathmandu, ready to board our pre-booked flight to Lukla, and I was in Bangladesh.

Two days later we finally met at Lukla airstrip and another problem had arisen.

'Your bag is not here sir.' And indeed it wasn't.

'We think it is in Namche Bazaar. Perhaps it will be here later. It will catch you up.'

Our porters were ready and waiting. What to do? It didn't help that the bag was a black holdall almost identical to so many other bags on the baggage carousels at Kathmandu. Waiting risked wasting precious days. And if it didn't turn up, or the wrong bag arrived, there wasn't a lot we could do about it whether we were in Lukla or further on. We decided to start the walk and cross our fingers.

It was cold and snowing heavily and I was very aware that my sleeping bag was in the missing bag. Accommodation for the night was an unheated building where we all slept together and Paul and I tried to share a sleeping bag. The night passed uncomfortably with much fidgeting. By morning Paul had declared me a bad bedfellow and the porters were staring at us intently.

The bag eventually arrived some days after we got to base camp, but by then we had dismissed our intended route as too dangerous. We made a half-hearted attempt at an inferior objective but gave up and went home early. It was not a great start to our Himalayan partnership.

All of this was very much in my mind as Steve, Ian and I arrived at Kathmandu airport. All being well Paul's flight should have arrived ten minutes before ours.

'There he is!' Relief flowed over me, prematurely.

'My bags are missing. Still in Delhi I'm told.'

The memories came flooding back. It was 9 a.m. and the next flights from Delhi were due at 1 p.m. and 4 p.m. With luck the missing bags would be on one of them, after which we had a fourteen-hour drive to the town of Nepalgunj, where we were booked on an 8 a.m. flight to Simikot. If the bags arrived at 1 p.m. we should have plenty of time; 4 p.m. would be tight, and after that we would miss the plane and possibly never see the bags again. Best not to think about that.

First though, we needed to go into town, see Mahesh and sort out various permits. After the disastrous earthquake scenes shown on television we wondered how Kathmandu would be faring five months on.

'Kathmandu is 100 per cent open for business. Here, look at our earthquake damage.'

Mahesh pointed to an inconsequential crack in a garden wall. He went on to explain that reports of ongoing disruption in Nepal had resulted in bookings being eighty per cent down on the previous year. Wandering around the tourist area of Thamel we were surprised to find that the tottery-looking buildings that hang over the narrow streets were virtually all intact.

The earthquake killed over 8,500 people and was an appalling disaster, but the impression we formed from news reports was completely false. It seemed clear that what our agent had told us was correct: Kathmandu was open for business and suffering badly from foreign office warnings and Western news reporting. What with earthquake damage and the huge drop in tourist numbers Nepal was suffering a double whammy.

'Please tell your friends to come,' was the clear message as we tackled the necessary formalities.

Back at our agent's office we met with Prem, the cook we had used on Mugu Chuli in 2011, and his son Lapkha who was to be our kitchen boy. To my surprise Julian Freeman-Attwood was also there. He was about to embark on an exploratory trek in Humla and, as much as we had been in touch before leaving the UK and knew that we might meet in Simikot, I had not expected to see him in Kathmandu. He was in the buoyant mood that tends to take him over when remote exploration is on the agenda.

He inspected our papers with a gleeful and critical eye.

'Ah yes – trekking permits. Wonderful documents.'

Aside from satisfying officials at remote checkpoints, I have never been clear what purpose a trekking permit serves. They were very formal looking and stated that we were Irish, presumably taken from our 'United Kingdom of Great Britain and Northern *Ireland* passports' and permitted us to trek in 'Simikot, Yari, Limi, Muchu, Tange Khola and Hilsa'.

'Those are not the areas that you will be trekking in,' laughed Julian.

I felt a pang of concern. Why was he laughing? This didn't seem very funny.

'But it's not a problem because all trekking permits for north-west Nepal say the same thing.'

Mahesh arrived at this point and confirmed this. Sometimes it seems best not to ask too many questions.

'Just your TIMS permit to go. These are for your safety.'

TIMS, it transpired, stands for Trekking Information Management System and is a relatively new permit introduced after a storm in 2014 in which over twenty trekkers died of hypothermia. Again it seemed a formality: hand over $10 each and receive a stamped permit form. The TIMS appeared not to come with any information about trekking, but did divide trekkers into two categories. Green category: 'Trekkers carrying own luggage and bearing all the liabilities and all the responsibilities individually.' Blue category: 'Trekkers using local facilities/expertise such as trekking guide/support staff and all the pre-booked facilities.'

'You are in the blue category,' advised Mahesh. 'I hope you enjoy the pre-booked facilities at your unvisited base camp.'

Having learned from my experience in 2011, we had decided to spare ourselves the long head-crunching public bus journey and hire a minibus for the trip to Nepalgunj. This would also save us a day as the vehicle would be faster than the bus, leave exactly when we wanted it to and, all being well, get us to Nepalgunj in time for the flight to Simikot. The vehicle was waiting outside the airport, and aside from the small matter of Paul's bags, our driver was ready to go.

The scene at the airport was one of controlled confusion. It seemed that about a hundred passengers on Paul's flight were in the same situation. Rumours abounded as to how the problem had arisen and how it might be sorted out. No one seemed to know for sure, but the most widely accepted explanation was that there was no fuel at Kathmandu airport, which meant that planes had to carry enough for the return flight meaning there wasn't enough weight allowance for all the baggage. We knew there was a fuel problem in Nepal, but we didn't fully buy this. But if it was true, it was difficult to imagine how an increasing backlog of baggage could be avoided. As the others waited outside the terminal, Paul and I somehow bypassed security and joined the throng of agitated passengers at the baggage carousels. Optimism levels were not high.

'YAYYY!'

At 4.30 p.m., after several hours of stressful waiting, the missing bags miraculously arrived. We piled them into the vehicle and were ready to go. Everyone was clearly relieved. Except for our driver.

'I've never driven through the night before,' he explained.

I couldn't recall ever having a Himalayan driver that spoke good English and contemplated that easy communication is not always a bonus.

'But I think we have enough fuel to get there,' he added in an appropriately reassuring tone.

It transpired that it had taken him seventeen hours to gather enough fuel to fill the tank. Nearly all fuel in Nepal is imported from India and a dispute had resulted in India halting deliveries. News reports indicated that over 300 fuel deliveries normally cross into Nepal each day, but as a result of the dispute fewer than five were getting through. The effects were obvious and queues for fuel were truly outrageous. I could readily believe that our driver was not exaggerating. He seemed a very likeable chap and I felt rather guilty that he was clearly stressed at the prospect of a full night of driving. Initially I thought he was refusing to do so, but it became clear that he just felt the need to make preparations.

'Is it OK for my lorry driver friend to come with us and sit in the passenger seat?' he asked. This sounded a very good idea, so much so that I wondered whether we should ask the lorry driver to drive.

By the time we had met the chap and got going time was tight for the Simikot flight. On the plus side, the fuel problems meant there was very little traffic on the road. Yet a few hours later we were stuck in a queue. We were in a small town and initially I thought nothing of it. Soon though, I became aware of a large number of people running past us on both sides.

'A serious accident,' our driver reported after walking up to find out the reason for the delay. Eventually, curiosity and a desire to assess how long we might be held up for led me to get out and see for myself what the problem was.

Crowds develop around accidents in the UK but this was on a different scale. A severely damaged minibus and an overturned dumper truck were completely blocking the road. I watched, fascinated, as a JCB hooked its bucket prongs into the lorry's wheel arch and started to tip it back on to its wheels. The force of the crowd pushing forward on the other side of the lorry was such that those at the front couldn't easily move back. As it crashed upright and threatened to roll, tragedy was only narrowly averted, but I could now see that two bodies had been under the lorry. I just had time to register that they wore police uniforms and looked very dead when the crowd surged forward and the night filled with the flash of mobile phone cameras. Soon an emergency vehicle arrived but, despite flashing lights and sirens, the crowds would not part. Meanwhile the JCB driver totally ignored the human throng and made fast and erratic efforts to push the lorry to the side of the road. From somewhere riot police arrived and with much shouting and baton waving some semblance of order was restored. It transpired that the two policemen had been directing traffic around an earlier accident when the lorry lost control and overturned on top of them. As the traffic began to flow again Ian looked out of the window and could see the two bodies now lay spread-eagled on a bank with a weeping young lady next to them. The atmosphere in our vehicle was decidedly subdued as we continued our journey.

We rolled into the car park at Nepalgunj airport with a few minutes to spare. As we parted company our driver said he was pleased not to have dozed off 'too badly' on the drive. It also became clear that he didn't know Nepalgunj and had no idea whatsoever how he might find enough fuel to return to Kathmandu. His lorry driver friend had clearly contributed absolutely nothing to the journey.

There were only eight people on board the Twin Otter flight to Simikot so it seemed an unnecessary luxury to have an air hostess on board. Mind you, she was delightfully friendly and offered us boiled sweets and earplugs served on the same tray. Simikot is the administrative centre of Humla region, but there are no roads and, although the straight-line distance from Nepalgunj is only just over 200 kilometres, the journey takes just under a week without flying. Driving hereabouts is so tortuously slow that I guess flying will always be the only realistic access option for most mountaineers and trekkers, but flights are totally weather dependant and there is always a risk of being stuck for days.

Simikot may be small and a long way from the road but it has plenty of traditional little shops and we were easily able to purchase lighters for our stoves. Ours had been spotted and confiscated by the eagle-eyed baggage handlers at Nepalgunj. This had not gone down well. The replacements looked identical to the ones I had bought at Heathrow. Ten lighters there had cost me £15, whereas here the cost translated into about £1.30. Understandably I was roundly abused and accused of wasting expedition funds.

Lighters are of course not the only items banned from planes. It was a bit frustrating that the carriage of gas cylinders for our stoves was prohibited. Being as the plane only flies at a little over 4,000 metres, there seemed to be a good reason to apply common sense – after all, some commercial airports in China are at over 4,300 metres. But then, as us civil servants know only too well, 'rules are rules' and common sense cannot be guaranteed to change anything. Luckily, we had clarified the situation in advance and paid for cylinders to be portered in from the roadhead before we arrived.

'How long did it take to get them here?' we asked our Mr Fixit man in Simikot.

'Oh, not long. They came on the plane,' he explained. Knowing the right people there was clearly very important.

While still in the village Steve was knocked off the track by a mule. He fell five metres through a bush and some brutal Himalayan stinging nettles and landed flat on sun-baked earth. Local people rushed to help, hoist him back on the track, apply mustard oil to his stings and generally pamper the poor old Westerner. Uncertainty prevailed. It had been a nasty fall and there was some question over whether he had been knocked unconscious for a short period. For a few minutes it looked as if it might all be over for him before we had even left Simikot. That would have been difficult to live down on the Peak District Wednesday evening scene.

The joys of the internet are such that we had been able to pre-order mules at an agreed price. We also employed a porter to carry kerosene and ferry kit to base camp in case our mules couldn't make it all the way. Somehow we ended up with far more mules than we needed but the muleteers did an admirable job of spreading the load in such a way that it was not immediately obvious how lightly loaded they were.

Mule tracks are the main roads of this part of the world and if one doesn't fall off them they allow relatively fast movement. We followed them through pleasing villages on day one; occasional shepherd huts, delightful old forests and precariously suspended solid wood beehives on day two, and by day three we were above the tree line and saw no more humans until the walk out.

It was on day four that the real adventure started. This was the day we left the main valley and turned into the left fork of a side valley, the Lacham Khola. Julian Freeman-Attwood, Nick Colton and Ed Douglas had been up the right branch on their Gave Ding attempt, but we had no real idea how far we might be able to make it up the left-hand branch. The plan was to have a base camp at 5,000 metres by a prominent lake that we had spotted on Google Earth. From what we had seen it looked as if an easy ablation valley could be followed to reach this point.

Sadly, Google Earth is not yet perfect.

'The mules can go no further.'

Prem was interpreting for the muleteers who were acting in a way that left little room for doubt. We were at about 4,500 metres and a long way horizontally from our intended base camp site. The distance was such that our plan to use a porter to ferry loads to the lake was out of the question. Prem and Lapkha offered to help but, although it was a setback, we concluded it would be easiest to have our base camp where we were.

For every meal on the walk-in Prem had laid a plastic sheet outside as a sort of table cloth. I had assumed this al fresco dining was something of an ad hoc arrangement to help him cope with all the unpacking and repacking hassle of the walk-in. It was something of a surprise when, in sub-zero temperatures, our first base camp meal was served outside. For reasons I cannot explain we allowed this to carry on and, even when the nearby stream froze over, nearly every meal at base camp was eaten outside on a bright blue plastic sheet.

The day after arriving, nine days after leaving the UK, the four of us ventured up the moraine that had stopped the mules and into the hidden ablation valley. It was time to find out whether our research and gut feeling was right – that exciting objectives were to be found here. After all the planning, preparation and anticipation it was a tense day.

We need not have feared. The north face of Gave Ding reared up in a complex line of Eiger-like walls crowned by a snow ridge that snaked up to a short but sharp headwall. Ice cliffs threatened both sides but there looked to be a single safe line in the centre going straight to the summit. We had struck gold. All we had to do now was climb it.

First though, some acclimatising was necessary and that became problematic. Directly opposite the north face of Gave Ding was a side valley ringed by unclimbed 6,000-metre peaks. On Google Earth this looked like an excellent spot to explore while acclimatising. Steve and Ian had hoped to find an inspiring objective here but as we gained a better sense of the area it became clear that much of the ground in this valley was tortuous rubble where water was a real problem. In fact, above the lake where we had originally planned to have our base camp we could find no fresh water at all. The glacier was completely covered in sun-baked moraine and no streams came down the mountainside. The valley was one of the most dry and desolate glacial basins we had ever seen. We managed to spend three nights camped on rocks at 5,300 metres or so, during which we punctured two sleeping mats. It was not our most successful acclimatisation outing. The end result was that Steve and Ian decided to try a 6,035-metre peak closer to camp while Paul and I consoled ourselves by noting that the face on Gave Ding looked hard, so we would gain height slowly and thereby acclimatise on the route. Positive thinking is important in Himalayan climbing.

After waiting out a couple of days of indifferent weather a full day of walking saw us camped under the face with seven days' food and four gas cylinders for the stove.

Our planned day one was to move together up a snow couloir and then traverse easily to a possible bivouac on a col between a pinnacle and the face. The traverse line turned out to be powder snow on slabs and very tricky in places, but even so by early afternoon we were at our planned sleeping place. The sharp crest sported no good spots for our little tent so for the first time ever we used Paul's snow hammock, basically a piece of fabric which could be secured at both ends and filled with as much snow as possible. The idea was to create an area of snow wide enough to pitch the tent on but the powder seemed reluctant to consolidate. We tried urinating on it in the vague hope that this would help freeze everything together. It sort of worked and we ended up with the tent floor draped over a fifty-centimetre-wide crest of snow. Boots and other heavy stuff hanging in the fabric on either side vaguely stabilised matters but the ever-possible chance of the whole show slipping off to one side did not make for the most relaxing of nights.

But before settling down there was work to be done. Since 2008 I have worked with Berghaus to help develop and market their Extrem range. As part of that work I promise to return from trips with video clips of prototypes being tested in earnest. This particular year two key products were being tested: a new ever-lighter, ever-warmer down jacket and a new ever-more-breathable, ever-better-designed shell jacket. How those technical and design people keep coming up with new and demonstrably better products is beyond me. But they do. Anyway, before leaving I had tested prototypes in the ice box at the King Kong climbing wall in Keswick in the Lake District. There, festooned in heat sensor technology, my job had been to climb up and down the ice wall and be thermally imaged at various points throughout the day. A cameraman had been employed to capture shots of the intrepid mountaineer grappling with the challenge of ten metres of steep ice.

'How long do you think you can go up and down this?'

'All day,' I heard myself say. It seemed the right answer from someone about to perform on a Himalayan face. By mid-afternoon though, the repetitive movement was such that my wrist had begun to hurt quite a lot – but I was too proud to say so. Fortunately, a recovery period presented itself when the cameraman decided that he would like to shoot a video clip from above. That involved him climbing up and hanging in a position where he could look down on top of me. A couple of top ropes were already rigged and he was tied into one and kitted out with crampons and axes. He was quite a large chap compared to the belayer, who I chatted with as he took the rope in. Soon all was not well. I suppose it could be said that my chatting was distracting the belayer, but the unexpected fall, complete with a loud clattering of expensive camera equipment, was more spectacular than is usual at a climbing wall. The second attempt ended in much the same way, but at the third attempt, the cameraman ended up hanging in a curious near-horizontal position at the top of the wall. It looked excruciatingly uncomfortable but videos were taken, all present declared themselves satisfied and my wrist was relieved of any further strain without me ever having to admit that anything was wrong.

I recalled all of this as I readied myself at the bivouac spot, hoping that our on-the-route video clip would proceed rather more smoothly. Action shots were not really practical and a short summary of my on-the-route feelings seemed the best way to approach things.

'OK. Go,' announced Paul.

The trouble with new products is that every item and every feature has a unique name which is difficult for the exhausted and altitude-fatigued mountaineer to remember. Consequently my gasping commentary was regularly punctuated by peering in a not-too-blatant way at a piece of paper reminding me of the names of the garments and the features. But I'm not complaining. The risk of wrist injuries was non-existent. Much safer than the Keswick ice wall.

Above us the face reared up in a series of blank walls broken by discontinuous white streaks. We had devised a plan and various fallback plans for this section. Plan A was a curling line of weakness leading to a distressingly steep section. If we failed on this, plan B was to abseil diagonally out of the steep section to a parallel line further right. And plan C was to traverse a long way back left to a line that, now we could see it clearly, looked harder – so plan C wasn't much of a fallback at all really.

A morning of awkward work on powdery mixed ground and delicate traversing put us above a huge drop below the main difficulties of plan A. As I arrived at the stance Paul was hanging out from the belay, craning his neck to get a good view of the tenuous line of weakness above.

'Looks hard. Might just go.'

The position had become outrageously exposed. The ground below overhung for several hundred feet, such that abseiling into plan B was clearly a non-starter. That meant we really had to get up the near-vertical mixed ground above – and it was my lead. Oh dear.

As much as I derive enormous amounts of retrospective pleasure from technical Himalayan climbing it is not often that the Fowler body yelps with delight at the time. Here though the situation was exceptional. The conditions were perfect, the protection reasonable and the climbing just within my limit.

'Absolutely brilliant!' I heard myself shouting to no one in particular.

It soon became apparent that the now-perfect conditions were possibly due to the consolidating effect of the large quantities of spindrift that intermittently poured down this part of the face. But nothing was going to detract from my enjoyment. Three fantastic pitches, including a memorable descent from a disturbingly unexpected cul-de-sac, led to an easing of the angle and a snow crest on top of a buttress which, almost uniquely in my experience of such steep faces, was soft and deep enough for us to quickly fashion into a platform that was only a little short of the size of our tent. It did collapse a bit in the night and bend a pole, but we had expected a sitting bivouac and a bent pole seemed a small price to pay for the relative luxury of tented accommodation.

Steep mixed ground led to another rock band cleaved by a difficult-looking line of weakness. By now we fully appreciated that we were very truly climbing a north face. We had had no sun whatsoever since crossing the bergschrund three days earlier and the temperature was stubbornly low.

Out of sight, Paul persevered as I shivered. Soon he reported that he was leaving his rucksack hanging on a runner. Never a good sign, that. We both like to avoid the faff of hauling sacks if at all possible. The problem was ice – too thin for secure protection – that stretched a long way up a near-vertical groove. Seconding on a single seven-millimetre rope I couldn't help but be aware that a) the rope looked very thin, and b) the sack being hauled on the other rope was making much smoother progress than me. It was a pity I couldn't get any photos of Paul leading such a spectacular pitch, but I did manage to snap a shot of his sack.

We were now well up the face with excitement levels growing. We seemed to have been correct in our judgement that the line was safe from objective dangers and the climbing was turning out to be even better than we had expected. In addition, the face had looked to be so devoid of good bivouac spots that I was expecting a whole series of semi-hanging nights. Indeed, the ground we were on led us to believe that we would end up spending the night in a sitting bivouac or, at best, on a nose-to-tail ledge cut out of the ice.

It was then a cause for great celebration when, at just the right time of day, we discovered a flat ledge where we could easily pitch the tent. Here we were on our third night and thus far we had managed to get the tent up every night.

Not far above us was the start of the snow ridge section which we likened to the upper Peuterey ridge on Mont Blanc. Not only would gaining the ridge mark the point where we would escape the steepness of the face, it would also be the first point on the route where, weather permitting, the sun would reach us. But reality fell short of expectation. The higher we climbed, the more the wind got up and its chill all but cancelled the warming effect of the sun. Already we were commenting that the conditions were the coldest we had experienced on our climbs together.

At the end of the ridge a twenty-metre ice wall gave access to a small hanging glacier below a 150-metre headwall of cornice-fringed, hard blue ice. But with the weather now looking to be on the turn, our priority was to get the tent up. Thus far we had had the odd evening snow shower but now, as darkness fell, the sky was grey and snow was falling heavily.

We had with us a walkie-talkie for evening chats with Steve and Ian, and with some reluctance I had bowed to pressure from insurance companies and borrowed an emergency beacon satellite device from the Alpine Club. I find this whole communication business and the fine line between adventure and foolhardiness is becoming an increasingly difficult one to tread. Nicki and I have always worked along the lines that 'no news is good news' and I have no desire to contact the family until I am off the mountain and safely on the way home. But I cannot deny that satellite phones are an extra safety tool. In 2008 for example, the Slovenian climbers Dejan Miškovič and Pavle Kozjek were climbing on the Muztagh Tower in Pakistan when Kozjek fell through a cornice and was killed. Miškovič was carrying a satellite phone and, after concluding that he was unable to descend alone, made a call back to Slovenia. A helicopter rescue was mounted – involving climbers who flew out from Slovenia! – and he was rescued. We are now at the stage where many insurance companies will not offer cover unless one is carried.

All this might make the man in the street think that it is irresponsible not to carry one. But then the other side of the coin is the spirit of adventure itself. What are we actually seeking when we climb in remote places? For many, the complete escape from everyday life is one of the attractions of greater-range mountaineering. There are those that argue that 'adventure'

Antarctic crossings are rather missing the point when they can summon a plane to collect them immediately if something goes wrong. I suppose it all comes down to the degree of risk we are prepared to accept and how that balances with the desire to fully experience the atmosphere of self-reliance in a mountain environment. At the moment I use excuses such as weight, cost and 'too much communication' to justify not carrying a satellite device on the route. Taking an emergency beacon to base camp is as far as I am prepared to go. What the future holds I don't know but I will always feel uncomfortable about the subject. I fear that the mindset that quashes adventurous spirits by trying to cater for every imaginable risk might creep into mountaineering. And to an extent I already see that happening. As a trustee of the annual Nick Estcourt Award, I recently reviewed a grant application arranged by students from two of Britain's leading universities. I quote verbatim from their 'risk register', which detailed the risks that they felt their expedition might face and the preventative measures they would put in place.

Risk	*Consequence*	*Preventative Measure*
Exhaustion	Lowered core temperature. Irritability. Possible stumbling.	Frequent and adequate rests.
Sunburn	Blisters. Open wounds. Snow blindness.	Wear sun cream, lip balm, sunglasses and sun hat.
Hypothermia	Uncontrollable shivering. Possible death.	Wear sufficient, warm, waterproof and windproof clothing.
Swept into river	Loss/damage to equipment. Drowning.	Take great care crossing rivers. Use poles. Cross in a group.
Slipping or falling on ice	Grazes or cuts or worse.	Always wear gloves on snow/ice. Use crampons/ice axes.
Falling in a crevasse	Cold, shock, possible death.	Careful route choice, rope up. Be competent in crevasse rescue techniques.
Road crossing in towns	Injury or death.	Take extra precaution while crossing roads.

There were another twenty-one risks listed. I found it sobering that these top undergraduates – the leaders and influencers of the future – were clearly being conditioned to approach adventurous projects in this manner, although I did find it slightly refreshing that the use of communication channels such as satellite phones was not mentioned at all in addressing any of the twenty-eight risks listed. And I couldn't help but smile to note that the risk of a serious accident in a remote and inaccessible spot was not even on the list.

But I digress. On Gave Ding our regular evening contact time was 6 p.m. As we battened down the hatches below the headwall Steve and Ian reported that the weather down at base camp was looking grim. I wasn't sure I wanted to know that. It didn't take long for the wind to pick up and the snow to accumulate such that the walls of the tent pushed heavily against us. I lay awake listening to the sound of the wind and snow; I didn't sleep well.

It was a relief when morning dawned clear and calm but bitterly cold. Around seventy-five centimetres of new snow had fallen and we could see that the snow line was way below base camp. We guessed the temperature could be as low as –30 °C.

'Nearly 80 °C colder than Saudi,' I pointed out.

We had been talking about Paul's time in Saudi, which sounded tough if lucrative. With summer temperatures exceeding 50 °C the main challenge outdoors appeared to involve identifying a line of shady spots ahead and hurrying between them. With security being a big issue, he was not allowed to leave the living compound for any reason other than to be taken to the site he worked on. There was a gym on the compound, but it was not very well stocked and his main activity over the last month had been on a step machine. As an outdoor man he was clearly unhappy about being reduced to stepping up and down in a gym. Conversely I found the thought rather amusing and enthused at length about a great rock climbing week that Steve and I had recently enjoyed in Scotland and the fell races that I had been running in my own effort to keep my body in condition.

'I'll come into my own if we have any steps to climb,' he assured me, grumpily.

With a good frozen surface it would have been a fifteen-minute stroll to reach the bergschrund at the foot of the final slope. As it was I have no idea how long it took, but it was certainly a long and very cold time. At times the powder was chest deep and as Paul took the lead I shuffled along in the trench behind him shouting the occasional supportive comment.

'Lucky you did all that step training.'

At one point I offered to go in front but Paul has seen how much that slows things down and assured me he would prefer to continue. Nicki would say that this incompetence technique is one I use to great effect at home in the kitchen. My take is that, despite all my fell racing efforts, I am still rubbish at walking. I shall not comment on my skills in the kitchen.

Meanwhile it seemed clear that a month of sweaty action on the step machine had not had an adverse effect on Paul's fitness and his was a fine, energy-sapping lead that pushed the trench all the way to the headwall.

'You should write one of those books about training for the Himalaya and peaking at the right time,' I suggested. I was left in no doubt that the first pitch on the headwall was mine.

The sheer effort required to climb blue Himalayan ice is almost impossible to describe. It is not that it is incredibly difficult technically, but that the ice is so hard that even with the most vigorous swings of the axes and the hardest kicks of the crampons it is only the extreme tips that bite into the ice. At one point the enormous force required to get a secure placement with my now-blunt axe ended with me reduced to clipping into it and hanging, sack-like, against the ice. Exhausting stuff, this Himalayan climbing. In addition, the temperature was such that this turned into the only climbing day ever where Paul, who seems largely immune to the cold, had worn a down jacket all day. The cold was becoming a slight worry. The expensive heated gloves I had purchased for the trip had performed so badly on our acclimatisation outing that I had rejected them and was relying on mittens with handwarmers. Now I was down to my last pair of handwarmers and, with a keen wind blowing and the temperature as low as I have ever experienced, I was very aware that my glove arrangement was at its limit and that I needed to take care to avoid cold injuries.

The summit crest came suddenly. After five days of hard climbing on the steep and inhospitable north side it felt like something of a release to pull into the sun and have a whole new panorama open up. To walk about freely on the relatively amenable southern slopes felt very strange, but the summit was easily reached and a firm summit hug seemed to be in order.

We pitched our tent in a good spot just below the top and enjoyed the last few hours of daylight soaking in the wonderful view of unexplored terrain and relishing the feeling of having completed the climb that we had dreamed of for the last year. We wondered how close the nearest other climbers were, and concluded that, other than Steve and Ian, it was a very, very long way away.

All we had to do now was get down. That took a further two days of complex glacier travel, twenty-five abseils from Abalakov threads and four absolutely exhausting hours crossing the glacier and descending to base camp.

Steve and Ian were lying in their sleeping bags wrapped in down jackets. Conditions on their climb had defeated them, but they seemed not in the least bit downhearted. Paul and I agreed it had been one of the very best climbs that we had done together. Prem set to work cooking a fine soup and it wasn't long before I had fallen asleep mid-mouthful and spilled it into my lap.

As we walked down through the changing seasons of old deciduous forests, I knew already that the retrospective pleasure of such a fine trip would stay with me for many years. Adventures in the remote Himalaya are difficult to beat.

Chapter 20

Sersank – Never Too Old

I sat at my desk pondering the future: 2016 was my sixtieth year and it was going to be a seriously busy one. A raft of forthcoming litigation cases promised a busy time at the tax office. My father was becoming increasingly frail and his bungalow and our family home were to go on the market, meaning a new place to live had to be found. My diary bulged with commitments, and somehow, within all this, I was determined to fit in more climbing, running and, most importantly, the annual greater-range trip.

I also needed to find a new Himalayan partner. It was approaching fifteen years since our first Himalayan trip together and Paul was increasingly keen to try some higher objectives, which I was less enthusiastic about. With a thirteen-year age gap between us it was obvious that we could not remain compatible climbing partners forever. After all, when I am seventy-two he will be the same age as I was on Gave Ding. And if he is still climbing at the same standard then he can count me out as a climbing partner. We had first discussed all this during the Hagshu trip, and although we had readily agreed to go to Gave Ding together, it was also amicably agreed that we should try going our separate ways in 2016.

As good fortune would have it, 2015 had seen a reunion with Victor Saunders. I first met Victor back in the mid 1970s when I recall commenting that I found him an irritating little squirt. But familiarity brought respect, our contrasting personalities fitted well, and we did lots of memorable climbs together throughout the 1980s. In 1987 we climbed together on my first Himalayan success, the Golden Pillar of Spantik in Pakistan. After that we largely went our separate ways until Eric Vola, a mutual friend in France, was so intrigued by our different writing styles that he decided that it would be a good idea to translate and merge sections of our books and publish them in France under the title of *Les Tribulations de Mick et Vic en Himalaya*. Knowing that the subject matter was over twenty-five years old and dubious about the exploits of two Englishmen being of interest to a French-speaking readership I thought this was a rubbish idea and was not exactly over-optimistic about a successful publishing experience. But Eric is a confident and persuasive man. He persevered with the translation and proved me woefully wrong when the book won the Grand Prix at the Passy Book Festival in France.

As Victor was resident in Chamonix and I was in the UK, the build-up to publication brought the two of us back in contact and prompted conversations about climbing together. And so, when Paul and I decided to go our separate ways, the search for a climbing partner didn't go very far.

Over the twenty-nine years since Spantik our lives had followed very different paths. Back then we were both based in London with 'proper' jobs. Victor was trying to convince himself that the work of an architect with Lambeth Council was to his liking while I was doing my best to summon enthusiasm for managing the tax collection and audit office in Balham. Ultimately Victor left to become a mountain guide and moved to Chamonix while I decided to stick with the office job and stay in the UK.

Both of us kept on climbing, me primarily through my greater-range trips and Victor through non-stop climbing activity of one kind or another. It was not until we got together in the run-up to publication of *Les Tribulations* that I fully appreciated that he had guided clients to the summit of Everest six times, sport climbed at F7a and spent much of his time guiding in far-flung spots such as Antarctica. Speaking to him made me feel that my work life of sitting in an office with occasional outings to tax meetings was not exactly adventurous. Mind you, if climbing had been my job I don't think I would have kept as motivated to enjoy my own climbing as Victor has.

When we last climbed together Victor was forever struggling to strike a balance between climbing, his first family, his second family, work and everything else that seemed to go on in his life. Maybe it was inevitable that getting him to commit to something was particularly challenging, and his well-used nickname of 'Slippery Vic,' or 'Slipper' or 'Slip' for short, seemed very apt.

One incident I particularly recall before Vic left for Chamonix was our boxing match in a seedy east London pub. The reason for this was to settle a disagreement we had over climbing partners but in reality that was an excuse for some memorable out-of-comfort-zone action. It was a mutual friend, Simon Fenwick, who had first alerted us to the existence of this unusual establishment. Simon is a bank robber's son from Essex and the fact that he described the pub as 'quite shifty' somehow conveyed the atmosphere admirably. The Kings at Ilford was a no-holds-barred kind of place where anything was acceptable. On a Sunday lunchtime a boxing ring would be erected in the dark and cavernous public bar and the place would be absolutely packed. The boxing alternated with strippers, with the atmosphere livened up by a commentator who appeared intent on being as racist and insulting as possible. For a time, the outrageous antics made it an interesting venue for our climbing group on those rare Sundays when the weather was judged too bad for climbing.

Despite the extreme racist language of the commentator, the resident boxer was black. The idea was that those keen for a box could either fight him or go in for a bout with friends or others. Any white person fighting the resident boxer could guarantee being supported by a stream of racist commentary blasted through the sound system. Usually the bouts with the resident boxer were tame and involved little more than him fending off overenthusiastic young men trying to hit him. Boxing between 'friends' was sometimes more action packed and female boxing, a rarity in those pre-Nicola Adams days, was always popular. On one occasion Nigel Benn turned up. Benn was known as 'The Dark Destroyer' for his formidable punching power and aggressive fighting style. He went on to win numerous titles and is now ranked by BoxRec as the fourth best British super-middleweight boxer of all time. Benn's entourage was large, black, short-necked and strong looking. Remarkably though the commentator stepped up his racist rhetoric and continuously expressed glee at the sight of two black men hitting each other. It was some surprise that no riot ensued and no surprise that the resident boxer ended up being carried into the car park to be revived. He returned some time later demanding a rematch but by that time the strippers had come on and no one was very interested. I later read that one boxer suffered a permanent brain injury after a fight with Benn so perhaps everyone got off lightly that day.

Anyway, The Kings seemed a fine spot for Slippery Vic and me to indulge in some rainy Sunday activity in pretence of settling our differences. Somehow the commentator had been told that I was a taxman and, with Victor's skin being darker than average, he had ample ammunition to rev up the crowd with abusive commentary.

A ringing bell indicated that we should start trying to hit each other. Vic later claimed that he had never hit anyone before, whereas I had at least tried occasionally at school and once threw a wayward punch at someone who tried to take a guitar jack plug from me after I caught it when it was thrown into the audience at a David Bowie concert. It was one of the first times that Vic had worn contact lenses, and as huge boxing gloves were strapped on to his hands I could see that he was having trouble seeing clearly. This was to give me a distinct advantage. The canvas ring was stretched inexpertly over the floor and having not noticed an obvious fold Vic stumbled badly. Taking the opportunity I hit him with my enormous gloves. He looked really surprised, tripped over and stumbled back on to the ropes. The baying crowd immediately pushed him back into the ring.

'I didn't expect you to hit me,' he commented later.

Once he was back in position I tried to get him again but Vic now held his huge glove-covered fists in front of his face, which made it difficult to hit him properly. Soon I began to tire and Vic emerged to throw some punches in my direction. The commentator hurled abuse, the crowd jeered and we gradually ground to a halt. The crowd's shouts changed from inciting action to calling for us to get off. All in all I sensed that our performance was not providing the best entertainment value.

'Get them off. Bring on the stripper.'

And so Vic and I were bundled to one side and the stripper came on until after a few minutes the commentator decided that another change was called for.

'Get her off. Any more boxers?'

But there weren't and the lunchtime was drawing to a close. An old man entered the ring and sort of danced and did his best to pick up all the coins that were being thrown at him. It was an unusual and seedily memorable place, The Kings.

By the time *Les Tribulations* was published many years had passed and us two sexagenarians (probably about the age of that Kings dancer) were keen to devote our attention to climbing objectives rather than boxing matches. Victor was sixty-six which, it struck me, was ten per cent older than I was. It somehow sounded much older than sixty. I couldn't imagine myself planning to climb a technical multi-day Himalayan climb with any other sixty-six-year-old.

An objective was needed. My box file came out, Victor shared his secrets and endless hours of deliberation began. We dithered and ultimately it was the British mountaineer Martin Moran who came to our rescue.

In 2011 he led a trek across the rarely crossed Sersank La pass between Pangi valley and Kishtwar in the Indian Himalaya and became one of the few mountaineers to see the north face of Sersank, the south side of which had dominated the head of our base camp valley on the Shiva trip. Subsequently he wrote that the face presented 'a mighty north wall' and a 'tremendous face of linked white spiders'. Victor and I knew Martin well enough to read between the lines. We contacted him, confirmed our suspicions and found our 2016 objective. It was time to grapple with bureaucracy and let the excitement build.

It seems a regular thing that I hurt myself in the run up to a trip. On this occasion just three months before departure an incompetent plummet from a climb at Matlock called *Darius* resulted in one of my ribs parting company with the cartilage. This left me with the curious sensation that my internal organs were floating around in an unsupported manner. The prognosis was that I should recover in time for Sersank but an unfortunate stretch while putting on my socks re-activated the problem just before we left. Add to this a seized back, a badly cut finger in a sandwich-making accident, and a cleanly cut nerve and artery after falling on to a bottle, and the list of ailments was uncomfortably long.

Naturally I never revealed any of these little difficulties to Victor and our pre-trip conversations always ended with positive confirmation that all was proceeding well. Later Vic admitted that he too had been having his fair share of pre-trip difficulties with a painful hip, memory loss concerns and the development of cataracts. With all this going on the Indian Embassy issuing X-mountaineering visas that expired the day before our return flights felt nothing more than a minor inconvenience.

With logistics all arranged through Kaushal, our ever-reliable agent in Manali, our first job was a quick drop in to the Indian Mountaineering Foundation in Delhi. Here we met Sanju, our liaison officer, and were subject to a mandatory briefing exercise. Mainly this involved officials staring intently at Victor and asking if we had a satellite phone. Victor squirmed uncomfortably. Denials complete, an air-conditioned sixteen-hour bus ride to the honeymoon town of Manali followed. This mode of transport sounds very organised but in fact catching the bus can be quite challenging. The problem is that the whereabouts of the pick-up point is an ever-moving feast. It seems that the official bus station charges a significant fee and so the bus owners arrange pick-up points elsewhere. This is all very nice but the authorities don't approve and so the pick-up point is likely to change at a moment's notice. How everyone manages to catch the bus remains a mystery. Anyway, after waiting for a long time at the side of a Delhi road, word of the new pick-up point somehow reached Sanju and after a short taxi ride we were on the way.

In Manali we met Kaushal and Devraj, by now promoted from kitchen boy to cook, before boarding the usual Force Traveller for crossing the Rohtang Pass into the heart of the Himalaya. Perhaps unsurprisingly, I noted that the tunnel under the Rohtang, due for completion in 2015, still appeared nowhere near finished.

Enjoying a 'snow experience' on the pass had become outrageously popular for Indian tourists. Even out of season the traffic queues were memorable. In spring, Sanju told us, there was now a restriction of 800 taxis per day ferrying people to the snow line. Before this limit was introduced the numbers reached as high as 6,000 per day. Judging by the level of congestion with a lot fewer than 800, we could hardly imagine what 6,000 would look like.

Signs urged us to *Keep Nerves on Sharp Curves* and pointed out that *Safety on Road (leads to) Safe Tea at Home* until, on the far side of the Rohtang, the atmosphere changed abruptly. A sign saying *Last Fuel for 365 Kilometres* captured the new remote feel. Downstream from here, in the Chenab gorge, the tarmac ran out and the road deteriorated fast. It took twelve hours or so from Manali before we turned off the route we had followed to Kishtwar Kailash and entered the Sural valley where, in line with so many of the valleys hereabouts, the roadhead had been extended to the last village, Sural Bhatori.

Mules were hired and never turned up, porters were engaged and after a halting two days of slow walking and negotiation, base camp was established in sight of the Sersank La pass and at an altitude of about 4,400 metres. Then, after a day of rest and sorting, two days of getting heavy sacks up the energy-sapping screes to the col and a further day of descending and traversing to a high vantage point, Victor and I were able to lie in our tent staring at the face we had come to climb. Actually, the stares were very intermittent glimpses through thick cloud. Most of the time we lay reading and sucking in the thin air.

All of a sudden Vic was searching around our very small tent with an increasing sense of urgency.

'It's my memory loss tablets,' he explained. 'I can't remember where I've put them.'

He had told me about these tablets earlier, but his reasons for having them were delightfully unspecific and I was never quite sure whether they were to stave off memory loss or treat asthma. Either way, he was delighted when they were eventually found.

Each tablet came in a separate compartment with the day written on it.

'What day is it?' asked Vic.

'Saturday.'

'Oh shit. I still have tablets for Thursday and Friday. I must have forgotten to take them.'

Arriving at the Sersank La pass was a crucial moment. Before leaving home our research had uncovered a photograph that made the face look very dry and dangerous. We didn't know at what time of the year the photo was taken, but it was a great relief for us to see that the face was coated with snow and ice. It looked safe and well frozen, but also distressingly steep. Acclimatisation could proceed in a more relaxed frame of mind.

'Blurghhh!'

It was the middle of the night and Victor awoke with a start. He knew immediately what was wrong.

'I'm so sorry ... ' he began, but it was too late. The liquid in our water bottle was most definitely not the refreshing water that I had expected.

Up until this point I had been snoozing contentedly in our little tent. Now I was very much awake and seized with a sense of spluttering unpleasantness. Victor was clearly dehydrated and, although I am no expert, my guess was that his urine tasted worse than average.

'I can feel the need for another bout in The Kings ... '

Vic chose not to respond. Perhaps his hearing was failing as well as his memory.

There was no water to flush the taste away so I fumbled outside to gather enough snow to melt. An hour or two earlier the weather had been grim, with snow falling steadily. Now the stars were out and an improvement looked to be on the cards. That made me feel a little bit better.

Our initial plan of accessing the face via a very steep chute was soon dismissed as too exposed to anything falling from above. But like-minds spied a single safe route accessing the face via a buttress to the left. It would add a few hundred metres to the climbing and no doubt increase the time it would take, but the fact that we both homed in on it was refreshing. Like-minded thinking in the mountains is important and we had both wondered whether we would still feel the same way after twenty-nine years apart. Our personalities have always been very different, but by the time we were settled into our acclimatisation routine the banter was flowing as freely as it had done in the 1980s – albeit with old man subject matter. Now our mountain judgement looked as if it was in tune too. Already we were agreeing that it was great to be back in the mountains together.

What's more, I was being reminded of Victor's wiry strength and enviable ability to plod through deep snow and carry huge loads at great speed. I had hoped that my fell racing efforts might have levelled us out in this respect, but that appeared not to be the case. Interestingly we had by now discussed our pre-expedition ailments and realised that they weren't really causing us any problems at all. We concluded that Himalayan mountaineering is good for mind and body. We couldn't wait to get going, albeit with some trepidation.

The buttress was steep, with powdery snow stuck to all but the very steepest rock. What looked to be straightforward from a distance was terribly precarious and painfully slow climbing that involved clearing perhaps fifteen centimetres of snow, hooking crampon points over rugosities in the rock and teetering upwards. It was not until early on our second day of climbing that the ground changed as we reached the knife-edge crest of the buttress. The pitch that Victor led to get us to this point was a heroic performance that left me in no doubt that years of commercial expeditions have not dented the Saunders ability.

The way forward now was to traverse a sharp crest that sported intermittent overhanging walls on either side. It wasn't the kind of ground that could be abseiled and if we should fail higher on the face it was clear that our descent would involve reversing these time-consuming pitches. I very much hoped we were good enough to get up.

'My stomach is not feeling too good,' said Vic at the end of our second day.

We had found a lovely little spot to pitch the tent, but as I took photographs of a fantastic sunrise the following morning it was clear that all was not well.

And by the end of that day, as we were buffeted by spindrift in a much more precariously positioned tent, the situation had obviously worsened.

'Got to get out!' came urgently from the far end.

Being of slight build and with minimal blubber Victor likes to wear a lot of clothes both in his sleeping bag and while climbing. We were testing various items of clothing for Berghaus and Victor was wearing them all: five layers and a harness. Sadly there was not enough time.

'Agh! Agh! Agh! Oh no! Oh no!' came from above my head as he scrabbled for the door. A full assessment revealed that Vic's favourite Calvin Klein pants had taken the brunt of the force.

'What shall I do?' he asked no one in particular.

With his harness and so many layers of clothing, taking them off was not possible without major spillage. Meanwhile I was keen to both stem the flow of spindrift into the tent and see a quick resolution to the odorous problem that was playing out above my head.

'Cut them off,' I announced unhelpfully.

To my surprise Vic produced an Opinel knife of the kind that I thought were only used for peeling vegetables.

'Great idea,' he announced, cutting away at his underpants.

For the rest of the night we lay with our own thoughts. The accumulation of spindrift was pushing the tent off the ledge but Vic's predicament was a more serious problem for us both. Four days out from base camp and three days into the face it was not the best position to have this kind of difficulty.

Come the morning there was no improvement, but Victor was irrepressibly positive.

'Looks brilliant ahead,' he enthused, 'but can you lead the first pitch while I get myself sorted out?'

One of the great things about Himalayan north faces is that the temperature is always below freezing. The accident of the previous night was well frozen but the ropes had suffered and I did not envy Vic as he fought to feed them through his belay plate.

The climbing was becoming brilliant. The conditions on this upper part of the face were much better than lower down. Every pitch looked uncertain but turned out to be just about within our limits. The ice was a bit soft which meant our ice screws were less secure than we would have liked, but progress was slow and steady. On this difficult ground it was interesting to note that I readily recognised Victor's distinctive way of moving from twenty-nine years before. He too commented that he instantly recalled my habit of resting my head against the slope when tired. The front of my lightweight helmet was becoming very dented, which perhaps said a lot.

A fantastic day ended with us at a little snow crest where we were able to cut two small ledges, one above the other. At my request Victor took the lower one. He was still not feeling well and the day had been punctuated with numerous stops, or 'natural breaks' as they like to refer to them in tax office conferences.

'I think perhaps it is the dehydrated food,' announced Vic, leaving most of his portion.

This was unfortunate, as aside from boiled sweets we didn't have anything else. It also struck me that Victor had told me that his usual weight was fifty-nine kilograms (compared to my seventy) and our pre-climb blubber comparison had suggested that I had more reserves. So, as I happily boosted my calorific intake by polishing off Vic's food, I couldn't help but mention that even he wouldn't be able to run on empty forever.

The man himself appeared not to be concerned. 'Not a problem. Perhaps it's just the evening meals, and the porridge for breakfast will stay down.'

Whatever the situation, it was becoming increasingly clear that finishing the climb and descending the far side would be considerably easier than retreating down the face and recrossing the Sersank La.

The porridge only partially stayed down, the 'natural breaks' continued and day five on the face proved both challenging and fine. By the time we had solved the difficulties of the headwall and had the cornice in sight, the Saunders body was surging forward. Where he found the energy from I do not know. Not once did he complain about a situation that would have ended the climb for lesser beings. At the age of sixty-six he was a truly remarkable man.

At 6.30 p.m. on our fifth day on the face some acrobatic heavy breathing in the last rays of the day saw us over the cornice and flopped out before a new panorama on the relatively amenable slopes of the south-west side of the mountain.

Hopes of being able to pitch the tent were quashed by hard ice, but a clear and cold night on thirty-centimetre-wide nose-to-tail ledges saw us through to a perfect dawn and a lazy 10 a.m. start. Unknown to us, Sanju and Devraj had their binoculars trained on us and were concerned at the lack of morning movement. But there was no need to rush; it was a beautiful cloudless day and ahead lay just the 150-metre summit pyramid and what we hoped would be a leisurely descent.

The summit pyramid itself had not been climbed. In 2008 a team of Japanese climbers and high-altitude porters had reached the foot via the glacier systems to the south-west but did not proceed further as local people had apparently asked them to leave the summit untouched. Knowing this, we had quizzed locals at Sural Bhatori who assured us that they had no objection to us climbing to the highest point.

From photographs we had seen, it looked as though the Japanese had approached the summit pyramid from a difficult side, but we faced no great problems and by 12.30 p.m. we stood on the top. Satisfying a childhood urge of mine, I built a little cairn to mark our passing. The panorama of the Kishtwar, Pangi valley and Lahaul peaks was inspirational. Every time I stand on a summit in this area I see exciting new objectives. It was a first for Victor in this area and he was like a playful puppy faced with an array of new chews. I took a little video clip:

'Those were six of the best days of my life.'

Moving words from a poo-covered man. I wondered what six of the worst days in his life would be like.

All that was left was to descend the glacier systems of the south-west side. Martin Moran had suggested the descent might prove easy. Let's just say he was wrong. After a day and a half of complex glacier travel and forced abseils through icefalls, we eventually escaped on to rocky ground. Vic removed his shell suit, four days of pent-up odour was released and we descended to a welcome tea meeting with Sanju and Devraj.

Two days later, on 6 October, I was able to upset Vic by telling him that I'd had my first crap since 30 September. By the end of the next day, Victor had fallen into two streams, our porters had ferried our kit down to Sural Bhatori and, three days later, we were ensconced in a local house watching satellite television. Bear Grylls was on the screen, eating a variety of insects and drinking his own urine.

'Appears to be more refreshing than mine,' concluded Victor as Bear licked his lips enthusiastically.

All we have to do now is agree a follow-up reunion climb – there's a lot to be said for them.

'I'll arrange the food next time,' said Vic.

Chapter 21

The Challenges Never End

'When are you going to retire?'

It was end-of-year appraisal time again and my boss was clearly concerned about her manpower budget. I had just completed thirty-nine years of working for the tax office. *Wow.* Said like that I sound really boring. The prospect of being a pensioner made me sound really old too. But then perhaps sixty is old?

It's odd this getting older business, and the way life changes and aches and pains come and go. One month it's my foot that hurts, then that inexplicably clears up and my back starts to ache, then that clears up and my hip starts hurting. And then I go to the Himalaya and everything is absolutely fine. All very strange and frustrating. It's almost enough to make me think that I should take up some sort of structured training programme.

Instead though, over the last few years, I have become a regular visitor to a physiotherapist in the weeks before an expedition. Matt is based in Nottingham and was recommended by some of the Wednesday evening crowd who explained to me that he hurt them a lot and so must be good. My first visit to him was after Nicki asked me to move a large pile of gravel from our driveway to the back garden just before I left for a trip. The result was gravel successfully moved but a crippling pain in my back. I have a natural aversion to spending money on things that I can't readily appreciate will improve matters and, although the sensible side of me knows otherwise, physiotherapists had always come into this category. Matt though, was different. What I had been told was correct. He hurt me almost as much as cupping at the Chengdu massage parlour, but miraculously my back problem was cured almost instantly and I have never been bothered by it since. It was a great initial success. That must have been five or six years ago and since then I have been a regular visitor just before an expedition, so much so that his usual greeting is along the lines of: 'You must be off again; where is it this year?'

And then he tries to engage me in normal conversation while inflicting great pain.

Although never repeating the resounding success of my first visit he has always told me that there is nothing seriously wrong and so I should stop whinging and get on with it. Paying £50 to be told this by a professional feels like money well spent. And so far he seems to have been right. Nicki has expressed some cynicism but I swear it is true. All those pre-expedition jobs at home that have had to be put off because of niggling pains have been deferred for good reason. Honest.

In 2015 I dropped to working three days per week but, as so many people had warned me, that didn't work very well as I just ended up working five days and getting paid for three. Now though, with the end of 2016 fast approaching, and with some prompting from my boss, it was time to ponder the prospect of fully retiring. George, my much-loved father, had died at the age of ninety-six earlier in the year, Tess and Alec were twenty-four and twenty-two, Nicki was keen to do lots of travelling and as much as I was OK about my job, I didn't love it enough to carry on unless there was a good reason to do so. For some time a recurring form of words had spun around in my head: 'Not many people die wishing they had spent longer in a tax office.' A decision was called for.

'Christmas this year,' I said to my boss.

But what would I do? After so many years of stressfully juggling my time the possibility of having free time lurked on the horizon. My mountaineering life would continue as before, that was taken as read. And I would try and improve my fell racing positions and rock climbing ability. But what about when I wasn't doing these things? I am not very good at just chilling out.

'Perhaps you could do more with sponsors?' suggested Nicki, who was clearly not keen on me hanging around the house.

It was true that I liked the idea of building on the design, testing and brand promotion work I had been doing with Berghaus. It often resulted in unusual and interesting experiences of a rather different nature than those experienced on climbing trips. I particularly recalled being asked to deliver a series of lectures in Japan. In the build-up I had been slightly bemused to be asked to forward a set of personal kit used on my last climb. I dutifully gathered together a selection of items and, as requested, prepared a short explanatory note for each one. What I could meaningfully say about some of these items I wasn't sure. For my spoon I wrote: *Used to eat from on numerous bivouacs,* and for my watch: *This cheap alarm watch is perfect for making sure we get up on time.* On arriving at the lecture venue I was intrigued to see a life-sized photograph of my face stuck on a full-size dummy dressed in my clothes. Nearby a queue of people waited to read labels attached to the selection of items I had forwarded.

'What does that one say?' I asked, pointing at the label attached to the pee bottle that I had rather mischievously included in my selection.

My host looked at it closely. 'Ah! It says this is a bottle that you have shared on several expeditions. It says you have never managed to fill it in one go.'

Those present seemed very interested and peered closely inside as if looking for some interesting feature that wasn't readily apparent.

The watch was a little more embarrassing. It soon became clear that my co-presenter for the evening was sponsored by Casio and my label suggesting that the cheapest-possible backlit alarm watch was ideal for mountaineering didn't sit too comfortably with the huge expensive multifunctional device attached to his wrist.

It was my first visit to Japan and I returned with a host of ideas, not least that it would be great if the British government could introduce a 'mountain day' bank holiday as the Japanese have done on 11 August each year.

Back home my clothing and accessories were returned safe and sound but I was rather perplexed to receive a cheeky invoice from HM Revenue and Customs asking me to pay £16 import duty for importing my own kit. Having just attended a pre-retirement course in the tax office I had learned all about tips for being more frugal. Nicki watched aghast as I entered grumpy-old-man mode and engaged in lengthy correspondence with HMRC. In the tax office those at the top forever encouraged me to 'put myself in the shoes of the taxpayer' and I took great delight in repeating this phrase ad nauseam to my customs colleagues. Eventually, after I asked for the matter to be heard by a tribunal, they backed down and £16 was saved. In total it only took a day or so of my time. Nicki was unimpressed.

'Oh my god. What the hell are you going to be like when you are fully retired?' she enquired.

'Perhaps there are voluntary positions you could take up?' she implored, no doubt thinking of my time as president of the Alpine Club. I took some time to think about this, but Nicki had already moved on to gleefully remind me of my track record of faux pas in posh gatherings when I had represented the club.

'The exploration and adventure gathering. Remember that?'

I did indeed.

In my role as president, I had attended a Buckingham Palace event for 'those involved in exploration and adventure'. It was hosted by the Queen and the Duke of Edinburgh, and, not having visited the palace before, I felt rather overawed by the surroundings. Being introduced as taxman first and mountaineer second appeared to cause Her Majesty some confusion, but mistaking Princess Beatrice for a waitress was rather more embarrassing. Personally, I thought it was entirely understandable. Everyone had name badges except for royalty and the waitresses and ushers. Princess Beatrice was not wearing a name badge and, not being an expert on the royal family, I didn't recognise her when our paths crossed.

'It must be a nightmare catering for all these people,' I commented, making small talk as awkwardly as ever.

'Yes, I think so. I see it a lot. It's my grandmother's place of course.'

She was fantastic and brushed off my faux pas with consummate ease. Meanwhile I covered my embarrassment by moving swiftly on to gulp down yet another glass of champagne and eat yet more canapés.

'You dined out on that one for months,' enthused Nicki, as if the lure of possible similar situations might help get me out of the house.

Try as I might I couldn't readily think of any voluntary positions that I might like to take on.

'You'll have to go climbing more then,' was her final observation.

I feared that she was right. After all, a happy husband is one who has had his fill of climbing. My objectives file still bulges with possibilities in the Hindu Kush, Chinese Karakoram, Tien Shan, Altai Republic, Andes, east Tibet and even Antarctica. And of course all the time there are wonderful opportunities for interesting adventures in the UK. It's a worry really that there is so much to be done and so little time.

With the issue of a retirement date out of the way my final HMRC appraisal returned to the normal format.

'So what can I record as your main achievements of the year?' asked my boss.

With my exit agreed and a bonus unlikely I had no hesitation in explaining that my main achievement of the year had been climbing Sersank with Victor.

The fact that she did not challenge this statement was not at all disappointing. A new era was on the horizon.

Epilogue

'You have cancer.' The consultant spoke with disturbing clarity.

It was my first year of retirement. Victor and I had spent the previous thirteen months planning a trip to Sikkim.

New eras do not always go according to plan.

It had all started so innocuously. I noticed one or two unusual-coloured faeces and a little weight loss but had slipped comfortably into a 'monitor the situation' mindset. It was easy to do. There was an expedition to organise, I had been doing more exercise than previously, my fell-racing results and rock climbing standards were improving and I felt fitter and healthier than for some time.

It was Nicki who persuaded me to go to the doctor. I had just been about a minor issue and hadn't even bothered to mention any other problem. I am embarrassed to admit that one reason I was reluctant was because I knew that I might be referred for tests that could continue for some time and disrupt the expedition. And I was looking forward to the trip so much. There probably wasn't anything seriously wrong, and anyway surely a few weeks wouldn't make any difference? Things would be clearer by the time we got back. It is always possible to dream up reasons for putting things off.

I was almost apologetic for taking up the doctor's time.

'I've not noticed anything unusual for a couple of weeks now,' I assured him.

He was unimpressed. A colonoscopy followed.

'How long will these tests take?' I asked.

Time was ticking by to our departure date and my fears were coming true. In truth, it was quick. The NHS moves fast when it needs to. And the journey was amazing. Watching a crystal-clear twenty-time-magnification exploration of my large intestine, right up to the inside of my appendix, was eye-opening. The nice lady operating the camera was very chatty.

'I've done over 10,000 of these. This is a lovely healthy intestine.'

And then when the camera was right at the anal sphincter she stopped.

'There's your problem,' she announced.

I peered at the screen. It meant nothing to me but the bleeding greyish polyp, magnified twenty times, didn't look good. Before the procedure started she had told me that any polyps would be removed. Now that she had found one she called for a second opinion. A lady who had done 10,000 of these was calling for a second opinion. That didn't feel like a positive step. It was decided that a biopsy should be done. Results would take a few days I was told.

Shit! This was starting to look serious. We were due to leave in just over two weeks. Should I warn Victor and everyone else involved in the trip? I decided not to. What's the point of spreading uncertainty when there are no answers?

By the time Nicki and I met the consultant for the results I feared the worst but still hoped that Victor and I could somehow still go to the Himalaya.

'You have cancer.'

It was both a shock and, in a strange way, a relief. The uncertainty was over. No more dithering. The trip would have to be cancelled. I would ring Victor immediately.

He was on the runway about to take off for a guiding trip to Mount Kenya. The connection was not very clear and the conversation halting.

'Vic, technical problem. I've just been told I have cancer so there's no way I can go.'

'No worries. We can do some climbing in the Alps instead.'

'No. No. You are not understanding. The treatment might be pretty hardcore.'

'Oh ... '

I had absolutely no idea what to expect. Cancer to me equated to ill-looking people with no hair connected to drips. But people kept telling me I looked well even though the doctors were telling me I was ill.

MRI and CT scans led to the discovery that the cancer had spread from my anus to my lymph nodes.

'You need a course of chemotherapy and radiotherapy,' explained the consultant.

This was not sounding good. It appeared that I was destined for some nasty times with no guarantee of a successful outcome. Driving back from the hospital I daydreamed about changing my will to leave bottles of whisky for the last ten finishers in the Jura fell race. It's funny the way the mind works in such situations. Perhaps I have an underlying jealousy of those good enough to win bottles of whisky under the current arrangements.

The staff at Weston Park Hospital in Sheffield were wonderful. I can't say they made it enjoyable to endure two weeks of chemotherapy and six weeks of radiotherapy rays being fired at my anus and lymph nodes, but they certainly made it bearable.

Each radiotherapy session started with dropping my trousers in front of two or three young radiographers. Usually it was the same young ladies and it took some time to feel comfortable doing this.

'Good morning ... ' Trousers down, top up and lie back on the radiotherapy table.

Although it became a regular routine it never quite felt a normal sort of thing to do. I couldn't help thinking it was the kind of behaviour that would lead to prosecution anywhere else.

Thereafter radiotherapy involved the machinery being lined up with the help of three pin-prick tattoos and lying completely still for fifteen minutes while huge lenses rotated, firing rays at me and doing their business. On one occasion I sensed a terrible internal feeling as if the rays had burned a hole in my bladder. Mostly though it was just like having a serious dose of sunburn up the bottom every day without enough time to recover from the previous day.

I was told there was roughly a two-in-three chance that the treatment would be successful but the consultant knew of my annual Himalayan holidays.

'Your body is used to being under strain for a month or so every year. It will just be a different kind of strain this year,' she explained.

Rightly or wrongly her words gave me hope.

'About nine months to recover as much as you are going to,' I was told. As it happens that was just about exactly the time to the planned Sikkim trip, which Vic and I had simply delayed by a year.

Chemotherapy did seem to drain the body of energy so, uncharacteristically, I felt I should be a little more gradual and structured than usual with my fitness preparation. The doctor had told me I should 'listen to my body' and start gradually.

I thought that a little gentle dog walking would be a good start and Jug Hole Wood near Matlock seemed a suitable spot. But, after not very long, a problem had arisen. Our twelve-and-a-half-year-old Labrador had disappeared. Seconds before she had been snuffling about in the depths of the huge entrance to Jug Hole caves. Now she was no longer to be seen. The seven-metre vertical shaft leading into the lower series was the only possibility I could think of.

The caving guide recommended a rope. Without one and with no light other than my mobile phone, the climb down was tricky and not helped by the warmer air in the cave steaming up my glasses.

The shaft led to a low horizontal tunnel where a pair of eyes glinted in the dark. Remarkably, a vertical fall of seven metres had resulted in a terrified dog but no obvious damage. The problem now was how to get a dog, which the vet subsequently weighed at 29.2 kilograms, back to the surface. Phoning home for a rope seemed a good idea but there was no signal. I could climb out and phone but then the dog might wander off into the cave system and fall again. I reviewed the possibility of climbing out. Perhaps if I was able to keep her on my shoulders I could use my body to fill the shaft below her and just kind of push her up and eventually over the final capstone. It was worth a try.

Twenty-nine-point-two kilograms is quite a weight to back-and-foot with, especially when the 29.2-kilogram package in question keeps struggling violently. The smart down jacket I was wearing for my gentle dog walk pushed hard against the mud and rock walls and my walking-boot-clad feet smeared awkwardly. The phone held between my teeth dimly illuminated the scene. It all felt rather precarious. Perhaps sensing this, the dog shat all over me. At least it was reassuring to recall that before telling me to 'listen to my body' the consultant had told me my immune system, weakened by chemotherapy, should be more or less back to normal now.

Initially the walls were fairly close together and I could brace myself quite well. Soon though the shaft began to widen and it was necessary to ram the dog's top quarters into depressions in the sidewall to take some of the weight while I udged up. The wider back-and-foot position and lack of good footholds made things far more strenuous and increasingly less secure than before. The wider shaft also increased the possibility of the dog falling past me. The exertions necessary to push the panic-stricken animal over the final overhang were of Himalayan proportions and left me gasping uncontrollably. I was absolutely knackered. It was by far the heaviest breathing I had done since my treatment started.

With a phone signal now, I phoned Nicki.

'The dog seems tired today. Could you pick us up please?'

The detail could wait until later. In the meantime I waited at the roadside in glorious winter sunshine assuring concerned passers-by that my bedraggled, mud-and-shit-covered appearance was not a problem and I was not in need of assistance.

Remarkably the dog suffered nothing more than severe bruising and I was left to contemplate that gentle dog walking had been a memorably frightening start to regaining my Himalayan fitness. If the timing had been different I could have recounted it in response to that 'what is your most frightening experience?' question.

So how do I feel now? Well, I feel fit, healthy and ready for Sikkim in two and a half months' time. And I am very aware of what a horrible disease cancer is. It creeps up on you quietly, showing no symptoms until it might be too late.

And creep up it does. As we go to print, after two clear scans, the latest monitoring visit has revealed that I am not in the clear. Much as I feel fighting fit, cancer is back. An operation is likely. Uncertainty prevails.

But at least I have answered the *Telegraph*'s request for assistance with my obituary.

And the dream of Sikkim is far from dead. Anything is possible.